ASHES
SUMMER

ASHES SUMMER

A Personal Diary of the 1997 England v Australia Test Series

Nasser Hussain & Steve Waugh

CollinsWillow

An Imprint of HarperCollins*Publishers*

First published in 1997 by CollinsWillow
an imprint of HarperCollins*Publishers*
London

© Nasser Hussain and Steve Waugh 1997

1 3 5 7 9 8 6 4 2

A CIP catalogue record for this book
is available from the British Library

ISBN 0 00 218801 5

Statistics supplied by Peter Byrne

Photographs supplied courtesy of Allsport,
Phil Brown and David Munden

Printed and bound in Great Britain by The Bath Press, Bath

CONTENTS

1 Turning Back the Clock   13
2 Prelude to an Ashes Summer *(Sydney–London)*   26
3 'The Tour Starts Here' *(Arundel–Durham)*   32
4 **Texaco Trophy One-Day Internationals** *22, 24, 25 May*   40
5 Building Up to the Tests *(Bristol–Derby)*   47
6 **First Cornhill Test Match** *Edgbaston 5–9 June*   59
7 Back to Reality   81
8 The Australians Regroup *(Nottingham–London)*   83
9 **Second Cornhill Test Match** *Lord's 19–23 June*   90
10 A Frustrating Week in June *(London–Southampton)*   103
11 **Third Cornhill Test Match** *Old Trafford 3–7 July*   110
12 Break for the Border *(Newcastle–London)*   128
13 The End of an Era   140
14 **Fourth Cornhill Test Match** *Headingley 24–28 July*   144
15 Thrills and Spills   164
16 Out West *(Taunton)*   167
17 **Fifth Cornhill Test Match** *Trent Bridge 7–11 August*   173
18 The Battle of Chelmsford
   (NatWest Trophy Semi-final, Chelmsford, 12 August)   190
19 Recharging the Batteries *(Londonderry–Canterbury)*   197
20 **Sixth Cornhill Test Match** *The Oval 21–25 August*   202
21 Carry on Captain   217
22 Lording It *(NatWest Trophy Final, Lord's, 6 September)*   221
Epilogue   227
Statistics   231

This book is dedicated to my dad, Joe, without whom I would never have got this far. Thanks also to Paul Newman of the Sunday Telegraph, an old friend, for all his help in compiling my side of the Ashes story.

Nasser Hussain
October 1997

1997 AUSTRALIA ASHES SQUAD

Captain: Mark Taylor – Tubs or Tubby
Vice-captain: Steve Waugh – Tugga
Wicket-keeper: Ian Healy – Heals
Darren Berry**
Michael Bevan – Bevo
Andrew Bichel* – Bic
Greg Blewett – Blewey
Matthew Elliott – Herb or Matty
Adam Gilchrist – Gilly
Jason Gillespie* – Dizzy
Brendon Julian – BJ
Michael Kasprowicz – Kasper
Justin Langer – Lang
Shane Lee**
Glenn McGrath – Pigeon
Ricky Ponting – Punter
Paul Reiffel* – Pistol
Michael Slater – Slats
Shane Warne – Warney
Mark Waugh – Junior
Shaun Young**

Coach: Geoff Marsh – Swampy
Manager: Alan Crompton – Crommo
Physio: Errol Alcott – Hooter
Fitness advisor:
    Steve Smith – Smithy or Tattoo
Scorer: Mike Walsh

1997 ENGLAND ASHES PLAYERS†

Captain: Mike Atherton – Ath or Athers
Wicket-keeper: Alec Stewart – Stewie
Mark Butcher – Butch
Andrew Caddick – Caddy or Ceefax
John Crawley – Creepy
Robert Croft – Crofty
Phil DeFreitas
Mark Ealham – Ealie
Ashley Giles
Darren Gough – Goughy
Dean Headley
Adam Hollioake – Smokes
Ben Hollioake
Nasser Hussain – Nass
Nick Knight
Graham Lloyd
Devon Malcolm – Dev
Peter Martin – Digger
Mark Ramprakash – Ramps
Chris Silverwood
Mike Smith – Smudge or Smithy
Graham Thorpe – Thorpey
Phil Tufnell – Tuffers or Cat

Coach: David Lloyd – Bumble
Fitness Advisor: Dean Riddle
Physio: Wayne Morton
Chairman of Selectors:
    David Graveney – Grav

* Players who left the squad during the tour
** Players who joined squad
† Including players chosen for Texaco One-day International matches

AUSTRALIA TOUR OF UK 1997

May

Thursday 15 Arundel
Duke of Norfolk's XI v Australia

Saturday 17 Northampton
Northamptonshire v Australia

Sunday 18 Worcester
Worcestershire v Australia

Tuesday 20 Chester-le-Street
Durham v Australia

Thursday 22 Headingley
1st Texaco Trophy One-Day International
England v Australia

Saturday 24 The Oval
2nd Texaco Trophy One-Day International
England v Australia

Sunday 25 Lord's
3rd Texaco Trophy One-Day International
England v Australia

Tuesday 27–Thursday 29 Bristol
Gloucestershire v Australia

Saturday 31– Monday 2 June Derby
Derbyshire v Australia

June

Thursday 5– Monday 9 Edgbaston
First Cornhill Test Match
England v Australia

Wednesday 11– Friday 13 Trent Bridge
Nottinghamshire v Australia

Saturday 14– Monday 16 Leicester
Leicestershire v Australia

Thursday 19–Monday 23 Lord's
Second Cornhill Test Match
England v Australia

Wednesday 25– Friday 27 Oxford
British Universities v Australia

Saturday 28– Monday 30 Southampton
Hampshire v Australia

July

Thursday 3– Monday 7 Old Trafford
Third Cornhill Test Match
England v Australia

Tuesday 8 Jesmond
Minor Counties v Australia

Saturday 12 Edinburgh
Scotland v Australia

Wednesday 16– Friday 18 Cardiff
Glamorgan v Australia

Saturday 19– Monday 21 Lord's
Middlesex v Australia

Thursday 24– Monday 28 Headingley
Fourth Cornhill Test Match
England v Australia

August

Friday 1–Monday 4 Taunton
Somerset v Australia

Thursday 7–Monday 11 Trent Bridge
Fifth Cornhill Test Match
England v Australia

Saturday 16–Monday 18 Canterbury
Kent v Australia

Thursday 21–Monday 25 The Oval
Sixth Cornhill Test Match
England v Australia

1

TURNING BACK THE CLOCK

NASSER HUSSAIN

The seventh of June 1996 will always be a special day in my life – when all the hard work became worthwhile and all the dreams finally became reality. For it was the day, in my first Test for three years (having played only seven Tests previously) that I recorded my maiden Test century. It was the moment, really, when I arrived as a Test cricketer and the one that I had been waiting for for as long as I can remember.

I suppose, in a way, it was fitting that the opposition for that Edgbaston Test should be India. My dad is Indian; I was born in Madras and I spent much of my early childhood at the Chepauk Stadium where my dad played first-class cricket as an off-spinning batsman. But I have always been English in my attitude, outlook and allegiance, hence the overwhelming feelings of pride and more than a little relief when I got to three figures in the first match of that Test series. The road to that point has often been rocky and more than once I wondered if I would ever fulfill my destiny.

Who knows what would have happened to my Test career if I had been given out by umpire Darrell Hair when I was on just 14 that Friday at Edgbaston and Javagal Srinath went up for a loud appeal for a catch down the leg side by Nayan Mongia. Yes, on the replay it did look as though the ball had flicked my glove even though I didn't feel anything at the time. I suppose you could say it was a pivotal moment in my career.

If I'd have gone then I would have been left with much to do in the second innings and at Lord's in the second Test where the ball did a bit, so it would have been hard work and I would have been under pressure. But you do need some luck along the way and, in the words of Jack Russell, you need more arse than class in this game, so I was determined to make the most of any luck I got and I went on to a century in difficult conditions, another at Trent Bridge and the man-of-the-series award.

No-one deserves more credit for that than my dad Joe. He is the one person I can thank for everything I've achieved in cricket. We have always been a cricketing family. Dad met mum, Shireen, in England but when I came along work had taken the family back to Madras. I can't really remember too much about my time in India but I do have vivid recollections of my childhood in Ilford, where we returned to live in 1975 when I was seven. Dad says that it was basically our education that brought us back, but there was no mistaking what future he had in mind for me. Every spare moment was spent on cricket. My older brothers, Mel and Abbas, already played and every weekend for me meant coaching at the Ilford indoor cricket school, which my dad now runs. Every Sunday morning without fail consisted of two hours with Bill Morris, a formidable character who has been a big influence on a lot of Essex cricketers' careers, particularly Graham Gooch.

Looking back now, it was pretty intense stuff for a kid of my age and all the pushing came from my old man. I just had a knack of bowling leg-breaks and my dad could obviously see the talent I had and he was determined I was going to make the most of it. When things were going well it was great because even at that age people wanted to know you but of course there were times when I wanted to go off and do other things and would occasionally wonder why I couldn't miss the odd spell of coaching to watch TV or just mess around with the other kids. But, to be honest, they were few and far between because I loved my cricket. And, looking back now, my dad's pushing is the best thing that ever happened to me.

I can remember watching my dad playing for the Ilford first team at Valentine's Park and in the summer I'd finish at the cricket school and go straight down the club. Mum and dad would watch me all over the country playing for Essex Schools, where I first met and captained a young Michael Atherton, even though mum was never really a big cricket fan. Her main priority was my sister, Benazir, the youngest of the Hussain clan and the person I was particularly close to during our childhood.

My mum and dad had earlier lost a daughter to cot death so mum was very worried about 'Benu' while she was expecting her and very protective of her after she was born. Then, as she grew up, mum would be as enthusiastic and intense about her progress as a ballerina as dad was about my cricket so I could empathize with what she went through. I'm sure there were times when she thought 'why do I have to go to the ballet every day' and 'why do I have to stay over at ballet school when I could be with my family' and I could relate to that but I could also relate to my mum because I knew she was giving Benu the best possible chance.

Of course, Benu went on to be a ballerina with the Royal Ballet Company and is currently in Perth with the Perth Royal Ballet and has done extremely well for herself. There are times when I've been at the Royal Opera House when Benu has been the only person on stage and everyone in the audience is looking for any little slip-up. Mum, meanwhile, is sitting there on the edge of her seat almost having a heart attack and I know what it's like because it's so similar to batting in a Test match.

I was very emotional when Benu moved to Australia early in 1997. I could understand why she went. The Opera House has been closed for a couple of years for renovation and she received numerous offers from other companies but she is married to Errol, who is half Australian, and Perth is a fantastic place to live. So there she went. She was living in a nice little flat in Hammersmith but now in Perth, for the same money, she's got a four-bedroom house with a swimming pool and a garden the size of her previous block of flats. I'm sure she'll be back one day because I know her well enough to know she'll miss home and mum's cooking. For the moment, though, she's enjoying Australia, the clean air and the nice people and who can blame her?

That is not to say me and Benu are the only achievers in the family. Far from it. Mel and Abbas have done pretty well for themselves too, another tribute to mum and dad. Mel, my elder brother, was an extremely talented cricketer. He still is. He had more talent than me at equivalent ages throughout and should really have gone on to a fruitful cricket career as an off-spinning batsman, like my dad. He was, in fact, offered a year's contract at Essex but at the same time was offered a three year deal by Hampshire and he took the Southampton option.

It turned out to be a mistake, basically because he was trying to break into a team which included Chris Smith, Robin Smith, Gordon Greenidge, Paul Terry and others but also because he didn't get on with the coaches at Southampton. There is more to being a professional sportsman than mere talent and maybe Mel didn't do or say the right things at times and it didn't work out for him, but he plays amateur cricket to a high level and has done very well in the Credit Suisse organization so he has no real regrets.

Abbas was different. He was always a jack of all trades and was pretty good at any sport he tried. He played second team cricket for Essex and also thrived at golf, football and even rugby league at Loughborough University. Basically, anything Ab puts his mind to he can do and now he's really excelling in business, having done very well in a pharmaceutical company and is currently living and working in India. Ab will end up as the rich one in the family, I've no doubt about that.

So much of my early life, then, revolved around sport, particularly cricket. But there did come a time when it all looked as though it might go wrong and that all the time spent at the Ilford school or Valentine's Park would be a waste. It was when I was about 15 and still taking stacks of wickets with my leg-spin in virtually every game I played. It was as though I couldn't do anything wrong until suddenly I shot up in height about a foot, almost overnight, and then the whole trajectory was immediately completely different. One day I was throwing the ball up from a low height and giving it a big loop and the next I was bowling the ball and it wasn't even spinning. I'd lost it.

I wish now that someone at that time who knew their leg-spin bowling had got hold of me and taught me how to adapt because it might have saved my bowling but as it was I was plunged into crisis. I distinctly remember a lad called Robert Pook, who spent some time on the Essex and Glamorgan staffs, tearing me to pieces in an Under-16 game and me just not having a clue what had happened. My dad was asking me what had gone wrong and I just didn't have any answers.

Before this time there were England Schools games in which I used to open the bowling with Athers and we'd both bowl 40 overs of leg spin and take tons of wickets. Now all that was in jeopardy but because everything in my life had been cricket I just couldn't give it up, so I just concentrated more and more on my batting until it had taken over.

In hindsight I should have tried to work at it because even if I was only a part-time bowler now it would have been a useful string to my bow but at the time I was just happy to still be in the game as a batsman and I just decided I would have to work my way up the order as quickly as possible. Before long I was an opener.

Luckily those dark days when my spinning days ended have never really been repeated. I went to Durham University after leaving Forest School, a great place, and continued making progress both as a cricketer and in my studies. I was playing second team cricket at Essex during the summers and I had met my future wife, Karen, who was studying at Durham to be a teacher. I didn't have a care in the world.

Before long I was getting involved in the Essex first team and I received a major break in my chances of progress when Keith Fletcher, who has gone on to be a tremendous influence on me, made the sort of unselfish gesture that every second team player dreams of. Fletch was still scoring more than his fair share of runs for the team but he had seen something in 'Nasher', as Fletch with his famous problem with names used to call me, so he decided to drop himself to give me every opportunity. It was an amazing thing for him to do.

This is an area, I think, that causes problems in English cricket. There are many older players who can still do an excellent job for their county but have given up any hopes they may have had of playing for England or reached the end of the international line. Meanwhile young second team players are forced to kick their heels awaiting their chance and have been worn down by the system by the time they eventually get in.

The best policy on this is a real dilemma for counties but I could have been in the same boat if I had come along five years earlier when Essex were particularly formidable or if it wasn't for Fletch. He has always been a good man and one of cricket's great thinkers and I will always be grateful to him.

This was in 1988 and less than a year later my name was being talked of in terms of England. I couldn't believe it. I'd been at Durham playing against teams like Newcastle and Hull universities when I was involved, in 1989, in a famous Benson and Hedges Cup run with the Combined Universities that first brought my name into the public's cricketing consciousness. It was a hectic time. We managed to get to the quarter-finals with a team which included, under Mike Atherton's captaincy, the likes of me, Martin Speight, Tim O'Gorman, Adrian Dale, and James Boiling and those of us at Durham had to get up, one day, at 5am to sit an exam and then travel down to Taunton for a cup quarter-final against Somerset. This was the game where I scored a century and we really should have won it but

Peter Roebuck bowled us out when we were virtually home and dry. The semi-final would have been against Essex too. I was absolutely gutted.

But it was a rare setback. I joined up full-time with Essex at a time when England were being heavily beaten by Australia. Then news broke of a second rebel tour to South Africa and I distinctly remember Goochie being furious when his name was linked with the trip when he wasn't going. Mind you, it was all over my head really until suddenly I got a phone call saying I was in the 13 for the final Test of the summer at the Oval under David Gower. I couldn't believe it.

That surprise call-up coincided with Essex's match against the Australians before the final Test and all their players, who had already won the Ashes, were looking at me in astonishment, as if to say 'is this the kid they're putting up against us?' I could see their point. I still had a lot of crappy gear from my university days and I was under a bit of pressure when I batted, but I did reasonably well and reported to the Oval soon after.

I went there with my county colleague John Stephenson, also called up for the first time, and they gave us a bag full of goodies including an England cap and sweater and for us it was like Christmas had come in August. Until, that is, Gower, a childhood hero of mine, told me on the morning of the game that they were going with 'Stan' Stephenson instead of me and could he have the cap and jumper back! I was more upset at handing my cap back than I was about not playing – receiving one of these is the ultimate.

Still, I earned around a grand just for turning up for two days, so I thought 'well, that's paid off my overdraft,' and then had to drive straight to Northampton to play for Essex. Fletch, always the wise old owl, told me not to worry and that missing out might be the best thing for me as a lot of people have played in the last Test of a season at the Oval and never been seen again. He was right as usual – Stan never played in another Test after that.

By now speculation had begun for the winter tour of the West Indies but I didn't think too much about it, even when Goochie, who I was driving around at that time, told me he wouldn't be coming up to Leicester for a game with me because he had to attend a selection meeting. It was the start of his reign as England captain.

Next morning, at breakfast in Leicester, Goochie put his arm around me and told me I was picked for the Nehru Cup, a one-day tournament in India, before the Caribbean trip. I was delighted with that, but then he added 'and we'd like you to come to the West Indies too.' I was 21. I thought 'this is it, fantastic.' I must have still been thinking that later in the day when I was dismissed by Jon Agnew for a duck but all attention was on another man at Leicester that day, one David Gower. Captain for the Ashes series, Gower was now excluded from the trip and I was, I suppose, going in his place. Luckily no-one really blamed me for that as most people were keen for youngsters to be given their chance but there was a lot of focus on Gower's omission and Goochie's role in it that day. In a way it deflected the attention away from me.

I was soon under the spotlight when we got to the West Indies. What better way to make a Test debut can there be than beating the West Indies on their own patch? That was my fate in Jamaica in early 1990 and it was typical of a great tour. Everybody got on extremely well and Goochie got us all together, working on our fitness and devising a plan to deal with their batsmen. Still, no-one actually expected us to win that first Test at Sabina Park. For some of the more experienced players it was the most incredible experience because they had played the West Indies a lot and never been on the winning side before. People like me and Angus Fraser, meanwhile, were more blasé about it because we'd never played them before and, perhaps, didn't fully appreciate the significance of it all.

Then, however, came another incident which was almost as damaging to my career as the loss of my ability to spin the ball. And I wasn't even playing cricket. There I was, thrashing Phil DeFreitas at tennis in Guyana during the washed out second Test to pass the time when I slipped and broke my wrist. Except I didn't know it was broken at the time and played on for the rest of that tour, taking part in the last two heart-breaking Tests of the series in Barbados and Antigua not knowing the extent of the injury. Of course, when I got back to England I'd done so much damage to it that I had to have it pinned up and ended up missing four months of the most batsman-friendly English summer on record.

Now I feel that must have been the biggest blip I've had. If that hadn't happened I feel I might well have played 50 or 60 Tests by now because I think I would have got into the side that summer, when seams were reduced and pitches had to start off 'straw coloured' and scored runs against India and New Zealand. Having said that, I've been pretty lucky with injuries since then so maybe that was my turn to suffer. I've seen good players have their career ruined by injury, so at least this wasn't the end of the world for me.

What followed, however, was six years of twists and turns, many ups but quite a few downs too before that fateful day at Edgbaston in June 1996 when I arrived on the international map. For a start, I got myself a 'reputation' for disciplinary problems which I insist to this day has been exaggerated out of all proportion.

On two occasions I found myself in trouble with the powers that be at Essex. And a former Middlesex player subsequently told me that if their players had been suspended for similar 'crimes' to those which landed me in hot water then they would never have got a team out on the field. The first incident came in 1992 and basically was a problem I had with Neil Foster. I felt the club shouldn't have left him in charge during our game against Kent at Tunbridge Wells when Gooch and Derek Pringle were absent. Now Fozzie was one of the best fast bowlers the club have ever had but as a leader of men I didn't think he set the right example. Just the previous week at Ilford he'd refused to bowl, saying his knees had gone and that he didn't want to bowl anymore and Goochie had given him an almighty rollicking.

Then, next game, he was captain and I didn't think that was a good idea. Sure enough he had a go at me about something and I was so angry when I got back to the dressing room that I ended up squaring up with Mark Ilott over something ridiculous. It was subsequently reported in some papers that my problem was with Ramble (Ilott) but that was a complete red herring. Mark and I are the best of friends and we were never going to come to blows. It was just unfortunate that my anger with Fozzie came out while he was around but people should remember that when professional sportsmen live with each other for six months a year they're not going to be kissing each other all of the time. There will be times when there are squabbles.

Actually, this has been the only time in my career that I've ever been disappointed with my team-mates for not backing me up. Firstly, Foster should never have been in charge and secondly it was a handbags at ten paces job and the other boys should have realised that. But word got back to Goochie and he told me that they had to do something about this and as it would hurt me more to be not playing rather than a fine he was going to leave me out of the next game. It was to be my first return to Durham since leaving university too.

It took me a while to get over that. The next time I saw Mark he came straight up to me and said 'I can't believe what's happened' and expressed his regret. But we've never had a problem. My problem was with Fozzie.

That was not the end of my disciplinary misdemeanors, but the other occasion when I was obliged to miss a game was more of a misunderstanding. It came in 1993 at a time when Goochie was under a bit of pressure during another poor Ashes series. I'd come off the field one Saturday night during a game at the Oval moaning about the way our bowlers had performed and Goochie said 'leave it to me, it's not up to you to say anything'. Then Paul Prichard told me Goochie wanted to have a word but he failed to tell me that the captain wanted to see me straight away. So there I was, on the Sunday, sitting in the dressing room when Goochie came up and said 'why didn't you come and see me?' and I replied that I didn't realise it was urgent. He then added 'too late, I've tossed up and you're out of the side.'

Obviously I was very disappointed but I feel that incident was not particularly serious and I must emphasize that Goochie has been a considerable influence and friend to me so these were very much isolated problems. But as far as the press were concerned I now had a temperamental label and it's been hard to shake off. Yet if you go and ask anybody in our dressing room about me they'll tell you that the only time to avoid Nasser Hussain is two minutes after he's got out. It means so much to me that for a short while after I've been dismissed people just must leave me in a corner of the dressing room demolishing my gear and effing and blinding at myself. That's my character. After that I'm fine and it's out of my system.

I can't say I was too perturbed at the reputation I was getting because I knew Goochie thought of me as someone he wanted in his side and I knew I wasn't a disruptive influence. I was just a bit fiery and perhaps some people were uncomfortable with a younger player who had opinions. Goochie, to be fair, always told me that I would have to channel that aggression and he clearly didn't hold that Oval incident against me because later that summer he was picking me to face the Australians.

So we were winning things at Essex and I was, on the whole, scoring well and getting involved in England A tours without managing to get back into the full side until that troublesome summer against the Aussies.

I came in at number seven when I was recalled to the side for the third Test at Trent Bridge but I got a seventy and an unbeaten 40 odd and was batting with a certain Graham Thorpe when he scored a century on his debut after four A tours. The other three Tests of that summer, during which time Goochie stood down and Atherton started his record-breaking reign, did not go quite so well for me but I averaged 31 in the four Tests, facing Australia for the first time, and was on the winning side at the Oval. So I was pretty pleased with that and was looking forward to being part of Atherton's bright new era of young players and continuity of selection. Little did I know, before we left for my second tour of the West Indies, that I wouldn't play another Test for three years.

That 1994 tour of the Caribbean was my most disappointing time as a full England player. I was the man in possession of a place but I made a bit of a slow start in my three first-class knocks before the first Test and found myself missing out. Now the captain and coach who made that decision, Atherton and Fletcher, were people I totally respect but they decided to go with other players so I had to accept that. I made a century against a president's XI and then England were all out for 46 in Trinidad but still I didn't get a chance. I kept myself going and didn't let my head go down. I got some stick for a poor shot in a tour match in Grenada but as far as I was concerned I just didn't pick a googly. It was hardly evidence of a poor attitude after being left out, I thought.

When we returned from the West Indies there was no indication that I had drifted out of selectorial thoughts. Ath put his arm round me towards the end of the trip and said 'this is the squad, we're going to stick with it. We're going to go the way of the Aussies and stick with the likes of you, Thorpey and Ramps (Mark Ramprakash).' That's really what Ath wanted but unfortunately by the time we came back things had changed above him and Ray Illingworth had come in and altered things immediately. The likes of Gooch and Mike Gatting were back and I was a long way from the side.

Consequently I had a very poor 1994. I let my head drop, didn't even get a thousand runs and missed out on a winter tour, so I made the decision to give it one more go. I got hold of some videos of myself and really worked at my game both at home with Fletch and Goochie and in South Africa in club cricket. I basically decided to analyse my whole game with the support of Karen, who was fantastic. I said to her 'look, there are two ways I can go here. I can either settle for being a good county player and earn a reasonable living or I can spend another winter away from you, this time in Cape Town, giving everything to get my game ready for Test cricket.' She said 'go for it, you'll regret it if you don't.'

So the hard work began. Basically, I was opening the face of the bat too much, something I've always been accused of, and I was moving around in the crease too much. I worked at both and had a great summer in 1995. It was not enough to get me on the tour of South Africa but I couldn't argue with their choice of batsmen on that trip and instead I had the considerable consolation of the captaincy on the A tour to Pakistan, where we had a successful and harmonious time.

By that time I was also vice-captain of Essex, having been appointed Prichard's deputy when Goochie stood down, so things were going the right way again. My call-up for the first Test of the 1996 season, and the chain of events after that, made all the hard work worthwhile.

*   *   *

I did not expect to be vice-captain of the 1996–97 England tour party to Zimbabwe and New Zealand. At the end of the 1996 season I was just grateful to be a regular member of the side and was more inclined to review my performances against India and Pakistan rather than worry about any higher office.

But there I was – again at Edgbaston, where it had all happened for me in June – sitting in my car during an end of season match between Warwickshire and Essex and listening for the winter tour parties to be announced. After Mike Atherton's name was read out I was expecting the next one to start with an A or a B but my name was read out, followed by the words 'vice-captain' and it took a while for it to click while the rest of the party was announced. When it did sink in I realised I was just an Atherton injury away from captaining my country and things like that tend to focus the mind a bit.

The feelings of pride, however, became somewhat mixed when we got to Africa because for a while in Zimbabwe we experienced absolute chaos and I, as the vice-captain, was in the thick of it. Touring can be hard work, make no mistake about that, and the whole business involves a lot more than cricket. We were on a hiding to nothing in Zimbabwe. The press had almost set us up before we went by saying that we were playing a poor side on good wickets but that just wasn't the case at all. It turned out that we were playing a good side in conditions that encouraged swing and, to compound that, it was the rainy season and we were without proper net facilities.

Add the fact that Dominic Cork, our main swing bowler, wasn't in the party in conditions that were made for him and you can see that this was never going to be quite the piece of cake for England that many would have you believe. Having said that, we played pretty well in the two Test matches and were just one ball away from winning in Bulawayo before rain affected our chances of victory in Harare. So what did we do particularly badly in the most important form of the game? I don't know.

In the one-day internationals we were dreadful. There's no getting away from that and we deserved more stick than we actually got for losing that series 3–0. But for many of the press guys to criticize us for not going out and for being insular was a bit much as far as I'm concerned. There would, rightly, be plenty of stick flying around if we were out drinking all the time and not taking our task seriously, but surely we shouldn't be chastised for being professional and concentrating on the cricket.

When the level of abuse that we were receiving starts flying around you can approach it in two ways. You can either say, well, the press have always been like that and ignore it, or you can take a bit of a stand and we decided on the latter course of action by not attending the press Christmas lunch.

The point was, almost all the papers were getting stuck into our captain who a year earlier had batted for a week to score an unbeaten 185 and save a Test in Johannesburg. Then he was the best thing since sliced bread, but now they were sticking turnips or whatever on his head, so we felt it would be wrong to pretend that we weren't hurt as a team by the flak our leader was getting. It wasn't even Ath's decision to miss the press lunch but he still got the blame for it. As far as I can recall he didn't even have a vote in the decision but it's fair to say a few people, like Jack Russell, felt we should go. I was among those who felt we shouldn't and I was in the majority so, after a vote, we didn't go.

It shouldn't have been that big a deal. We were simply saying that we as players have to look at ourselves when things are going badly and that perhaps the reporters should look at themselves occasionally too. A lot of the press guys took it the right way but some took it so badly they slagged us off for weeks afterwards. That's life.

A lesser man than Mike Atherton would have thrown it all in during the darker times of that trip. I kept him going a little bit by occasionally reminding him that the boys were completely and utterly behind him even though almost all the papers were calling for his head. I used to tell him that he was the one we wanted and that once we got to New Zealand everything would be fine.

And, as anyone who knows their cricket should have anticipated, once we got to New Zealand everything was indeed fine and the captain was back in the runs. If we could only have bowled Danny Morrison out in Auckland we would have won the Test series 3–0 in New Zealand but as it was our little squad and David Lloyd were still able to prove the doubters wrong.

I felt so sorry for 'Bumble' (Lloyd) when he was copping just as muck flak as Ath. The players desperately want a coach who is on their side and the one thing you know about Bumble, unlike some people from the past we could mention, is that he's totally behind us. He's got an obligation to deal with the press and he doesn't mind providing them at times with quotes that they can have a field day with, but he's behind us and when he speaks we'll go out there and give everything for that man.

We played some good cricket all the way around New Zealand, but from a personal point of view I was unable to complete my winter target of a Test century in each of the countries we visited. I'd recorded my third Test century in Bulawayo and played well, but opportunities were restricted in New Zealand because we were doing so well and, even though I got a big hundred in a warm-up game, I couldn't do the same in any of the three Tests.

I should have done so in Wellington when I was 60 odd overnight and needed to start again the next day but my mistake was in trying to cut Daniel Vettori too early on and I snicked him. That was my big chance. Also, by this time, I'd been back in the Test side for almost a year and, playing so much intense cricket, you find yourself without too much time to analyse any problems you may have with your technique. I found myself moving around in the crease too much towards the end of the tour, an old problem of mine, but I was reasonably happy with my winter performances and an at times difficult trip was completed for me when I led the side in a one-day international in Auckland when Ath was injured. We won, the boys gave me total support and whatever happens to me from now on I can say I've captained my country in an international fixture. That's a very rewarding feeling.

When I got back into the side at Edgbaston in 1996 my only objective was to still be in the team for the next two or three matches. That's the only target you can really set yourself in those circumstances. But, at the start of the 1997 season, I wanted to go a stage further than that. Now I wanted to become something close to an automatic choice and to get my Test average up in the forties and to be an Atherton or a Thorpe – basically, a highly respected Test player.

This meant I had to keep working on my technique. We all knew, after our successes in Wellington and Christchurch, that the team for the first Ashes Test would be pretty much unchanged but that did not appear to be the way some people were viewing it. I turned on the television during one early season match to hear Bob Willis questioning whether I should be in the England team. It upset me because at the time I'd played in 10 Tests since returning to the side, had scored three centuries and was averaging close to 50, so I didn't think my place should be questioned at all. I thought, 'Hold on a second. I've done pretty well here. What's his problem?' I think, to be fair, Sky TV want Bob to be the one who questions things and stimulates debate but it did spur me on a bit. I thought 'I'll show him at Edgbaston.'

The first real setback of the summer for me was the naming of the one-day party to face the Australians in the Texaco Trophy. Beforehand I'd decided I wasn't going to get too upset if I missed out providing they picked the side I expected. After all, I'd been left out of the one-day team last year against India and Pakistan and I half expected it to happen again, even though I feel I have much to offer as a one-day player. But the thing that did upset me a bit was that, when they did announce the side, I was the only member of our successful winter top six who wasn't in it. That made me think I had something to prove.

That something I have to prove is that I am a good one-day player. 'Grav' (David Graveney) rang me before the party was announced to tell me I wasn't in the squad, but he softened the blow a little by telling me that I'd definitely be in the first Test. The Ashes, as far as I'm concerned, are the number one priority this year but I still asked Grav if I could have a talk with him at some point during the summer about my one-day chances. I'll remind him that I average in the forties in the Benson and Hedges Cup, forties in the NatWest Trophy and thirties in the Sunday league which, considering I've spent most of my career down the order on Sundays, I'm quite content with. Add my fielding and I feel I should be in with a shout. Having said that, I really need to bat in the top four in one-day cricket because I'm not the type of player who can slog in the lower middle order, so I can appreciate that there's a lot of competition for places.

It's just something I'll have to work at because there's a World Cup coming up in England and I want to be in it. While the one-dayers were being played and people were justifiably getting excited about England's performances, I was at Gloucester with Essex where the pitch, for the most part, stopped us playing at all. That was difficult for me. I wanted to be with England and the Gloucester rain just rubbed it in that I wasn't.

Of course, the 3–0 series win was tremendous. For one thing it gave me the chance to wind up Stuart Law but it also got us off to a perfect start in what was always going to be a huge summer. And the selection was spot on. Each choice paid off, notably the arrival in tandem of the Hollioake brothers. Ben's innings in the third match at Lord's was the stuff of dreams and he clearly is a very exciting prospect. I don't know him too well yet, but looking at him play I think his bowling will develop to the point where he could be pretty quick. He can obviously bat too and is a very confident lad, so there's no reason why he shouldn't cement his place in the one-day side in the build up to the World Cup.

Adam, of course, was also spectacularly successful, so did it ever cross my mind that the selectors might get carried away in the euphoria and pick these guys for the first Test? No, not with the current batch of selectors at the helm. They're very clear cut and decisive about what they want and so far they've delivered everything they've promised, so I wasn't concerned that they'd go back on the promise Grav had already given me about Edgbaston.

I was slightly concerned that the press would get carried away and take this as a sign that we've got the measure of the Aussies because one-day cricket is not an accurate guide to the outcome of the Ashes but what the selectors, captain and coach have succeeded in building up is a great atmosphere within the team and that can only be enhanced by the one-dayers. This is the first time that I've ever thought of myself as being a member of two teams. When I leave Essex now I'm going to play for my other team – England. Before, when you arrived for a Test, you almost had to introduce yourself to the players you didn't know too well, and almost felt that you had to prove yourself to your team-mates. It was almost something of a relief to get back among your friends at your county after a Test but that's not the case now. Of course, we have to keep on performing to earn this continuity and I know, for instance, that Bumble is very keen for everyone to be pushed hard for their place. But if we keep playing well we know they'll keep on picking us and I, for one, feel secure about that.

I knew my Test place was never in doubt so it was just a case of being mentally right on the first morning of the first Test. That can be difficult if you haven't got many big scores or haven't seen much of the opposition bowlers and the opening matches of the season with Essex weren't fantastic for me. We'd played on some spicy wickets and I hadn't had that many innings so I was hardly ecstatic about my form, but I felt fairly happy with the way I was hitting the ball. The fact, however, that 67 was my top score for the season before Edgbaston did concern me enough to have a chat with Fletch about the way things were going. I'd worked very hard with Goochie, who was a tremendous help with my technique, but I wasn't kicking on to centuries and I could see Stuey Law getting big scores on the same pitches as I was playing on, so I asked Fletch for his advice. As ever it was spot on.

He told me that I was right to work on my technique but that I should never forget that I'm a natural player. He said, 'Yes, you do hit the ball with a bit of an open face and, yes, you do hit the ball a bit inside out but you're not going to become a different player now. Just remember that your style is your strength.' It was timely advice because I'd perhaps been worrying a little too much about my technique in the early county matches but Fletch encouraged me to still hit the bad balls in the way I've always hit them because that's how I get my runs. Ronnie Irani was good about this too, telling me that I should never forget that I'm a flair player and that, coming from a team-mate, helped my confidence. Meanwhile, the big day was approaching.

2
PRELUDE TO AN ASHES SUMMER

STEVE WAUGH

10 May 1997, Sydney to London

Even after 12 years on the international cricket merry-go-round, encompassing countless overseas tours, I remain something of a novice when it comes to packing bags with any sort of authority. A final 30 minutes of mayhem invariably sees me scavenging through my compact discs to try to narrow the field down to my favourite 20 or so, followed by a double, and then triple-check on my cricket kit to make sure all the essentials are safely tucked away in my monstrously-proportioned, 'Coke'-emblazoned cricket coffin. Then there's the mad scramble to locate that always-elusive passport. And then there's a final scout around, which more often than not leads me to my toiletry bag, standing there all alone like a scorned child in the corner of the room, begging for a berth on the upcoming tour.

These final moments at home are always emotional ones. Hurried goodbyes to family are not exactly the way you want to part company, but life as a modern-day cricket professional is full of them. For me, each tour becomes a little more difficult, particularly as I am now the father of a nine-and-a-half-month-old daughter, Rosalie, who I miss desperately on each and every day I'm not with her. And, like me, my wife, Lynette, is no better at saying goodbye than when I first toured for Australia back in early 1986 (to New Zealand) and the tears still flow when it's time to head off.

Lynette doesn't come to the airport any more, where we don't get any sort of privacy, particularly with camera lenses everywhere sweating on players showing any affection to their loved ones. As well, there are countless interviews wanted and needed by the television and radio stations and a stream of autograph hunters desperate for a scribble on any piece of paper they can lay their hands on. This is a far from ideal environment to bid a proper farewell, especially for a tour that lasts longer than the usual winter season.

At the airport, I found the boys in a jovial mood, although the fun was tinged with a touch of apprehension and a dash of excitement. This, after all, is the ultimate tour, the pinnacle for any Australian cricket player – an Ashes tour. The group that assembled in front of the Cathay Pacific business-class check-in is the

33rd Australian touring party to the UK, and as such has a chance to enhance the legend of the lads in the baggy green caps. It is a huge honour to have this opportunity and I quickly realised that everyone on board appreciated this fact.

It was great to catch up with the lads once more. It almost feels as if the family is back together again. For some, this is a new test of their characters – Justin Langer, for example, is leaving his six-week-old daughter, Jessica, for the first time. Knowing how proud and doting he is of her, the initial week or two away will be torture for him. But Shane Warne has probably the most difficult situation to leave behind, as his wife Simone is only six weeks away from delivering their first child. Not long after we got through customs, he mumbled to me, 'Leaving this time was the hardest thing I've ever had to do.'

For Michael Bevan and Andy Bichel, this tour will be a new experience – they're travelling as married men. They have been sampling married life for just 13 and 14 days respectively. But, as we all know, we are also married to our profession and 'give and take' is essential for both marriages to prosper.

Marriage is not the only thing new to our squad; appearances have also changed. Fast man Jason Gillespie has returned to his 'Australia's Most Wanted' look, with the goatee making a reappearance, while Michael Slater has gone for a 'George Clooney' haircut. Slats has also added a couple of fashionable highlights that he thought wouldn't be discovered by the boys – how wrong he was! Brendon Julian's new short back and sides has given him an angelic choirboy look. And coach Geoff 'Swampy' Marsh has continued his remarkable weight loss campaign, which began during the just gone Australian season when a caring spectator asked, 'Hey, Marsh, have you swallowed a sheep?'

Without doubt, though, the biggest news of all came from Glenn McGrath, who informed the troops that he is now the proud owner of 34,000 acres (Pigeon said 'acres', not 'hectares') of terra firma, located about 100 kilometres north of Bourke, just short of the Queensland border. This, apparently, is a mere 1000km from Sydney. Being a country boy, originally from Narromine, his love of the bush will only be enhanced every time he wanders till his heart's content. It is vitally important to get away from cricket during your time off, to clear your head and get back to reality. I find that it makes you refreshed and ready for the next challenge, and it also helps to put everything in perspective.

Pigeon has already asked Swampy whether or not we can have our pre-season camps out on his new property. However, this idea doesn't sit too well for the city boys – our 'living off the land' skills are about as good as Pigeon's cover drive.

In all, the squad has 79 pieces of luggage to be checked in and out throughout the tour. Plus there are our carry-on-board items, which all adds up to a major operation every time we move to a different venue. As for the flight to Hong Kong? The days of drinking and rowdiness on plane trips are long gone, so the journey was a tame affair. The only incident was Jason Gillespie's not insignificant nose bleed due to the change in air pressure, which needed a napkin as well as tissues to stem the flow.

12 May, London

I felt like a rookie on my first overseas trip when we touched down at Heathrow, at 6.05am. Such is my excitement at being back for my third Ashes campaign. I must admit, the boys looked remarkably smart in their new dress suits, so distinct from the usual pin-striped blazers, as we made our way through customs accompanied by the ever eager press photographers. All were desperate for a shot of Warney, who remains big news over here. I'm sure his every move will be monitored during the next four months, to the point that if he wants any privacy, he'll have to become a virtual prisoner in his own hotel.

It is good to be back at the Westbury Hotel, our home away from home for all of my Ashes tours. Just being here makes things that bit more stable for us. We know we can trust the staff and the management know what our requirements are.

Our first official duty was the traditional media conference, scheduled for 10am in front of every cricket-related journalist, presenter and commentator in the land. Each team member had been prepared for the obvious questions, thanks to a two-hour media training session in Sydney before we left. Issues such as the captaincy and vice-captaincy controversies were bound to crop up, so Mark 'Tubs' Taylor and I had worked out our replies in order to prevent unwanted or unwarranted headlines. Surprisingly though, the normally voracious appetites of the notorious Fleet Street tabloid journalists for ineffective answers to provocative questions weren't evident. The whole affair ran smoothly, partly perhaps due to the presence of Michael Parkinson, who handled proceedings. And he was clearly expecting the worst – when he declared question time was open, he remarked, 'Okay, let the bun fight begin.'

The rest of the morning was spent shopping around London and getting our bearings. This was important, as we will be spending a fair proportion of our tour here and it's vital to know where all the good pubs are and, of course, where all the 'golden arches' are as well.

We knew, though, that it wouldn't be long before Steve Smith, our fitness guru, inflicted some anguish upon us. This afternoon we found ourselves sweating it out on the treadmills and bikes, barely a couple of hours after unpacking our suitcases. For me, the scariest thing was that I almost enjoyed the exercise, while the swim and spa definitely made me feel a tad rejuvenated. Mind you, there was no way I was going to let the human equivalent of an energiser battery know any of this!

This being our first night together in London, we all headed off for a feed at a favourite hang-out of previous tours – a Mexican restaurant called 'Break for the Border'. But what had initially sounded like a good idea turned out to be a somewhat foolish one. Jet lag was beginning to set in, and we all struggled to get through the meal without falling asleep at the table.

13 May, London

I knew I didn't feel that flash when I woke from a restless night's sleep. The answer was simple. I squinted at my bedside timepiece, which read 5.36am. Unfortunately, there was to be no more shut-eye, as my body insisted it was a reasonable hour back in Australia and, as such, my day had begun. I resigned myself to the fact I couldn't win the battle. Anyway, there wasn't much point considering fitness session No. 2 was scheduled for 7.30am. The routine this morning consisted of a 15-minute walk to Hyde Park, followed by a one-minute run, one-minute brisk walk, 10 push-ups, 10 sit-ups, each repeated eight times over.

A spot of breakfast was sneaked in before we headed off for our first training session at Lord's (a place that was totally foreign only to Jason Gillespie among our squad). It's always special to get back there and Geoff Marsh summed it up perfectly when he mentioned to me, 'I'm more excited to be here as a coach than when I actually played here.'

Training was low key, the idea was to get all the travel stiffness out and develop a feel for the tour and what lies ahead. These early sessions do have special significance for Tubs Taylor, though, as he has virtually told everyone that he has a month to get his batting right or else he'll drop himself. In this event, of course, I'd take over the No. 1 job.

That scenario is something I haven't given much thought to, which I'm sure many would find hard to believe. One thing I have learnt from playing at this level is that you can't think too far ahead. Nothing is ever guaranteed, so it's always best to play for the moment and not the future. Sure, I would love the top job, but I also hate seeing fellow players performing poorly, as I know how much playing and succeeding at this level means to them and what they've had to sacrifice to reach this level. And Mark Taylor has been not only a team-mate of mine for over 15 years, but a very good friend, too.

The way I hit the ball in my net session was a genuine surprise, considering that I hadn't picked up a bat in three weeks. Most balls found the middle in a morale-boosting session for me, but others were not so fortunate, especially Bevo, who turned in perhaps his worst net session ever. Not that this means anything, because the first week of a tour such as this is basically a period where you need time to adjust to the different conditions. But if, after a week or two, you're still struggling … then you have to take notice and rectify things. One slight downer for me came afterwards – Smithy must have noticed the extra girth on my waistline after the three weeks I've just spent in the tuckshop and ordered me to undergo another visit to the gym for 25 minutes of bike work and a spot of swimming.

Tonight's team meeting provided an opportunity for the ground rules for the entire tour to be laid down, and for us to briefly discuss and clarify our team goals for the Test series. Everyone is in great spirits, particularly after this afternoon's individual meetings between players and the captain and coach, which from all accounts went exceptionally well. I believe this is potentially a great squad, not just because of the talent available but, more importantly, because all these guys are great blokes. I believe we can create a team spirit that will see us virtually unbeatable over here. Interestingly, today's press comments have been almost gushing in their praise for us. This was nice to read, though I couldn't help thinking that they are building us up, but hoping and praying they will get the opportunity to tear us apart at some stage in the near future.

The day's formalities weren't over just yet, as the tour sponsor, Coke, were hosting a function for us at the very hip 'Cafe de Paris' restaurant-nightclub in the centre of London. In booking this venue I'm sure the Coke management had more than admirable intentions, but the meal of Spartan proportions, backed up by unknown sauces and extravagant concoctions was not what the boys fancied. My fellow diner, Jason Gillespie, was mortified by the entree of raw tuna in a pepper-based sauce, and refused to even acknowledge its presence on the table. The side salad of 'Lord's grass clippings' and Parmesan cheese received a token stab of the fork before Dizzy dismissed it as being 'absolute crap'. Happily, the situation was somewhat saved by the main-course – fillet steak – although the quantity wasn't what us Aussies are used to. But it did satisfy the taste buds and that, on the night, was a first for most of us.

14 May, London

Times have certainly changed since I began my international career back in 1985. This is typified by the fitness regimes that are now in place. There once was a time when all the players would be curled up in their sheets, dreaming of a nice English breakfast to start off their day, but not any more. Instead, we found ourselves in the foyer of the Westbury Hotel at 7.30am, marshalled together in preparation for a team workout involving running, walking, sit-ups and push-ups.

The greatest benefit from this exercise was just being out in the fresh air and open spaces of Hyde Park instead of the stale recycled air of our hotel rooms. Not everything has changed during my career though, I thought, as I tucked into the bacon and eggs on offer at the breakfast buffet. But then I noticed that most of the younger brigade were settling for muesli and a selection of fruits.

Training was once again on the 'hallowed turf' of Lord's, with all the boys trying to step it up a cog or two. I was disappointed with my own form today, and in particular my lack of concentration and application during my net session. I vowed to myself it wouldn't happen again, bad habits are like a cancer that can spread quickly and affect your whole game before you can get it under control. On a positive note, Mike Kasprowicz bowled with excellent rhythm and movement in an impressive spell that augers well for his tour prospects.

Smithy continues to hammer me about my midriff, and demanded another extra session this afternoon – 25 minutes on the stationary bikes, followed by a swim and (thankfully) a spa to round off the occasion. When these tasks had been completed it was time to start preparing for tonight's MCC dinner, held in our honour at Lord's – a thought that didn't exactly have us all eager with anticipation. Most of the lads find these dinners hard work, as we are split up, one to a table, and required to entertain a circle of up to a dozen guests. The gents at tonight's function are a part of the elitist Lord's membership, a club limited to males and with an average age on the wrong side of 55. Consequently, you feel like a school kid in their presence.

I was lucky to have a 'modern thinking' group who were quite entertaining. But the downside came after my nearest companions had extracted enough information about topics ranging from our tour prospects to the England side's make-up; they departed to be replaced by a new group who fired exactly the same queries at me. After three hours I was a shell of a man.

Some of the other lads copped a bit of a blast. Take Andy Bichel, whose table partners suggested, 'You Aussies take this sledging to a new level, you do it far too often.' Bic, of course, came back strongly on our behalf, but it was to no avail. 'It's always in the papers,' he was told, 'so it must be true!' This is always a topic that brings heated debate, and it's hard to break the stereotype that allegedly began back in the Chappell era. To be honest, I always find it amusing that people reckon we need to resort to these tactics. In my experience, sledging is born of desperation and we certainly haven't experienced too much of that sensation in recent times.

But the night was far from awful. Mark Taylor certainly won over the members with his tribute to the great Denis Compton, while our manager, Alan Crompton, gave a detailed account of the great significance of the Ashes in a speech that was probably one of his life's highlights. Crommo enjoys a genuine love affair with this game. The chairman of the recently-formed ECB (the England and Wales Cricket Board), Lord MacLaurin, then gave an insight into the future of English cricket in an eloquent and sometimes eye-opening address, before the audience got down to some serious cigar smoking.

3

'THE TOUR STARTS HERE'

STEVE WAUGH

15 May, Arundel

Australia 235–5 (Slater 50*, M Waugh 46, Taylor 45) defeated the Duke of Norfolk's XI 122 (Gillespie 4–21) by 113 runs.

The tour's opening fixture had us pitted against the Duke of Norfolk's XI at the majestically impressive ground located next to Arundel Castle. The only downside was the two-and-a-half-hour bus trip to get there, much of it on long winding roads that had our bus swaggering along like a drunk in the night.

Even at this early stage of the tour the guys have all laid claim to certain seats on the bus, with the front stalls being occupied by team management. Behind them is the '500' card school of Taylor, Warne, Bevan and Elliott, who are seated opposite Langer, Julian and S Waugh. The remainder of the team are up the back of the bus, separated from the front by a fridge and a microwave. A toilet is down the back. The bus also has three televisions, which come in very handy on the long hauls, especially for those who aren't keen book readers or card sharks.

An Ashes tour always ignites British spectators' interest in the game, and this was quite evident by the mid-week crowd of over 10,000 that eagerly packed the Arundel ground to catch a first glimpse of the touring Aussies. Michael Slater's impressive unbeaten half-century at the death of our innings signalled not only that he was 'back' but, more significantly, helped exorcise some personal demons that can prey on players who have to come back from being dropped.

Ominously for England, Dizzy Gillespie claimed a wicket with his first delivery on British soil when he ripped out the off stump of a disbelieving county professional. Many more, I'm sure, will suffer the same fate, as this guy is something special. In fact, Glenn McGrath and Dizzy may even form one of the great opening bowling combinations.

Significant contributions also came from Mark Taylor, who showed glimpses of a return to form, and Mike Kasprowicz ('Kasper'), who bowled impressively. My innings was brief, but the 27 runs I scored were made with some authority and I was pleased with my efforts.

16 May, Northampton

The vice-captaincy is a huge honour for me. And with it comes a single room as a little perk on the side. However, with this extra privacy comes more time for contemplation and I am already finding I regularly flick through photo albums, and think of home and, in particular, my wife and daughter. There have been many times over the past few months, and especially in the past few days, when I've wondered whether it is really worth it all, whether being away from home so much and missing seeing my little girl learn new things is the right way of life. But I guess you can't have it all. I am doing something I love and the thing I do best ... and getting well paid for it.

On a positive note, when I do get home we inevitably spend a lot of full days together. For us this is quality time, and an opportunity that not many families get.

Back to the real world meant preparing for the first One-day International, which is less than a week away. Practice today was more like it – I was more switched on and came away from the net session feeling in control of my game. However, with this confidence boost came the disappointment of breaking my favourite bat. This bat was the one that scored 160 in the recent first Test against South Africa, in Johannesburg, so it was special to me. But all is not lost, as it will make the journey back to Australia and end up living in my memorabilia room at home.

A testimonial soccer match for the benefit of the former Coventry City defender, David Busst, was being played only 30 minutes away from our shack for the night (the salubrious Swallow Hotel). Busst had suffered a horrific double compound fracture of his lower leg while playing for Coventry against Manchester United eighteen months earlier. In fact, so grotesque was this injury that players from both sides needed counselling to overcome the nightmares, while Busst has, to date, had to endure fifteen operations just to enable him to walk again.

On a typical misty, icy cold evening, a packed crowd at Coventry's home ground, Highfield Road, saw the great Eric Cantona for Manchester United and Glasgow Rangers' Paul Gascoigne, as a guest for Coventry, exhibit their freakish talents. Their displays left us (Taylor, Julian, Langer, Gilchrist and S Waugh) feeling privileged just to be in the same stadium. There is something special about seeing geniuses in action, such as a Maradona, a Viv Richards or a Shane Warne. Invariably a hush comes over the crowd, with everyone anticipating a moment of greatness and no-one wanting to miss it, otherwise it will be lost forever.

Tubby safely navigated the boys home in pouring rain, as we continued to talk of the magic we had just witnessed. And as the windscreen wipers stayed at full speed, it became more and more apparent that a day off tomorrow is a distinct possibility.

17 May, Northampton

Australia 232 (Taylor 76) defeated Northamptonshire 134–5 (after 35 overs; Loye 65*) on a faster scoring rate.

Once again, I wasn't woken by the booked wake-up call but because my body thermostat had overheated due to the absence of air conditioning (instead, stifling hot air is continually being pumped out, to please the locals who seem to appreciate the extra warmth).

Outside, though, the temperature did look on the coolish side. A thick mist made it impossible for the sun's rays to penetrate – the type of day an Australian cricketer dreads. And I couldn't help but notice the abundance of rabbits darting about in the adjoining grassland.

Being one of the reserves for today's fixture meant that I, along with Blewey, Heals, Pigeon and Bic, had to make good use of the facilities available to keep us in good shape for the games ahead. So, while the playing team did their usual 20 to 30 minutes of stretching and warm-ups, we hit the nets. The practice wickets were excellent and the time spent on them was invaluable, particularly for we batsman who like to feel the bat on ball in a match-like situation, which can only occur when good true practice wickets allow it.

Years ago, the reserves would have put their feet up and completed no more than routine tasks, such as organising drinks, making sure the autograph bats were signed and generally just checking to see that the guys on the field were happy and ready to play at their best.

The reality of today, though, is that you must do extra work – whether it be in the gym, on the running track, a brisk walk or even some boxing or swimming. If you've completed these tasks you might be asked to go to a sponsor's box, to talk to some valuable clients, or perhaps do a spot of commentary for the television stations covering the game. I managed all three tasks today and have now come to the conclusion I'd much rather be out on the field playing than 'watching'.

The ominous looking weather finally did what it had threatened to do all day, and the game ended prematurely. On the day, though, the better side gained the win, which doesn't always happen in these situations.

One couldn't say we were convincing winners and, to be truthful, we made a lot of basic mistakes, including bad calling between the wickets and some sloppy fielding. Good performances were turned in on the batting front by Gillespie, Slater, and Waugh junior, but the most significant was from Mark Taylor, who occupied the crease for 126 balls in scoring his 76. Statistically, this might be classed as a bit laborious, but it was compiled on a testing wicket. Tubs held the innings together, which was invaluable from our team point of view. When you are out of form there is only one way back and that is by occupying the crease until your feet movement, shot selection and timing gradually come back to you. Judging from today's efforts, our captain is returning to form.

Encouraging signs in the bowling department came from Brendon Julian, whose rhythm looks great at present, and Warney, whose tempo and control of delivery appear to be nearing the heights of twelve months ago.

Thankfully, our next destination of Worcester was only one hour away, but it did require a pit stop for food. 'Huey', our bus driver, pulled off the motorway and then gave us the bum steer of the year when he cheerfully told us, 'This place sells good food.' That may well be the case if you're looking to add a couple of thousand calories in one sitting, but *that* I do not need to do!

18 May, Worcester

Worcestershire 123–5 defeated Australia 121 (Haynes 4–40, Leatherdale 5–10) by five wickets.

It's always good to see a fellow Aussie professional cricketer over here and none is more popular than today's opposition captain, Tom Moody, a man who only a few months back was in national colours, playing in the Australian one-day team during the 1996–97 World Series.

Everything about today's game was typically English – from the cathedrals in the distance to the lush outfield, the manual scoreboard, the overcast dull conditions, the chicken curry at lunch and, devastatingly for us, Worcestershire's little 'dinky' medium-pace bowlers who combined to make us look like schoolboy novices.

Arguably the Australian team's biggest weakness in recent years has been our inability to adapt to variances in wickets that we're not used to. This was our nemesis here, as not even one of us came to terms with a seaming wicket against bowlers who on flat wickets would be classed as 'cannon fodder'. Today they were world beaters, or made to look so, due to some lazy and ill-advised strokeplay.

Only Justin Langer had any sort of excuse, for he was 'triggered' (as in, robbed by umpire). These types of decisions seem to follow some players around. It appears commonplace for a player of high standing to be given the benefit of the doubt while players who are trying to make names for themselves are given the rough deal. This is certainly a testing time for 'Lang', who is away from his newborn child and, after many overseas tours, still trying to force his way into the first XI. Mental strength will be needed for him to succeed on this tour.

We managed only 121, and the depth of our plight was highlighted by the knowledge that the destroyer for Worcestershire, David Leatherdale, wouldn't normally get a bowl in a Chinese restaurant. However, owing to injuries, he got a chance and tomorrow morning will be able to start filling up his scrapbooks with the newspaper reports of his miraculous deeds.

The news wasn't all bad, though. Kasper bowled beautifully, gaining regular movement in the air in much the same way Terry Alderman did in 1989, and we all know what Alderman accomplished with these attributes.

Big 'Moods', though, was the hero of the day and the town, leading from the front in compiling 32 and marshalling his troops for a famous victory. From the way the crowd was going off at the finish, you would have thought the Poms had won the Ashes, but when you've been starved of success it does make victory much sweeter when it happens. Hunger is something that will definitely motivate the England side this summer and could well be a crucial element in the overall outcome of the series. For the team that is the most desperate usually wins.

The English squad was announced today. It appears the selectors have changed their priorities and finally plumped for youth. The choice of Surrey's Ben Hollioake in the squad, at just 19 years of age, after only half a dozen first-class games, is a watershed selection and signals that talent will be recognised and appreciated much earlier by the three 'Gs' (the new English selection committee of Mike Gatting, Graham Gooch and chairman David Graveney). Their squad is full of players I've never come across – Dean Headley, Ashley Giles, Graham Lloyd, Adam and Ben Hollioake, Mark Ealham and Chris Silverwood. This probably gives the home team a slight advantage, as we don't know many of their players' strengths and weaknesses while our game is well known to them.

The full England squad is: Atherton (captain), Crawley, Croft, DeFreitas, Ealham, Giles, Gough, Headley, A Hollioake, B Hollioake, Knight, G Lloyd, Silverwood, Stewart and Thorpe.

After a week of full-on cricket and commitments it was time to let the hair down a bit. We began tonight's proceedings with a team feed at an Italian restaurant, followed by a thirst quencher or two at a local establishment. It was there that I made my thoughts clear to Malcolm Conn, the journalist who is covering the tour for *The Australian*, who wrote only a couple of days ago that this series was no longer the ultimate for an Aussie cricketer and that we were putting on a facade to try to enhance this 'myth'. How wrong he is. This is still the ultimate tour, steeped in history and tradition. It will always be special.

19 May, Durham

Our first task for the day was not to pay our room bill or to indulge in a spot of breakfast, but to sign 300 cricket bats for the Test series sponsors. I can assure you there is a distinct difference between the first signature and the 300th scribble. In fact, some players had resorted to initials only as they neared completion.

Our trip to the next port of call, Durham, in the north-east of England, presented us with the longest leg of our adventure so far – four hours from Worcester. Lang, as he always does, looked after the team and purchased a handful of videos that served as a saviour once boredom set in (about 20 minutes into a trip). Meanwhile, the quartet of Elliott, Bevan, Taylor and Warne had just about reached the stage where they would have been eyeing a spot in the *Guinness Book of Records* – for continuous card playing. I can't recall a solitary moment of road travel that hasn't involved a hand or three. It was with some relief that we finally reached our destination, and once we had checked into our rooms, the lads all headed off in various directions for some R&R. Some took to the local golf course, which I viewed as a brave option considering the obscenely cold temperatures, while others went walkabout down the cobblestone streets in search of a bargain or two. The toughest ventured to the gym for a workout with Steve Smith, who was going cold turkey after not pumping iron or wearing out a treadmill for the previous couple of hours. My task, along with Swampy and Tubs, was to pick the side for the first One-day International and to have a chat about our initial thoughts on the Test team line-up.

After lengthy deliberations on various options we eventually settled on a combination for the first one-dayer which I'm sure (as always) will leave at least some of the omitted players disappointed. We'll be keeping our decisions to ourselves until after our one-dayer with Durham tomorrow, in case someone puts up a big case for selection against David Boon's new side.

My situation as a selector is a little awkward, as Tubby's ordinary form over the past two years is a topic that just won't go away and one that must be discussed. As a good friend for over 15 years, I'm not comfortable with the fact that I may be the one to end his run in the team, as I will have the deciding vote if Tubs and Swampy don't agree on the right thing to do.

I really can't see how the team will benefit if, for instance, I leave Tubs out of the one-day side. Then, two weeks later, Tubs will be captain again for the Tests and I will be his vice-captain. This, to me, is not an ideal working environment, as we are in positions where we have to not only trust each other, but also work closely and give each other support.

In my opinion, the selectors back home should be making these hard decisions. My great hope is that Tubs makes some runs and finally squashes all the repetitive talk about his form. The constant speculation is starting to damage the morale and spirit of the side, simply because the issue is one that nobody is able to dodge.

The bottom line is that we would all like to see Tubs play every one-dayer and Test – he's the tour captain and should lead the team.

There are always two sides to any argument. In this case, we have the world's best Test-match captain, who also possesses an outstanding personal record which includes 14 Test centuries. On the other hand, Tubs hasn't reached 50 in his last 20 Test innings. I know quite a few journalists think he shouldn't be playing Test cricket. The dilemma is not an easy one to solve. Realistically, Tubs is the only one who can do it – by scoring plenty of runs. I hope he does.

Warney's tally of Margherita pizzas is mounting by the day, with another two added with ease tonight. Afterwards, it was great to catch up with David and Pip Boon for a quick drink in the bar. After his early-season efforts with the County Championship newcomers, Durham, Boonie has already been labelled a legend in these parts. Apparently, he has already added some toughness and professionalism to the squad. In due course, I'm sure, he will also enlighten them on the merits of fine Australian red wine.

20 May, Chester-le-Street

Australians v Durham, match abandoned.

As soon as we arrived at Durham's home ground, the impressive Riverside complex at Chester-le-Street, we knew that there would be no play today, despite the best efforts of the water guzzling 'super sopa' that was busily trying to devour the pools of water that lay all over the outfield.

For Durham, this was to be a day of celebration, with the revered soccer great, Kevin Keegan, due to officially open a new section of grandstand, while the local team would have obviously benefited from the experience gained in such a fixture. From our point of view, quite a few players needed a run to gather some momentum and form. But it was not to be, and the game was officially cancelled even before the scheduled starting time of 10.45am, much to the disbelief of the considerable crowd that had gathered.

It's quite amazing, though, what a few autographs can do to appease a crowd and one sensed that they were now all going home quite satisfied with the day's entertainment. I also felt I had achieved something out of the morning, after I confronted a well-respected journalist and former player, Simon Hughes, about a recent column he wrote, which I believed was out of line. In this article, he gave all the Australian team ratings for 'Style', 'Sledging' and 'Stamina'. It just so happened that I was labelled as not entertaining, a major sledger and not fit, leaving me as the only member to fail in all three categories. Initially, I saw the humorous side to this tongue-in-cheek piece, which, of course, duly found its way into all the Australian papers. I did take exception, though, to the non-entertaining tag and told him so when I spotted him at the ground. Looking very sheepish, he began to try to justify his ratings before changing tack and agreeing he was wrong. He ended up preferring to point the finger at the editor who had told him to spice the articles up a bit. I was glad that I had made my point and he seemed relieved to get his grievances off his chest. The end result, a form of truce if you like, was that I am now the proud owner of a signed copy of his just-released book, *A Lot of Hard Yakka*.

Confronting a journalist can be a hazardous exercise – generally there can only be one winner and that's the person with the pen in their hand. But sometimes I reckon it can be justified. These occasions are when the comments are not backed up by fact, or when the criticism is not constructive, but even then a player rarely comes out on top. As a rule, it is better to remember that one day the story will be wrapped around some fish and chips, while you'll still be out there batting on.

Upon our arrival in Leeds, we were greeted by sunshine overhead, so we immediately dumped our gear at the hotel and headed for the nets at Headingley. It's always nice to return to a ground where you have experienced success; it was here that I scored my first Test century, in 1989, and again reached three figures in 1993. So I made a beeline for the same position in the dressing-room I occupied for those two matches, to make me feel even more comfortable and confident.

Training today was excellent, with everyone realising it was time to up the ante and start switching on. This was best exemplified by Pigeon, who had easily his best-ever net session with the blade, keeping the lengthy queue of bowlers that always seems to congregate in his vicinity wicketless for the first time in his entire career.

Tonight's confirmation of the team for the game in two days' time wasn't easy, reflecting the difficulties we faced when we first discussed the side in detail back in Durham. Very few of us are able to say we are in good form, and some are carrying a variety of ailments.

On the batting front, only Taylor and Slater have any runs on tour to speak of, so both became easy selections. On the bowling side of things, Mike Kasprowicz has been the stand out so far, and he gained the third bowling position, just ahead of Brendon Julian, who has also been quite impressive but is carrying a niggling neck problem. Kasper, a laid-back gentle giant, has benefited from the enforced layoff imposed on Andy Bichel due to a back injury. Many say this is fair recompense for events at Bic's recent wedding, where Kasper performed the best man's duties with distinction.

Greg Blewett just made the team despite a dodgy knee, while Michael Bevan hasn't bowled yet due to a cortisone injection he had in his groin before he came on tour. Consequently, we might have left ourselves a little exposed in the fifth bowler department and slightly underdone in our preparations, yet at least on paper we'll start as favourites. The full Australian team is: Taylor (captain), S Waugh (vice-captain, batting No 3), M Waugh, Bevan, Blewett, Slater, Healy, Warne, Kasprowicz, Gillespie and McGrath.

It was off to the cinemas tonight for the boys to watch the cult hero of the team, Jim Carrey, starring in his new flick *Liar Liar*. He has been a favourite of ours since we watched *Ace Ventura* and *Dumb and Dumber* endlessly during our recent trips to the Indian subcontinent. Glenn McGrath reckons the Waugh boys are Dumb and Dumber, but I believe if they are looking to make a sequel they should base the story on Pigeon and Dizzy.

Well, on second thoughts, perhaps not Dizzy!

4
TEXACO TROPHY
ONE-DAY
INTERNATIONALS

STEVE WAUGH

21 May, Leeds

The famous sports bookmakers, Ladbrokes, this morning offered the most generous odds ever posted on a sporting event when they quoted 'M Walsh' at 5–1 to score the most runs for Australia tomorrow in the first One-day International of the summer. Being the official Australian tour scorer, Mike Walsh is bound to score the most runs and all from the comfort of the scoreboard. But before anyone could cash in on this scam it was revealed to be a printing error – 'M Waugh' at 5–1 is correct. Still, not a bad bet.

This morning's practice session was conducted in moustache-snapping conditions that sent a burning sensation through our lungs with each intake of air. Each breath out was accompanied with a puff of mist, as we struggled in vain to get the circulation moving. Even Tattoo's warm-up routine didn't get the usual moans and heckles. It was so cold that we were revelling in his guidance and grateful for his input – maybe the cold had begun to affect our judgment.

My pre-game routine was pretty much as usual – a reasonable haircut (£12) and a massage (£25) to get me relaxed and feeling fresh for tomorrow. Blewey, though, wasn't so lucky in his search for a decent cut. In fact, he suffered the double blow of handing over £35 and then having to wear a style not unlike the one he had for his first day at school. Needless to say he copped a pasting from the lads all night, many of whom broke out into spontaneous laughter each time his new spiked crew cut came into view.

Generally, before a game the team dines together, just to get that bit closer and tighter as well as to enjoy each other's company. Would you believe it, tonight our chosen restaurant was also frequented by Messrs Atherton, Gough and Croft from the England side, who looked more than a little outnumbered by the 20 or so in our party. As luck would have it, we were seated right next door to them.

22 May, First One-day International, Headingley, Leeds

England 175–4 (Thorpe 75*, A Hollioake 66*; McGrath 2–34) defeated Australia 170–8 (Bevan 30, Blewett 28; Gough 2–33, Ealham 2–21, A Hollioake 2–22) by six wickets, with 9.5 overs to spare.

Breakfast on match days for me is generally a couple of juices, toast, tea, eggs (either scrambled or fried), tomatoes and baked beans – more than enough to see me through to lunch time in the game. As usual, the last of the tea had to be rushed down, as the bus was waiting …

Not unexpectedly, there were extensive queues already forming outside the ground by the time our coach pulled up at Headingley's gates nearly two hours before the scheduled starting time. That time went like a rocket – it was good to be back playing top-level cricket – and after Mark Taylor called incorrectly, we found ourselves getting first opportunity to put a few runs on the board.

Our batting performance was indicative of our preparation, with each player struggling to come to terms with the slow seaming pitch. My innings, despite the nature of the wicket, strangely felt like the first of the season, with the ball hitting the bat quicker than I expected. This was due to a couple of reasons – one being the pace of Darren Gough, which was much quicker than anything we'd come across on tour so far; the other was the grey sky and dark dreary colours the crowd were wearing. It all seemed to form a blurry picture. And just when I felt as if I was gaining some momentum and confidence, I played across the line of an outswinger from Mark Ealham.

It was much the same for all the batsmen. The statistics told the story – our top scorer was Michael Bevan with 30 as we stuttered to our final total, which was 50 runs short of what we had hoped for at the start of the day. For England, Gough and Robert Croft both impressed. It is already quite obvious that this whole summer is going to be much harder than many English critics would have led the public to believe.

With one-day cricket anything is possible and it appeared, especially when we reduced England to 40 for four, that we might pull off a memorable victory. It was then that Adam Hollioake, a guy who learnt most of his cricket in Oz, strode to the wicket to partner the gifted Graham Thorpe. If there's one thing that gets an Australian side fired up more than a Pommie walking to the wicket, it's an ex-Aussie in Pommie colours walking to the wicket, but on this occasion his desire, application and determination proved too much for our attack. In a *Boys Own Annual* finish he dispatched Gillespie for a pulled six to win the match, before swiping the three stumps for souvenirs and careering into the ecstatic swarming crowd as he ran from the ground. To make it even sweeter, unbeknown to him or his brother Ben (who was left out of the England XI), his mum and dad had flown over from Perth to see the game. One can only imagine how proud they must have felt.

Adam Hollioake was named Man of the Match, but I was even more impressed by the composure and self-assurance of Thorpe, a guy who has always had immense natural talent without ever quite supporting these gifts with runs on the board. Hopefully this won't be his summer!

It's always at least a little disheartening to lose when playing for your country, but there is more than enough experience in our squad for us to get too down about it. Rather, we have to work on improving our game quickly, so we can fight back in the next two one-dayers, to be played in London on the weekend. To this end, we decided to make the four-hour journey back to the capital straightaway.

We're still all in good spirits.

23 May, London

Twenty-four hours can sometimes put a better perspective on things. I now realise that England held a slight advantage over us going into the first one-dayer. The fact that we hadn't seen a lot of their players in action, and as such didn't really know their strengths or weaknesses in order to exploit or avoid them, was a bigger plus for the home side than we first thought. Tomorrow we will be better prepared.

The numbers for training today, at The Foster's Oval, were down to 14, with BJ, Bic and Blewey all unable to take part. Blewey's knee flared up yesterday and is of great concern, especially for the moment, as it throws the balance of our one-day side out of kilter. He, along with Bev, has become our fifth 'bowler'.

Once again the practice wickets were painfully slow and once again the press were hounding Mark Taylor about his form. It must be like the film *Groundhog Day* for Tubs at the moment, with the same questions being asked, the same pressures being applied and the lack of privacy continuing on and on. Quite clearly, captaining your country and failing with the bat is not the ideal mix, because you always have to front the press. At the moment, we are trying to unburden him of some of the team's obligations by sharing the media responsibilities.

After training it was time for another selection meeting, with the urgent matter of a replacement for Blewey top of the agenda. And there was the ever-present matter of Tubby's form. It was decided that Adam Gilchrist would be given the nod, replacing Blewett on the back of his encouraging efforts in the one-dayers in South Africa. The remainder of the team has been given the chance to redeem themselves.

The main concern within the team for us at the moment is the constant conjecture and discussions about Tubs's lack of runs in the big matches. I guess it's only human nature, considering it's always in the news, but it has to stop or else we'll self-destruct.

The best way for us to get things back on track is to make the senior players aware of their obligations to the team and make sure they kill off any whingeing and discussions of selections as soon as they hear them. The non-sighting of a member of the Australian selection panel, Steve Bernard, is a little intriguing, as we assumed that he would be around to have a chat and exchange ideas. Steve is following the cricket around and I was told he'd been informed by the chairman of selectors, Trevor Hohns, that he may be needed.

24 May, Second One-day International, The Oval, London

England 253–4 (Atherton 113*, A Hollioake 53*, Stewart 40) defeated Australia 249–6 (Bevan 108*, Gilchrist 53) by six wickets, with 10 balls to spare.

There was no change to Mark Taylor's recent run of bad luck, as the toss once again went England's way and we found ourselves strapping on the pads first for the second time in a row. When the game began, the wheel of fortune continued to plot against us. First to suffer the dread of any batsman – the run out – was our captain, who was stranded after a succession of disjointed calls. Three balls later, the Waugh boys were at it again when Mark hesitated for a split second and subsequently expired at the hands of an unlikely exponent of the art of direct hits … Robert Croft. And there were to be a further two calamities of this nature before the innings was complete!

In between these disasters, Michael Bevan produced another masterpiece of mixed dabs and exquisite flourishes, to score an undefeated hundred, while Adam Gilchrist further enhanced his already impressive reputation by scoring 53 at better than a run a ball in a crucial period of the game.

My innings, again, was terminated just when I felt I was about to let the clutch out and accelerate into third gear. Continuing the driving analogies, my dismissal was like being involved in a pile-up on a motorway, where you try to stop hitting the car in front but you can't. I played a perfectly good defensive shot that decided to spin backwards and clip the top of the off stump. In both situations, you do nothing wrong but have to pay the price.

Our final total of 249 looked impressive enough, but we could tell by the English team's body language that they were happy to restrict us to that score. Taking into account the lightning fast outfield and docile wicket, which was getting better to bat on with each ray of sunshine that beamed down from above, you couldn't really blame them. A total of 280 was what we really had in mind, but in One-day Internationals anything over 230 is usually hard to get – especially so if you lose early wickets, which was obviously the key to our chances.

Strike early we did, but our joy was short-lived as Mike Atherton and Alec Stewart slayed our attack at a rate that easily exceeded what they needed for victory. Once again, things weren't going as we had planned, with run out opportunities and tough catches being missed while the bowlers were unable to obtain a consistent line and length. Consequently, we couldn't exert any sort of pressure. By the 20-overs mark, the game and the series had already begun to drift away from us and we couldn't regain any control. In the end, we had succumbed to a player who had been written off as not good enough for one-dayers at the start of the series (Atherton, who answered his critics with a classy century) and a relative unknown (Adam Hollioake, who plundered another 50 before racing off with even more souvenir stumps).

Today's loss was much harder to swallow than our defeat at Headingley. This was because we didn't compete as strongly as we should have. We didn't have enough fight in us, and that is not the way we normally play. Probably the best thing for us was to be present at the handing over of the Texaco Trophy, in front of a crowd cheering for the English and jeering at us. It hit home that this is not how we want the Test series to turn out.

The first task for Geoff Marsh, Mark Taylor and I was not to conduct a post-mortem of the game, but to pick a side for tomorrow's 'dead rubber' one-dayer at Lord's. Thankfully, Tubs saved a potentially uncomfortable situation by volunteering not to play. This gives Matty Elliott a chance to gain some touch before the Tests, while Justin Langer will come in for Slater, partly because we feel Lang has a chance to bat No. 3 in the first Test. Slats, I'm afraid to say, now has little chance of making the first Test XI.

The unlucky one at this stage of the tour is Ricky Ponting, who hasn't had many opportunities at all. But when the touring party has nine batsmen (including Adam Gilchrist), which is one too many I feel, it makes it impossible to accommodate everyone. Fortunately, Punter is a class act and will get his chance at some stage. And knowing his determination and positive mindset, once he gets it, he'll succeed for sure.

For me, the ultimate honour awaited – a chance to captain Australia at Lord's. As soon as I could I rang home to tell Lynette and, of course, to chat to baby Rosalie. I'm missing them so much and wish they could be here for tomorrow's game.

25 May, Third One-day International, Lord's, London

England 270–4 (Stewart 79, B Hollioake 63, Crawley 52, Thorpe 45*) defeated Australia 269 (M Waugh 95, Gilchrist 33; Gough 5–44, Ealham 2–47) by six wickets, with six balls to spare.

Lord's is definitely the place to play cricket – you'd only have to ask Justin Langer to confirm this. Lang has visited but never played here before and, judging by his enthusiasm in the warm-ups, he was always going to have the time of his life today.

My two-up skills have always been average at best, so it came as no surprise when my call of heads ended up face down against the batsman-friendly-looking strip. Mike Atherton stayed with his winning formula, electing to have a bowl after including young Ben Hollioake (to make his debut) as well as John Crawley and Chris Silverwood. Two of these guys – Hollioake and Silverwood – were unknown quantities to us and as such posed a threat.

Our batting today was another stop-start affair, with runs coming at a quick rate but, significantly, wickets tumbling at regular intervals. Each time we looked to be gaining the ascendancy, courtesy of a decent partnership, we would lose the initiative through a careless shot or lack of attention to detail. The only exceptions were my brother Mark, who was excellent, and Adam Gilchrist. Once again, I failed to capitalise on a promising start, falling victim to every batsman's curse – a premeditated stroke, this time an ill-advised cover drive that was caught quite brilliantly by the hot-and-cold Thorpe.

Our final tally of 269 looked formidable, but in truth we should have made in excess of 300 on what was the ultimate batsman's paradise. And the outfield was so slick that Torvill and Dean would have felt right at home.

Another highlight at Lord's is the lunch. It's little wonder Mike Gatting continues to run around for Middlesex in the County Championship. Each time I play here my admiration for the kitchen staff grows, with today's offering akin to the Last Supper. Dishes ranged from curried prawns and rice to silverside and hot vegetables, to lamb chops and a variety of salads and pastas. Then, to cap it off, fresh fruit salad or apple pie was on offer for those with any room left. I would love to have been one of those who didn't expect to have to perform deeds of speed or endurance after the interval.

Warney obviously didn't share my sentiments about the quality of the fare on offer. At one point, I saw him tucking excitedly into a roll that had brown stuff oozing out the sides. I soon realised he had helped himself to a makeshift sandwich, complete with a thick coating of butter and topped with a mountain of HP sauce.

Back on the field, things looked to be on the up when Michael Kasprowicz accounted for Atherton early on, and after 10 overs we had restricted them to around four runs per over. But then, rather than increasing the pressure on their batsmen, we went to sleep. Consequently, we drifted out of the game in a rather tame and meek manner. I'm not sure why this happened, but all I know is that it has occurred far too often in One-day International cricket during the past 18 months. Answers must be found.

I keep coming back to the fact that we aren't aggressive enough and don't seem to have that edge that all hungry teams have. In the end, we only went down with an over to spare, but in reality we were dead in the water from around the 20-overs mark. What is needed in the future is enthusiasm and a ruthless streak, combined with the belief that we have the talent and the courage to express ourselves without fear of reprisals if we fail to come out on top.

As captain, I had to attend the after-series media conference, which was attended by around 50 journalists. It was like being set upon by a firing squad, with questions coming at me like poison arrows. I think I repelled most of them and even had them thinking when I said, 'We are missing five per cent of an indefinable quality that is at present holding us back.'

At the conclusion of any series it's always good to have a beer and a chat with the opposition, so we headed down to the English rooms for a cold one. It was at this point that we realised how different their situation is to ours. There was no

45

sign of a party. In fact, their whole team were about to head off in their different directions, to prepare for their domestic Benson & Hedges one-day quarter-finals. If it were us, we'd have been merry and looking at a worthwhile celebration. It's imperative that you enjoy your success and let some steam off.

The successes are the times that provide lifelong memories. It's what makes playing so enjoyable. For the life of me I can't understand why they don't realise this. I guess it's their loss. In time I'm sure they'll regret it.

After a defeat it's always easy to mope around and feel sorry for yourself, or lock yourself in your room and get depressed. We decided to take an alternative approach and go out and have a drink together. As luck would have it, we ran into Allan Border, who is over here commentating as well as performing duties as a supporters' tour group leader. He said that, from the sidelines, it looked as if we lacked our normal aggression. If we were to get back on top, AB reckons, we have to revert back to the way things were. I agree.

AB also told us the story that one of his tour party was so disillusioned with our first two losses that he refused to go to Lord's today, as a personal protest against us, even though it was more than likely his lifelong dream to be there. And it had cost him a packet to get to the UK, too. It's more than a game to some people. When you play international cricket you're not only representing yourself, but also millions of supporters. Because of this simple fact, we have a huge obligation to always perform to the best of our ability.

5
BUILDING UP TO THE TESTS
STEVE WAUGH

26 May, Bristol

At a selection meeting this afternoon, Mark Taylor, Geoff Marsh and I had to make a few tough calls so that we can best prepare for the upcoming first Test. We found it nearly impossible to select a starting line-up, especially as the squad has nine specialist batsmen in the ranks. In picking the team for our upcoming match against Gloucestershire we tried to pick as close to what we think will be the first Test team. If we didn't and the next and last match before the Test (against Derbyshire) was washed out, we would go into the Test with one (or maybe more than one) batsman who hadn't played a first-class game on tour. Also of major concern is our mounting injury toll. Andy Bichel remains hampered by a lower back problem, Greg Blewett's knee has flared up again and Brendon Julian's neck ailment won't improve.

Taylor's lack of form was again discussed, although not at length – it isn't a healthy situation to continually put doubts into someone's mind, which is exactly what happens if we go on about it even if that's not our intention. To his credit, Mark has been very upfront with his situation. He has given himself two county games and one Test match to 'do the business', otherwise he will stand down. I really feel for Tubs at the moment, as he must be continually questioning his self-belief and deep down he must be feeling lousy. However, it's amazing what a few runs can do to turn things right around. Whatever happens, he has acted in a humble and noble fashion. And that, in the long run, is perhaps most important of all.

When we finally completed our deliberations, it was the richly-gifted Ponting and Slater who were unlucky. Our selection strategy means that they will probably not get a chance until after the first Test to show what they have to offer. The one thing we all agreed upon was to inform the guys who miss out exactly why they've been left out, and to try to keep a good solid communication set-up in place. We desperately don't want anyone to become disillusioned.

27 May, Bristol

Australia 249 (S Waugh 92, M Waugh 66; J Lewis 4–89) v Gloucestershire.

As the team's No. 5, I'm normally calmly foraging through my belongings, trying to restore some sort of order to my cricket coffin, when our openers face up to that first ball of the day. However, this morning, during the first day of our match against Gloucestershire, I was forced to speed up this procedure. Sadly, our captain was on his way back to a room which only minutes before had given him best wishes and hopes for a long stay at the crease.

You could almost hear the journos reach for their notepads or begin typing tomorrow's story about how Tubby has once again failed to post the big score needed to extinguish everyone's curiosity on the subject. We, though, had other things to worry about, for both Justin Langer and Matthew Elliott soon succumbed against an attack that, at best, you would call 'honest'.

The wicket was playing as slow as any I've ever seen, which for us was no surprise. It's common knowledge that the local curator was told to produce something along these lines, for two reasons. One, so as to not allow the Australian batsmen to achieve any real form or timing (because the ball won't be coming onto the bat with any pace) and, two, so the Australian bowlers can't get any encouraging zip or movement from the pitch. These 'pudding' types of wickets are made for unattractive cricket – they don't do the players or the spectators any favours at all. And to think that the groundstaff only have to roll the pitch for a few more hours to harden it up and make the cricket a much more attractive proposition.

My main concern when I first went in was to fire myself up and not to fall into the complacency trap that is so often associated with these fixtures. Not surprisingly, the lack of atmosphere that results from a relatively small crowd being scattered around a barren-looking ground can make you feel uninspired at times. But this is when you must dig deep and put your professional hat on.

Despite my best intentions, I did carelessly waft at a few innocuous deliveries early on. I realised I wasn't totally focused on the job, but gradually began to find concentration, and by lunch Mark and I had assumed the ascendancy, to the point that it was some surprise when Junior perished for 66, and then the elder twin for 92. I was a little aggrieved not to make the magical three figures, but my time at the crease augured well for the big matches ahead.

Our total of 249 was, to be truthful, very ordinary and one that must be improved upon in the second innings. Many of our dismissals came from a distinct lack of toughness and discipline – two key areas in the art of batting and things that all genuine top-liners should be accustomed to.

Having scored 92, and with Tubs again under close scrutiny, I obliged the throng of media at the conclusion of the day's play. Once surrounded, I soon realised that my innings was of no real concern. The scribes are totally and utterly obsessed with Mark Taylor. Questions flew thick and fast …

'Will Taylor play in the first Test?'

'Is the team that played today your first Test team side?'

'Will you have to drop him?'

'What's the feeling like in the camp?'

The inquiry seemed to be never ending. It was about halfway through that I realised what is was like for a sheep to stumble into a paddock full of foxes!

Tonight's dinner conversation was much more stimulating than the day's deeds on the field. Justin Langer, Michael Slater, Andy Bichel and I sat down and tried to analyse each other's approach to the game. This is the *X Files* area of professional sport and, in particular, Test cricket, a game like no other …

Test cricket is an adventure that is long in duration (30 hours over five days), with ample time between each delivery for the mind to wander. Lang, Slats and Bic all gave an insight into their make-up, as did I. We all learnt something and drew inspiration from each other. At one point, Lang suggested that if you want a clear and focused thought, then the obvious way to achieve this state is through meditation. I found his thoughts extremely interesting, because it is common knowledge that when you perform poorly it is almost inevitably due to the fact that you became distracted by previous events or by events you think might happen or you want to happen. The ability to switch on and off when needed is such a tremendous asset to have.

One reason I found Lang's observation so interesting is that, after scoring 170 against Sri Lanka in Adelaide in early 1996, over a post-match beer and chat two of their players asked, 'Do you study yoga and meditate?'

I asked them why they thought this might be possible, to which they replied, 'Because you looked like you were in a trance when you were out there batting.'

Concentration is a part of my cricket that I've worked on and my success in this area is, without doubt, the main reason for my success of late. The Sri Lankans' mention of the word 'trance' was interesting, as this is exactly the way I feel when I'm in control and focused. In sport, this situation is known as being 'in the zone'. As far as I understand, it is something that is achieved by very few to a high level.

It's a state I try to get myself into when I'm out in the middle. And when I manage to get there, I feel as if I'm 'looking in on myself' when I'm batting – almost as if what is occurring at the crease isn't real. But at the same time I'm totally in control.

28 May, Bristol
Australia 249 v Gloucestershire 350 (Trainor 121, Cunliffe 61; Warne 4–97).
Predictably the tabloids had a field day at Mark Taylor's expense. One tasteless example was an article that featured a mocking story of Tubs which had him being presented with a metre-wide bat to help solve his problems. This particularly trashy publication even had the temerity to ask Mark whether he'd be prepared to have a photo taken of him with this cardboard cut-out of a bat. Of course, the answer 'No' didn't stop them pursuing the issue and when we arrived at the ground this morning the cameras began clicking as soon as we hopped off the bus. Surprise, surprise, the guy standing right in front of us was holding up the bat, just at the perfect angle so that Mark appeared to be in possession of the item. I was so

unimpressed at this crass piece of work that I confronted the photographer and gave him a gobful, before handing him over to Alan Crompton. I was delighted to learn later that our manager had eventually extracted the offending roll of film from the photographer's camera.

Today, in the south-west of England, had been designated as 'Wrong Trousers Day' – everyone was expected to pull on a pair of inappropriate strides to raise money for charity. We agreed to this request and were duly kitted out in some of the worst threads imaginable. Kasper had the sheepskin daks, while Lang donned a three-legged variety that would have been of more use to at least one West Indian fast bowler I could think of. Tubs chose some 'joker pants', which more than one team member suggested was an improvement on his normal attire. I settled for some 12th-century battle leggings that smelt and felt like they'd not been washed since the day they were created. Never one to miss a photo opportunity, the press boys were immediately licking their lips in anticipation of a good 'mickey take' at our expense. They didn't miss!

This, unfortunately, was as good as the entertainment got. The locals grafted their way to a comfortable first-innings lead, as our bowlers toiled gallantly away on the lifeless track. Here was further confirmation that we had batted very poorly on the first day. No one bowler stood out, but there were encouraging signs from all three quicks (McGrath, Kasprowicz and Gillespie), while Warney enjoyed an extensive bowl that could only help him discover the rhythm he needs.

One ball that stood head and shoulders (if you'll pardon the pun) above all others was an evil bouncer that Dizzy produced out of nowhere. The game was meandering along with none of the quicks really producing anything too lethal when this brute of a delivery reared like a startled cobra and crashed into their opener's helmet. Such was the ferocity of this collision that the ball then cannoned into the advertising boards in the blink of an eyelid. You know a delivery is genuinely quick when your team-mates turn to each other with looks of disbelief that quickly turn into broad grins. Everyone knows it's much better to watch such a ball, rather than face it. This boy will be something special – he's got the quiet composure of an assassin and the steely glinted eyes of a man on a mission.

It's funny how opposites can attract. The close friendship of the Gloucestershire and England keeper Jack Russell and our own Ian Healy is not unlike the bond between the characters from *The Odd Couple*, Oscar Maddison and Felix Ungar. Heals is of course the meticulous one, fastidious in his neatness and cleanliness of his clothes, whereas Jack Russell comes out to bat in gear that could have been acquired at a garage sale. Jack is a man who some say is eccentric and is somewhat of a recluse. Do you know that his Weetabix has to be soaked in milk for exactly 12 minutes? Apart from this meticulously prepared cereal, he exists on baked beans, rice, potatoes, jaffa cakes and digestive biscuits, all washed down daily by at least 20 cups of milky tea. His phone number and home address are known only by immediate family, and he protects his privacy to the extent that a story has been told of a few of his team-mates being blindfolded as they travelled in his car to his home – so that they wouldn't know where they were when they arrived, or how they got there.

The common thread for these two is, of course, wicket-keeping. In my opinion, they are the best two custodians in the game today. Whenever their paths cross, they can regularly be seen talking about the game, exchanging ideas and checking out each other's gear. Heals is a keeper who regularly changes his gloves when he thinks they have lost their feel and support. In contrast, Jack at one stage had a pair that had been on the circuit for a full 12 years.

Jack has more than one string to his bow and is, in fact, a well-respected artist specialising in the military and sporting fields. So it was with great enthusiasm that we accepted his offer of dinner at his art gallery. The first thing that struck me when I entered the impressive 'Jack Russell Gallery' was the quality of paintings that hung around the walls. This wasn't a complete surprise to me, as I have half a dozen of his prints proudly hanging in my home (a limited-edition sketch of Sir Donald Bradman being a particular favourite). Many people might think that his work only sells because of his sporting fame, or even through sympathy, but once you've seen how good the final product is, you realise that he is a first-rate artist who plays a bit of cricket on the side. He even suggested that cricket is now almost a 'hobby' for him, that painting has become his main form of work.

His art has become so popular and respected that recently he rejected an offer of £25,000 for one of his cricket works. His sketches, most of which are done during spare moments on overseas cricket tours, start at £750 each.

Inevitably, the talk around the dinner table centred on his paintings and how he became interested in this difficult pastime. The good news for all of us was that it was only 10 years ago that he began as a complete novice. I can accept the argument that if you work hard at something you have some basic talent for, then you can be a success. But then he suggested that it would possible for anyone to reach his standard through simple hard work. I found this statement to be bordering on ludicrous. For a moment I sat there, thinking how I could become the next Picasso, but then I recalled the anguish and embarrassment of many a disastrous performance during family 'Pictionary' games. I quickly and sadly concluded that unless stick figures, cats and houses with chimneys are going to be recognised as strokes of genius on canvas then I was destined to continue as another frustrated would-be-if-I-could-be artist.

Some of the well known, if unbelievable, facts about this intensely shy and introverted man were confirmed during the evening. Dinner for the eight Aussie guests was a buffet of cold meats, salads and quiches. Jack, meanwhile, tucked into a full plate of rice and baked beans, washed down by a couple of cups of milky tea. He also explained that the rumour that he has asked that, upon his death, his hands be embalmed is 100 per cent correct. That said, he would also like to continue playing for at least another 10 years on the first-class cricket circuit.

Many say this guy is from way out left field, but I always find him a very interesting and, at times, inspirational character – a man whose personality adds spice and life to the cricket world.

29 May, Bristol
Australia 249 and 354–4 declared (Langer 152*, Elliott 124) drew with Gloucestershire 350.
Following Smithy's advice, I found myself floundering in the swimming pool first thing this morning. The reason? I was trying to open my puffed-up eyes, which, due to a mixture of the hotel air conditioning and the ever-present high pollen count that inflicts me with nasty bouts of hayfever, had closed during the evening. While I found the swim quite invigorating (eventually!!), the highlight of the morning's activities was undoubtedly the relaxing plunge into the warm spa that followed and then lasted much longer than was originally planned.

Our effort on the playing front today was very encouraging, with Lang and Matt Elliott ('Herb') doing a great job in each compiling much needed hundreds. This was not only good for the guys concerned, but also set a tone for all the other batsmen, who until now have been getting starts without going on with the job. Quite often, when someone makes the breakthrough, achieving goals becomes easier for those next in line. It was particularly pleasing for Lang to do well, as he is on the fringe of Test selection – this 'living on the edge' can cause more pressure than being a certain starter. His innings reeked of determination and commitment, and he showed the selectors he's ready and willing to claim a long-term Test batting spot.

The form of Herb was also very encouraging, especially because he has had little cricket so far on tour. Despite his lack of time in the middle to date, we see him as a vital part of our top-order. He has a technique that is as good as anyone's.

When two players are involved in a lengthy partnership, the rest of the lads tend to relax a little bit more in and around the dressing-room. Recalling last evening's inspirational words from Jack Russell – 'anyone can be an artist, you just have to start somewhere' – the lads decided to give their skills a try. With pencils in hand, Messrs Bichel, Healy and Slater began their sketches of the county ground from high up on the players' balcony, while Kasper attempted a portrait of our long-serving baggage man, Tony Smith. Within 15 minutes you could have been mistaken for believing a group of pre-school kids had moved in. Slowly, but not so surely, some images did come to life, amid a succession of jibes and hints that rang through the air. The main culprit was Swampy, whose tips were as useful as an ashtray on a motorcycle.

Even the cricket action has produced a few laughs, with the unfortunate Richard Davis, formerly of Kent and Warwickshire, being the centre of attention. Now here is a man with many lifelong scars. In 1993, Davis became a victim of Mark Taylor's bowling, an event which led to the stinging of a journalist who had backed Tubs not to take two wickets on that year's Ashes tour. Tubby and I both did very well out of that little wager. On the 1989 tour, Davis had to suffer the indignity of having one of his looping left-arm orthodox deliveries fly over the boundary ropes … from a stroke from the sweet caressing blade of Tim May (who had previously never hit a six in any form of cricket, from backyard matches to Tests). Dean Jones had offered 50–1 about this freak event ever occurring. Disastrously for Deano, Ziggy Zoehrer had £10 on it, but one had the feeling the embarrassment of the shot caused 'Dicky' Davis even more pain than that suffered by Deano's wallet.

When Davis strode to the crease, we had to let these skeletons of the past out of the cupboard. It was Lang, fielding at short leg, who began loading the bullets. He turned and asked across the pitch to me at silly mid-off, 'Isn't this the guy Tubby got out? And didn't Maysie hit this bloke for six?'

The strain of nursing these catastrophes for four lonely years began to show on Davis's face. I could contain myself no longer, and quipped: 'I wonder what the trilogy of disaster is going to be?' At this point, he finally cracked and began to laugh aloud under his helmet as Warney approached the crease. I think the release of the pressure did him the world of good, and he proceeded to take more than 30 precious runs off our bowling, and helped Nick Trainor to his maiden first-class century.

After the match petered out to a tame draw, largely due to the sluggish nature of the pitch, Jack Russell came into the room to judge the efforts of our debutant artists.

These were his reactions to each masterpiece …

The effort of Andy Bichel – 'What is *that*?' (Jack was pointing at one of Bic's 'trees' at the time.)

Ian Healy's – 'Is this Heals'? Brilliant … 9 out of 10.' (It's pathetic the way keepers stick together.)

Michael Slater's – 'Is this abstract?'

Michael Kasprowicz's – 'This is the best: definitely some talent here.'

After these brief appraisals, Slats was the only one who appeared to be disillusioned. 'I was disappointed with his reaction,' he moaned later. 'But everyone's got to start somewhere.'

30 May, Derby

Another selection meeting had been called, to determine the side to play Derbyshire tomorrow. Our main objective as a squad is to win the Ashes – and we must try and get the Test line-up in good form. The problem of too many batsmen and too few warm-up matches before the first Test has made it tough on a number of players, with everyone feeling the disappointments of those desperate for opportunities. I only hope this situation doesn't lead to any divisions within the squad.

31 May, Derby

Australia 362–6 declared (Elliott 67, Blewett 121, Bevan 56) v Derbyshire 68–1.
Under normal circumstances, the ten-minute drive to the ground would have been a relaxing part of the day – perhaps spent browsing through the papers or having a chat with the boys. But not today. Flicking through the business section of the broadsheet, the *Daily Telegraph*, I noticed a headline featuring my name.

What was in print underneath, I couldn't believe. It had been reported that I had been involved in an argument, in a bar room in Bristol at 4.30am, with a top Marks and Spencer's executive.

This was a straight lie. Not only had no such argument ever taken place, but on the night the affair was supposed to have happened, I had gone to bed at 11pm. This report demonstrated, once again, how too many people over here never let the truth get in the way of a good story.

When we arrived at Derbyshire's home track, the Racecourse Ground, we discovered that their fast bowler, Devon Malcolm, who looks certain to be part of the English attack for the first Test, had been ordered to sit this game out by the chairman of England selectors, David Graveney. It is quite clear they didn't want us to have a close look at Big Dev before next Thursday. We all found this a little strange, especially as he's well known to all of us and, now that he's not playing here, he will not have had a bowl in a match for two weeks before the Test begins. I guess only time will tell whether his 'resting' is a smart move!

One thing that is certain is that Derbyshire's captain, the Victorian and former Australian batsman, Dean Jones, was furious when he learnt that his No. 1 strike bowler was out. Deano is desperate to win against us, not least because each county has been offered the incentive of a £9000 cheque if they defeat the Aussies. Our purse for victory is a less impressive £2500, which doesn't go far split between 17 players. But at this stage we'd be very grateful to receive anything, as the amount of cash in the pool at present is £0.

On yet another slow seaming wicket we elected to bat first. Again, we were in immediate trouble, as the steady local attack accounted for Justin Langer and Mark Taylor before either could reach double figures. Thankfully, though, Greg Blewett and Matthew Elliott steadied the ship to have us nicely placed at the luncheon interval, with both players improving with each minute spent at the crease.

This was a day full of surprises, and the biggest came during the lunch break, when we were served an excellent curried chicken and rice dish. This easily eclipsing the gourmet delights we were offered in 1993 – a baked potato with bolognaise sauce on day one, a slab of pizza on day two, and a spartanly-proportioned cold meat salad on day three. The club was experiencing financial problems at the time.

For most of the afternoon the bat dominated the ball, as most of the lads gained some confidence-boosting form. Blewey drove with such precision and grace that even the locals rejoiced in its splendour. Matty Elliott continued his important learning process on these wickets, which are so much slower than the ones he's used to at home.

My 43 was compiled in a competent enough manner, but my dismissal was an example of poor shot selection and poor concentration, which disappointed me greatly. My shot was premeditated and speculative, which meant that the outcome was virtually guaranteed. I guess I should be able to learn from what was going through my mind in the lead-up to the shot ... and hopefully not repeat the mistakes again.

It was good to see Bevo and Heals also make worthwhile contributions that completed a pleasing day for most of our batsmen.

Our quick scoring enabled Tubs to declare with a little under an hour left to play, which gave Andy Bichel an opportunity, bowling alongside Brendon Julian, to compete for the third fast bowler's spot in the Test team. However, both bowlers looked underdone, with the very obvious result being quick runs from the Derbyshire blades. Bic appeared to be suffering at the moment of delivery, falling away marginally and not following through with his usual gusto. Perhaps this was because he's a little wary after his problems and doesn't want to incur another setback. For his sake, I hope this is the case and that his problems today are not indicative of a more serious ailment.

BJ claimed the only wicket we took before stumps, but he wouldn't have been overly happy with the blend of good and bad deliveries he offered. But that mixture can be his strength, as he regularly produces a wicket-taking ball just when a batsman thinks he has his measure. BJ is known in cricketing circles as a 'wicket-taking bowler' and, as such, is a very valuable commodity.

1 June, Derby

Australians 362–6 declared and 148–2 (Taylor 59*, Bevan 58*) v Derbyshire 257–9 declared (May 67; Julian 3–88).

We received unfortunate news this morning – Andy Bichel has experienced more problems with his lower back and the top of the buttock area, which have ended his role in this match and also destroyed his chances for a spot in our side for the first Test. One thing that did cheer us up a little was the weather. The blue sky and mild conditions were much appreciated, especially here at Derby, where a cold wind on the open ground can make life very uncomfortable.

It has been said that you never know how good someone is until they are given a chance. This theory was confirmed today by the Derbyshire opener Michael May. During the 1996–97 English off-season, May tried his luck at St Kilda, Warney's district club in Melbourne, where the selectors placed him in their third-grade line-up. Three months later, here he was taking on the Aussie new-ball attack and putting up a formidable display. He split the field with some beautifully timed square drives, albeit among a few flashy play-and-misses, but the bottom line was he was having a go and making a good fist of it. His dismissal, however, was followed by one of the most bizarre incidents I've ever come across in my 13 years as a professional cricketer.

The culprit was the new batsman, Chris Adams, an opener with credentials that clearly warrant monitoring by the English selectors. The incident occurred when Warney pushed through a quicker leg break that skidded onto the batsman, forcing him to hurry an attempted leg glance. The result was a flurry of bat, pads and ball being interwoven into a split second – in fact, Adams probably managed to get the faintest of edges onto the ball, which then raced away to the fine-leg boundary. However, from the bowler's end, it appeared as if the ball may have struck the pad before the bat, hence the confident appeal for lbw from Warney and the decision of the umpire in favour of that appeal.

Adams, who had been running what he thought was a legitimate single, stopped dead in his tracks not far from the umpire. The poor bloke then begged for some sort of pardon from the ump, continually pointing to his bat. Finally, he began to dawdle backwards towards the pavilion, but not before stopping next to our huddle to ask, 'You're not going to take that, are you? Aren't you going to call me back?'

The reply was not the one he was looking for. It went something like this … 'No way, you're out, it's the umpire's decision. See you later.'

Like a little boy scorned he replied with, 'You cheats! You Aussies are all cheats!'

If Adams wasn't sure about his chances of a recall, after that remark we made sure he was quickly made fully aware of our stance towards his dismissal. Finally, he began the lonely walk off the ground, somewhat slowed by the tail between his legs that dragged along the ground. Getting what you think is a bad decision is always hard to accept, but the way you accept the umpire's verdict generally says a lot about your character. Although we all have our moments, common sense says that once you've been given out you may as well go quickly, because the decision will not be reversed. Any objection makes you not only look ridiculous, it also damages your reputation.

To Adams's credit, once he had some time to think about his behaviour, he did apologise to Mark Taylor during the luncheon interval, and in doing so won back some admiration from all concerned.

This wasn't the only notable incident of the morning session, with the other belonging to Greg Blewett. For a man blessed with abundant natural talent, Blewey has of late been catching with a style similar to that of a blind beggar asking for cash on the streets of Bombay. His attempt today to reel in a top edge left him with nothing more than a handful of high pollen count and an ego that may not be able to take much more ridicule from the boys. Needless to say, Blewey was pretty timid and decidedly quiet for the remainder of the session; no doubt he was deep in thought, trying to come up with some excuse for when we probed him over the luncheon table.

However, he had nothing inventive to say while we tucked into a pasta dish of moderate quality. The best he could do was that oldest of all excuses, 'The sun was in my eyes.'

The afternoon session was another reasonable one for us. All the bowlers snared a couple of 'poles', but, as it had been in the morning, it was not the actual cricket that provided the entertainment. This time we found ourselves closely observing the unusual mannerisms of Derbyshire's keeper, Karl Krikken, while he was at the batting crease. I've never seen a guy fidget with his gear more than this guy, so Warney and I decided to put a count on his touches between deliveries. His best effort was an extremely impressive 23, with his protector and helmet coming in for the harshest of treatment.

Our second innings began somewhat shakily, with Herb and Lang barely troubling the scorers. However, the most notable incident came when Dean Jones dropped a straightforward catch at first slip ... from the blade of Mark Taylor when Tubs had only a single to his name.

This missed catch may well prove to be the most crucial single moment of the entire tour. Mark finished the day unbeaten on 59, and it appeared that his confidence and strokeplay were improving as each ball passed. Another failure here would have seen our captain go into the Test under enormous pressure to succeed, without him having enjoyed any reasonable recent time in the middle.

During the day, the English squad for the first Test was announced. There are no real surprises, perhaps with the exception of uncapped Mark Butcher instead of Nick Knight at the top of their batting order. In my opinion, it looks a well-balanced and in-form squad.

The full squad is: Atherton (captain), Butcher, Caddick, Crawley, Croft, Mark Ealham, Gough, A Hollioake, Hussain, Malcolm, Stewart, Thorpe and Tufnell.

2 June, Derby

Australia 362–6 declared and 265–4 declared (Taylor 63, Bevan 104*, Julian 62) lost to Derbyshire 257–9 declared and 371–9 (A Rollins 66, Adams 91, Jones 56; Warne 7–103) by one wicket.

In an effort to make a result possible, we raised the tempo during the morning session. Michael Bevan effortlessly compiled another hundred, while Brendon Julian gave all present a demonstration of his prodigious ability by slamming 62 from only 49 balls. The result was an equation that left the locals chasing 371 off 66 overs, on a batting-friendly wicket and with a slick outfield to help them.

We were confident of gaining our first first-class win of the tour, even though we were without the services of Bichel. However, after just a couple of overs we were missing Gillespie as well, after he complained about a sore foot. But though these guys were absent, we should have played much better than we did. From very early on we appeared in trouble, as shoddy fielding, undisciplined bowling and poor body language strangled our cricket.

To me, it feels as if the team is operating like a car being driven around with its hand brake on. The result was a history-making win for the home side and a soul-searching loss for us, with the only good news to come out of our display being Warney's seven wickets. Strangely, in the end, despite our numerous lapses, we still had many opportunities to grab a victory. But although only one wicket separated the teams at the end, we know we have to re-assess our approach to our cricket, or else it's going to be a long tour.

The atmosphere in the change rooms at stumps wasn't exactly the way brother Mark and I had intended to celebrate our 32nd birthdays, but our mood was cheered up a little by the cakes presented to us by our tour sponsors, Coke. Later on, during what was a fairly subdued evening journey down to Birmingham, Geoff Marsh and I had a bit of a chat about the current state of affairs. We agreed that the squad lacked a bit of hunger and, crucially, that the team's spirit seemed to be lacking that little bit of something that, when it's there, you don't try to think about what it is.

Later in the trip there was some hilarity, though, when Herb relived the catch in the outfield he took off a no ball during today's play. Unaware that he had taken an 'illegal' catch, Herb began to celebrate by mockingly raising the ball in triumph towards the commentary box. He was aiming specifically at the former England fast bowler and now commentator, Bob Willis, who had earlier made reference to Herb's fielding by remarking that 'Elliott's been to the Phil Tufnell school of fielding'. Rather embarrassingly for 'Bill Lawry's love child', his animated celebrations gave the Derbyshire batsmen an opportunity to scamper through for a second run before the 'pill' was finally returned to the keeper. At the time we all found it quite amusing; retold again it was doubly enjoyable!

6
ENGLAND v AUSTRALIA
FIRST CORNHILL
TEST MATCH

Edgbaston, Birmingham, 5–9 June

NASSER HUSSAIN

3 June

Last year, would you believe, I was late arriving for the Edgbaston Test even though you would have thought I would not make such a mistake in my first Test for three years. I made sure I didn't make the same mistake this time, leaving home in Little Leighs at 9am to head for Birmingham. I drove up alone and was feeling quite relaxed.

Sometimes you can go into a match with a lot of things on your mind which can make you a little airy fairy in your approach, but this time I made a conscious decision to be absolutely focused in everything I did in this Test. That's going to extend to me staying in the hotel at night even though some of the boys like to go out, and I thought I'd get a video machine in and watch some film of the Aussie bowlers in action.

One of the first things that happened on arrival at the ground was the receipt of my new cap which for me means the end of the road, at least at international level, for my trusty 1990 tour cap. I knew the writing was on the wall when I saw Alec Stewart wearing the new one in the one-dayers, and I thought, 'That's it, it's time to change.' Next came nets and the first taste this summer for me of genuinely quick bowling. Not only was Devon Malcolm there but also Surrey's Alex Tudor and a variety of leg spinners including a young lad I recommended from the Ilford Cricket School, Saqib Mahmood, brought in to copy Shane Warne's action, so it was a very useful exercise. I'd had Monday off so I was very keen to have a good net and I was also keen to get some good fielding practice in as I had only taken one slip catch for Essex all season.

Devon was firing in the nets and bowled really quickly. You know when Dev is on form by his run-up and he was clearly well up for the challenge ahead. Meanwhile Alex Tudor, who was brought along for the day to experience the England atmosphere, looked a good prospect. It must be right to bring along players of genuine promise like this and I'm sure it won't be long before Ashley Cowan of Essex will be asked to do the same. I remember the atmosphere of my first Test being completely alien to me and this way you can integrate players who could well be featuring before long.

There has been some conjecture about our batting order with Jon Agnew, I think, speculating that Thorpey could go in at four ahead of me. So Bumble made a point of taking me aside and telling me that the order would be the same as in the winter and that helps in making you know your role in the match. I did, of course, go in at three last year and became the first English batsman for some time to make runs there but the decision to move me to four was made for sound cricketing reasons.

Once it had been decided, at the start of the Zimbabwe tour, that Stewie would be keeping wicket it became clear he would have a problem opening the batting. So Ath and Bumble thought it best if he went at three where his natural game is more suited to taking on seamers rather than spinners at the start of his innings. I understood that and, as soon as I got a century in Bulawayo in my first innings at four, I was happy with it, but maybe I wouldn't have been quite so pleased if things hadn't gone my way! It is, in fact, not that different to bat at three or four in a Test match.

One of the first people I saw at nets was Mark Waugh, a good friend from our days together at Essex and he was absolutely brilliant. He was surrounded by his Aussie mates but as soon as he saw me he greeted me like a long lost brother and asked me over for a cup of tea and a chat. Much was made in the press about those comments from Mark before he left Australia, saying that he always considered facing England to be like facing a group of individuals rather than a team. He told me that his quotes had been taken out of context. As a player I could see what happened. It was part of a long magazine interview he'd given some time before in which he'd talked about English cricket in general. Then his comments had been rehashed before the tour so he was always going to attract a few headlines over it. A few things he said rang true but he also said that England players can be selfish and that's certainly not the case with this current team. I know the bloke and he plays hard but fair like any Aussie and his comments were not an issue as far as I was concerned. I'm pretty sure the other players weren't fussed about them either.

Mike Kasprowicz is another great lad. In fact, he's almost too nice to be a fast bowler and he was popular with everyone at Essex when he played for us in 1994. Ridley's breweries, who sponsored his car, are always asking after 'Kasper' and telling me to pass on their regards if I see him. Unfortunately, I didn't get the chance to speak to him today but I'll catch up with him at some point.

It's been decided that we will not have team dinners on the eve of Tests this year unless the players want them, so we were free to spend the evening as we wanted. For me, as I've said, that meant an evening in my room at the Swallow Hotel watching videos. Video nasties? Well, if you consider watching Shane Warne and

Glenn McGrath in action in South Africa nasty then I suppose they were, but for me it was valuable homework.

I'd already spoken to Stuart Law at Essex about their bowlers and, while he didn't want to give too much away, he provided me with a few tips and the basic message that most of their bowlers hit the pitch hard so it's worth hanging back a bit when facing them. Jason Gillespie was a relative newcomer so I ordered my Indian takeaway through the helpful hotel concierge and sat down to watch him and the others. Gillespie looked pretty sharp so I made up my mind not to lunge at him; McGrath bowled back of a length so for him I'd be hanging back before I committed myself to the shot and Shane Warne looked to be bowling a little slower to how I remember him from 1993. But I was wary of that because when it's Warne you don't want to go into the contest with too many pre-conceived ideas. You just have to give him every respect and play him on the morning of the match as you see it. If you make a judgement on him you always feel he could have something up his sleeve to surprise you

Kasper was the one I was most familiar with and I knew he was mainly an outswing bowler so I'd be looking to get forward to him. The only one I couldn't work out from the video was Michael Bevan and I just decided I would have to play him on instinct. I don't think he knows where the ball is going, so as a batsman you certainly don't.

As well as Tudor we also had to say goodbye to one member of our nominated 13 today and as expected it turned out to be Phil Tufnell. Ath told everybody that he'd been told he must release somebody on the Tuesday night so that they could go and play for their county so 'Cat' (Tufnell) made a joke of it and ran into the physio's room saying 'please don't let it be me.' He probably knew it was him because Edgbaston was always likely to see only one spinner and Robert Croft has done exceptionally well in recent times. Cat is a very good friend of mine and I'm sure he'll come into the equation soon enough. He still feels involved in the set-up.

I don't think Adam Hollioake has ever been part of something where he doesn't feel involved in the set-up. He is a confident lad and was a huge part of the one-day success and he has been in at the heart of things today on his first Test call-up. It will be a close run thing between him and Mark Ealham, I imagine, for the final place in our side.

We always have single rooms at home Tests – I gather Lord MacLaurin plans to extend this to future tours, too – and it's up to us to decide if we want our partners with us during a game. Personally, I don't like Karen coming up at the start of a Test because I need to get my mind right. Sometimes during a Test you'll wake up in the middle of the night going over some aspect of the day's play and if you've got your wife with you, you can hardly turn the light on or make a noise. I prefer her to leave it for three days and come up at the weekend and as usually she's teaching this fits in perfectly with her too.

4 June

Today I did a bit of mental work out in the middle. I like to get my eyes adjusted to the light and the background out there and imagine what it will be like when the game starts. I don't know what it's called – I'm sure a psychologist could tell you – but I imagine we're 20 for two and I stand there picturing each bowler running in at me. The idea is basically tuning your mind to the Test. That way, when you do get out there for real you've been through everything in your mind and you think 'I can cope with this'. Sometimes it's actually better for your game if you really do come in at 20 for two because it concentrates your mind on the task in hand and it's a fact that many of my big scores have come when my side has been in trouble.

STEVE WAUGH

All 22 of us – players and support staff – assembled in the 'gers' room at 8.30am. The purpose of the meeting was to spend time thoroughly assessing our opponents, via a highlights tape that our management had acquired for quite a hefty sum. We also witnessed one of the best motivational speeches I've heard, from Ian Healy. It turned out to be one of the longest team meetings I've ever been a part of, but it was also one of the most searching and probing, as we attempted to dismantle the opposition, exposing their weaknesses and recognising their strengths. Only time will tell whether we tried to cram too much information into our skulls or whether such a process will prove to be a masterstroke. All I know is that, in Test cricket, it takes discipline and patience to come out on top. Combine that with a thorough knowledge of what the other side can and cannot do, and you can't go too far wrong.

Training sessions the day before a Test match tend to take on extra significance, as the players involved try to duplicate what will be expected of them come match day. This is part of the process of trying to peak at the right time, which isn't as easy as one might think. You want to feel as physically fit as possible – perhaps by taking it a little easier at practice or by making sure you get exactly the right treatment for a niggling injury. Cutting down on alcohol and making a big effort to eat correctly can also give you that little extra edge that could make the difference.

For a batsman, this is time to switch on, to get those feet moving a fraction of a second quicker. In the nets, you might think about where the fieldsmen are likely to be, and then try to hit the ball into or through the gaps. For a bowler, the day before a Test is when you want to be slotting into a nice rhythm, and pitching the ball into the 'danger areas' on a regular basis. Finding the right length is the key for most bowlers.

Sometimes, for various reasons these objectives are impossible to achieve – a batsman might be hindered by poor practice wickets, for example. Unfortunately, this is exactly what we encountered at the nets this morning, with balls deviating in unplayable fashion, complemented by every batsman's nemesis. Uneven bounce. All such conditions do is deflate a batsman's confidence and also give the bowlers an unrealistic view of how they're performing. But, despite the lousy conditions, I was happy with my form and, most importantly, came out of the nets feeling more positive than when I went in.

One player who did turn in an unusually poor net session was brother Mark, who got out a number of times and seemed ill at ease with the whole situation. To be fair to him, his turn came late in the practice, by which time the wickets had deteriorated to a very poor standard. It will be interesting to see how he fares after such a negative experience the day before such a big match, and whether he can just turn it on when he has to.

The press from home has once again been very negative and extremely hurtful. Both Ian and Greg Chappell and, to a lesser extent, Bob Simpson have written less than favourable articles about the situation Mark Taylor is currently facing.

Tubs is not quite his usual positive self, although he remains very determined and anxious to turn in an inspiring performance. During a brief breakfast conversation, I suggested to him, 'Don't worry too much about the outcome and remember whatever happens, it is meant to be!'

Tubs agreed and replied, 'I'll just try to really enjoy the game, and not put too much pressure on myself.'

5 June, Day 1, First Test

Australia 118 (Warne 47; Caddick 5–50, Gough 3–43) v England 200–3 (Hussain 80*, Thorpe 83*).

I slept well last night and I actually didn't feel any different this morning even though it was an Ashes series and people were expecting us to do well. It was a Test match and the game doesn't get any bigger than that and I felt the same as I did before I faced India or Pakistan. When it really hit me was when we went out to field. We'd already had that nice little ceremony where Mark Butcher was presented with his cap as a newcomer and I was quite pleased we were in the field. As a batsman it gives you a bit more time to get used to the environment and, on this occasion, I thought it was a good toss to lose. Before Ath went out for the toss I told him I would probably bat first even though the ball was likely to swing because the Edgbaston wicket is known to deteriorate and he agreed but said we would have to bat well. Luckily Mark Taylor felt the same and he called correctly. 'Ealie' (Mark Ealham), meanwhile, got the nod over Hollioake as the bowling all-rounder.

I saw Kasper for the first time this morning but it wasn't a repeat of my meeting up with Mark Waugh. He was on the outfield bowling at Ian Healy and I was checking the pitch. I shouted over to him to say hello but the moment to do that had gone and by this stage it was, in his mind, too close to the start of hostilities to be really pally. So he sort of half acknowledged me – he is too nice to ignore me –

but made it clear that the time for friendship was over and that he'd see me in the middle. That's fair enough. It was going to be only his third Test and he hadn't taken a wicket in two earlier ones against the West Indies so he was clearly focusing on the task ahead. So I just left it and walked off.

Then we went out and the roar from the Eric Hollies Stand on our right was amazing. There was a bit of noise here when we came out against India but this was something else and the people were so clearly behind us. Butch turned round to me and asked, 'Is it always like this? This is a noise and a half,' and I had to admit I'd never known anything like it.

It was the same when Goughy bowled the first ball of the series to Taylor. The roar when he beat the bat made me realise just how crucial this was and then began the most incredible couple of hours in which we reduced the best team in the world to 54 for eight. After each wicket I turned to Thorpey at slip and said, 'Is this really happening?' All I could think of were those times in recent Ashes series when people like Taylor and Geoff Marsh had batted all day without the Aussies losing a wicket and I had to pinch myself after they kept on losing one after another.

We had a plan and it worked like a dream. Now earlier Bumble had decided that perhaps it had been a mistake to play loud music and pump everybody up before the start of a Test because the plain truth was that our bowlers had bowled badly on the first morning of recent Tests when we've inserted the opposition and conditions were in their favour. Maybe it's pumped them up too much and they've gone out and thought 'we've got to do the job' and ended up spraying it around. So this time he decided to play it much more relaxed. That's what coaching is all about – man management. Once again, though, it's very much down to the individual. Jack Russell loves his patriotic tapes and Churchill speeches booming out everywhere. Others like to compose themselves. Whatever, on this occasion our build-up proved exactly right.

It was very humid and the bowlers had to pitch it up. To their credit they bowled in exactly the right place and got prodigious swing. The Aussies seemed to nick everything and it all went our way. For instance, the plan was to bowl short to Bevan and across him and it worked like a dream. We'd also decided that you had to pitch it up to Mark Waugh and that worked perfectly too in getting him out. It was also decided that the best way to get Steve Waugh was to pitch it up too to finally explode this myth about him struggling against the short ball. Sure, he might not look too comfortable against the short stuff but he rarely gets out to it. We don't want to make him look uncomfortable – we want to get him out. And we did. Mark Taylor was to receive the ball well pitched up and across him and that worked too.

There was a slip catch for me during a passage of play that was typical of Goughy. He had bowled Greg Blewett with a no ball – the umpire Peter Willey called it and then told Goughy 'you'll just have to get him next ball' – so Goughy said 'Okay, I will', went back calmly to his mark and, as the TV cameras later showed, said 'f*** me', turned and got Blewett to edge to me, diving to my left the very next ball.

When we went up to congratulate Goughy he was just standing there, in mid-pitch, saying 'No problem. I was always going to get him that ball.'

When Kasper came in Ath asked me how we should bowl to him and I pointed out that at Essex he used to run himself out every time so we should bowl for a run-out! Mick actually played quite well and hung around for a while in company with Warne. Did I say anything to any of them from slip? No. Against those boys I try not to go in for sledging because they're the kings of it and you're sure to get it back worse when you come in.

At lunchtime the atmosphere in our dressing room was electric. We put the news on and there we were among the leading items but by this time the batters were starting to think about our turn in the middle. Normally if you lose the toss you resign yourself to a day in the field but already the time was approaching for us to face the music. I started getting my gear out at lunchtime because you must always tell yourself you'll be batting soon so that you're ready when it comes. I was saying to myself 'Nass, your bit's coming up' and the best thing in that situation is to get the remaining wickets quickly and get on with it. That soon happened and 'Caddy' (Andrew Caddick) had completed a 'five-for'.

So now it was our turn to bat and I forgot I wasn't at number three because it was the first time for a long while in a home match that I had been lower. I rushed in and started putting my pads on before I realised I didn't have to, but Butch was soon out and I then had to get ready for real.

Luckily or unluckily, whichever way you look at it, I was in quickly at 16 for two when the captain was out and I wasn't really nervous. I just remember saying loudly to myself 'come on' because I felt pumped up. Kasper's first ball to me was a bouncer which was not entirely unexpected. I knew from his reaction to me this morning that he was fired up. Then he bowled me a couple on my hips which I pushed away so I was off and running.

I wear a contact lens in my left eye whenever I'm on a cricket field now. I always knew I had a dodgy left eye but I was never sure if it affected my batting. So, when I was in Cape Town a couple of years ago, this guy Ken West, an optometrist and cricket expert, told me it wouldn't hurt to wear a lens. I also do a few eye stretches before I bat and then put a finger in front of my eye and focus on that for a while. It all helps.

I also now wear a grill on my helmet, something I had never done before last season's series against Pakistan. I knew I was going to play Test cricket for a while and that meant facing the world's best bowlers and I wanted to reduce the risk of any injury keeping me out of matches. So I tried a grill in a county match against Derbyshire and Devon Malcolm and it felt fine. I lost the occasional ball but that just meant I needed to adjust the grill a bit and since then it has always been part of my equipment.

It was reassuring to face McGrath for the first time because he was exactly what I expected, a hit the deck , back of a length bowler. I was feeling fairly comfortable but the question which was always at the back of my mind was 'when's Warne going to come on?' I knew his introduction would be a big moment in the Test and I also knew that the crowd would be waiting for it and the commentators would be building it up.

But first came Gillespie. Everyone had said he had got some wheels and, yes, he was quick but I thought 'I can play this bloke', so that was reassuring too. Three of their bowlers had been on and I felt I could play them. Then came the big moment. Shane Warne was on. Luckily, Thorpey was facing him first up – Stewie had gone by then, surprisingly after looking a bit nervous and pulling a ball he might not have done if he'd got a few under his belt – and I was able to observe from the non-striker's end.

After that first over Thorpey confirmed my impression from the South African video that Shane wasn't bowling it as quickly as normal but we kept on reminding each other to keep an eye on him to check if he was getting any quicker and which variations he was employing. We were also keeping an eye on Kasper, who is usually a big swinger of the ball, expecting him to swing it more, but on this occasion he didn't really do so. Certainly their bowlers weren't swinging it as much as ours.

In that sort of situation, with your team losing two quick wickets, I feel you just have to play naturally. People watching might have felt that Thorpey took the attack to them while I was more technique orientated at first but basically we just did what felt right. Having said that, we knew we had to try to be positive because there were some difficult balls flying around, any one of which might have your name on it, and I decided that if they dished out any wide balls to me I was going to hit them and if they were going to give me any drivable balls I was going to drive them. There's a thin line between knowing what to hit on the off-side and what to leave alone but I wasn't going to miss any scoring opportunities.

And my policy against Warne? Well, it was not pre-conceived for him, it's just the way I play spin. I like to get my right leg right round behind the ball when I'm defending against spin and try to play with the bat rather than the pad as much as possible. I've been praised for this method but that wasn't the case during the winter when I was batting in Wellington against Daniel Vettori and played him in exactly this manner. Yet Willis was saying on Sky that my technique looked dreadful against spin, particularly the way my back leg was coming round! This came from a bowler whose bowling technique was not exactly textbook telling a batsman that his method against spin is wrong when I think I play spin pretty well.

The thing is, at this level, you're facing bowlers who are the best in the business and they are always looking for ways to counter your method, so I'm sure Warne will go away at the end of this Test and think about how he can get me out. It will then be up to me to rise to the challenge. I'm virtually certain Shane will decide that the way to bowl to me is a bit straighter because when he was giving me a bit of width I was able to cut and drive him. If he strays to the leg-side, of course, I can try to sweep him but they had obviously done their homework on me and know I like that shot because they had someone on the 45 for me as soon as Shane came on. But in doing that they opened up some other scoring avenues for me, so it didn't do me any harm.

When I last played against him, in 93, his flipper was his biggest weapon. It's difficult to pick because you can't see it in his hand but you can see it coming down at you, so as long as you remember when you get one that it's a flipper and not a short long hop you should be all right playing it by instinct. If you think it's a short ball and try to hit it for four you're probably knackered. You may get a short one but then he'll go for the double bluff and bowl a quicker one next time. That's why you must always be wary of him.

Facing Shane Warne really is one of the ultimate challenges. You have to watch him all the time. As he runs up you're saying to yourself 'watch his hand, watch his hand' and it became tiring after a while because he didn't bowl many variations at all on this occasion. We'll have to monitor this throughout the series because he's such a key figure, but at the moment I can honestly say there's been hardly any flippers and no googlies, not even to the left-hander, Thorpey. Whether it's his shoulder or not I don't know, but there must be more to come from Warne.

As time went on I realised I was playing quite well and Thorpey, who doesn't usually say a lot, came down to me and said, 'Nass, you're hitting the ball really well.' Whenever I looked up at the scoreboard we always seemed to be on almost exactly the same score and that was great. We spent much of the early stages talking about cricket but as time went on we were talking about anything.

Meanwhile the crowd were fantastic and I really didn't want the first day to end. I kept on thinking 'I can't give it away because I'd let everyone down and with these Aussies if you give them a sniff they can roll you away.' I knew that maintaining concentration was paramount. Most times, when you play Test cricket, you're playing for yourself and the team but I think today, for perhaps the first time, I felt I was doing it for the whole country. It may sound melodramatic but that's the way it was because everybody so clearly wanted us to win. Even the press were supportive which makes a big difference and really does give you a lift.

So, at the end of the first day, Thorpey and I returned to the dressing room, both in the eighties and with England in a strong position. Everybody was patting each other on the back but that's where the coach and captain come in. Ath came and sat with me for five minutes, emphasising that we had to start again in the morning and that we had to kill these people off while they were down. Then Goochie rang me in the evening saying virtually the same thing. He told me I hadn't got enough and that England had been in these positions before without finishing the job off.

But I knew all this myself. I knew that it would only take a good ball the next morning and then a poor shot in the second innings for me to finish with 80 runs from the match and feel disappointed. Karen rang me and I said how nice it would be to get a hundred and she told me not to be too disappointed if I didn't get it and not to put too much pressure on myself. I had a long soak in the bath and wondered what Friday had in store.

STEVE WAUGH

If anyone had said that after 18 overs we would be 54 for eight they would have been sent straight to a shrink. Mind you, the way we played we certainly needed help of some kind, and it was only due to a fightback from Shane Warne that we managed to scramble past the 100 mark. Six overs after lunch and the embarrassment was complete. All out 118.

It was a highly professional display by the English attack, backed by a hunger in the field that I have rarely seen from our Ashes adversaries in recent times. Capping off their inspired performance was the execution of what appeared to be an overall strategy that involved different game plans for different individuals.

For England, Caddick walked away with a 'five-for'. He bowled intelligently, swinging the ball away from the right-handers and also took advantage of the extra bounce that his height allows him to generate. However, the bowler who really fired things up was Gough, who charged in, hit the wicket hard and varied his pace cleverly. Perhaps most importantly of all, he revved the home supporters up with his theatrical appeals and animated celebrations. This created the most impassioned support for an English cricket team I've ever heard on English turf.

Thorpe and Nasser Hussain played superbly. Their aggressive outlook continued on from their team's performance in the field earlier in the day, and a lead of 112 to the Englishmen, with seven wickets still in hand, was a fair indication at the end of the day of the difference between the teams.

Sitting in the change rooms after play, it felt as if we'd been had by a pickpocket. In all my years in the Australian side I couldn't remember a worse day, or one where we had been so comprehensively outplayed. Geoff Marsh brought some sanity back to proceedings when he commented, 'Today's over. Let's concentrate on having a better day tomorrow. Let's get back into the game then.'

There was one bloke even more dejected than the rest of us. Sitting in the corner, icing his damaged hamstring which he had pulled chasing a ball around the boundary, was Jason Gillespie. His injury is a real blow to us, not only leaving us a bowler short for the remainder of this match, but leaving him in serious doubt for the second Test. A muscle strain of this kind takes a minimum of 10 days to recover from.

6 June, Day 2, First Test
Australia 118 v England 449–6 (Hussain 207, Thorpe 138).
The two important factors this morning were that the new ball was looming and McGrath had his tail up and was bowling a good spell at me. It actually helped me

concentrate and made me go back to thinking about technique and which ones to play or leave. The pitch? Well, it was a case of one ball an hour taking off and hoping it didn't get you when it came along. There was no use playing each ball as if that was the one that would misbehave. Yes, it was a bit worrying when it was happening on the first morning but the pitch didn't get any worse and, if anything, got better.

So I was stuck down at McGrath's end and Thorpey was down at Warne's end. Not that it mattered to Graham. He got stuck into Warne in a big way and raced along to his hundred while I was still in the eighties. There was Thorpey, saluting the crowd, and I thought, 'Lucky bastard, I wish I could hurry up and get there,' but I felt delighted for him. He's got three hundreds in his last four games now after going a long while getting out between fifty and a hundred and he deserves every success. He's done bloody well against the Aussies whenever he's played against them and you're talking about the best in the world, so no wonder he had a big smile on his face when he walked down the wicket for me to congratulate him.

Then I had to think about myself again and getting through a patch when I hadn't been scoring. There was a big shout when I was on 82 for lbw when I left one from McGrath that hit my back pad and if that had been given I couldn't really have been too annoyed with myself because I had built my innings on my judgement outside off-stump. As it hit me I thought 'that's close'. It flipped the top of my pad but I was a long way back. When Steve Bucknor turned it down Healy asked me how many innings I wanted and I looked up at the big screen to watch the replay and realised that it certainly was close. Thorpey confirmed it at the end of the over and gave me the impression he would have given it so I thought 'you might easily have gone there. Now cash in.'

Soon after that I suddenly went boom, boom, boom and got to my hundred too. They'd brought Bevan on and, as I've said, he's difficult to read and I tried to sweep him on 96 and missed it. I decided not to try that shot again because he bowls it so quickly and gets a bit of bounce so there was always a chance I might top edge it. Then, on the same score, he bowled me a long hop and I went to hit it so hard that I got an inside edge and almost dragged it on. So I was stuck in the nineties for a bit and after two or three balls from Bevan I was on 99 and had lost the strike. I didn't want it to go into the next over because McGrath would probably bounce me and make it that much harder for me to find a single but then Thorpey nurdled one to leave me with one ball from Bevan left in the over.

It was a half volley and I thought 'this is it' – I didn't know which way it was spinning but that didn't concern me – and the moment it left the bat I knew it was four. It was a difficult moment to describe. It's all the things you've worked for. It's against Australia. It's for all those people making so much noise in the Hollies Stand. That's why I lifted my bat to them very quickly. It was a huge moment against the best side in the world and a lot of great cricketers were watching. All the pressure seemed to be lifted from my shoulders so that I could enjoy the rest of the game. By this time Thorpey and I were talking about anything. He asked me how Brian Lara could possibly have batted for as long as he did and we were both definitely feeling tired. But I knew by this time I was batting as well as I'd ever done. The ball was getting a bit old, Steve Waugh was bowling and it was a question of 'don't get out to this'. Steve doesn't bowl much these days, but he was forced into action because the Aussies' fastest bowler, Gillespie, was off with a hamstring injury. Our position was a strong one. Before I knew it I was up to 150. The crowd had gone up when I hit a four before I realised the landmark I'd reached and it didn't seem that long after I'd got to a hundred.

Maybe it was the pressure being lifted. Maybe they bowled a few bad overs. But it was going like a dream. At lunchtime Ath came up to me and asked me to keep an eye on Thorpey because he could see him doing something a bit silly. Sure enough, soon after lunch he flicked at one and got out. It happens. It was one of his shots, but this time it went to mid on. He had done a tremendous job and we had set a new England third wicket partnership record against Australia.

Thorpey's dismissal had the effect of switching me back on, especially when John Crawley was out cheaply. I knew I had to kick on again. When Ealie came in he dropped one down on the leg side to try to get off the mark but I sent him back. If the throw had hit he'd have been out and I admit I'd been caught on my heels a bit but I was a bit tired now and I apologised to him. Then Justin Langer, the substitute fielder for Gillespie, started chirping at me 'you only want your own runs' so I replied 'at least I'm playing and not driving the bus around like you.' It wasn't the first time during my innings that the Aussies had got stuck into me. When I was in the fifties Shane bowled me a succession of good balls and, out of instinct, I nodded at him as if to acknowledge a good ball. But when I did it a third time I thought 'I shouldn't be doing this, he's going to think I' m taking the piss.' Sure enough he let me have it, shouting 'stop f***ing nodding at me. I know it's a good ball. Who do you think you are?' Then later when I was well into a hundred he gave me some stick over the fact that I've got my name on my bat saying, in his best sarcastic voice 'I must get one of those Nasser Hussain sabres. Would you autograph it for me?'

McGrath, too, is an angry young man. He and Thorpey have had a lot of fall outs in the past and luckily a lot of his aggression this time was channelled at Thorpey and they were having a few words, stares and stuff throughout. Steve Waugh lost his rag a couple of times also, reminding them it was a Test match and asking 'is anybody out here working?'

As a batsman it's nice to hear this sort of thing. I thought 'we've got them here.' Then, on the best possible stage, I reached my first ever double century. I was on 188 and Shane bowled me a loopy one on leg stump which was almost a yorker and I clipped it to mid-wicket for four. Then he bowled me a flatter one and I was determined to get there quickly so I hit that for four too. The next one was almost a carbon copy but it was stopped in the field. Now came the big moment. He bowled me a flipper and I picked it straight away and played it accordingly. It raced for four and I didn't know what to do with myself. I thought I'd better take my helmet off because you get letters of complaint if you don't and I made sure I raised my bat to the whole crowd, particularly that fantastic stand. Mark Waugh and I have a good rapport on the pitch. He calls me a curry muncher and I call him burger arse because of the size of his backside. It's not meant to be offensive on either side, just our way of joshing on the field. Now, when I got to two hundred, Mark came over and said 'well played, now f*** off and get out because we've seen enough of you.'

Sometimes it has crossed my mind what I might do in these circumstances but when it happens it's just whoosh and the natural emotion takes over. You can also feel self-conscious and worry that you might be over-doing the celebrations but you get stick if you don't raise your bat enough so you can't really win.

Now I'd run out of goals. When I was 150 it was 'let's go for 200' but this was now completely new territory and I didn't have a clue what to set myself. So I thought, let's go up in tens because I can hardly set myself 300. As it turned out I didn't get to 210 because, on 207, I got a good one from Shane, tried to turn it to leg-side and nicked it. If I'd played it straighter I would probably have been okay, but I could hardly be disappointed. In fact, it was the first time I can remember being content after getting out and it was the closest I have got to the perfect innings. Usually, if I get out between fifty and a hundred, I spend the whole journey home telling myself I should have got a hundred. Then, when I get a hundred, I find myself spending all evening saying 'I wish I'd gone on to a really big one.' This time I was satisfied but it didn't stop me throwing my pads and box across the dressing room on my return, swearing to myself about getting out to Shane Warne. I didn't want it to be him.

I soon calmed down and just sat there, not believing what was happening to me. I looked at the scorecard on television and saw all those low scores and then massive ones next to my name and Thorpey's. Someone, I think it was Goughy, said to me 'just think, you were only another 168 runs from becoming a millionaire,' but Brian Lara's record was the last thing on my mind. Wayne Morton, the physio, soon came in congratulating me and said 'I don't often do this, but I'm going to give you a rub down.' So I had a shower and then went into the physio's room still in a state of shock. Theo, our dressing room attendant, soon joined us and asked Wayne if he could have a go so he's got his hands on my back while Wayne was giving him a lesson in massage so he could try it out on his Missus that night!

It was actually a good laugh and Theo, a great lad, was thumping my hamstrings a bit because I'd got him running around earlier. There was, though, the problem of my tennis elbow which had been bothering me since the winter and which has required pain killers each time I bat. I've kept it quiet in case it looks like an excuse if I don't do well, but it was very sore after all that batting and Wayne had a look at it for me.

After an innings like that everybody wants to know you and then came a hectic round of interviews with the press, Sky and BBC radio and television. I also walked past Bob Willis on my way to the Sky box and he said well played. I also had to remember the new dress code and put my England jumper over a T-shirt before I joined Thorpey for a BBC interview with Tony Lewis. I was trying to look smart but soon after Bob Bennett said to me 'you have to wear a collar and tie for interviews', so I'm afraid I got that a bit wrong. The press conference was fine even though I got a couple of silly questions. One bloke – I think he was a *Sun* news reporter – asked if my Missus was pregnant while all the Aussie boys were asking if Shane Warne had lost it. I had to be careful what I said. I was trying to get across that we were confident but that we were not writing them off.

By this time I was looking forward to seeing Karen. She said she would come to the ground if I was still batting at lunchtime on Friday. As I was she set off but as she got to the outskirts of Birmingham I was out so instead she went straight to the hotel. It was a nice feeling, as I walked along the hotel corridor, knowing my wife was waiting in the room having not seen me since Tuesday morning and she just put her arms round me and said 'I thought you were going for a hundred – not two!'

The occasion called for a celebration meal and we went to Shimla Pink's, one of the best Indian restaurants in the country. A lot of people came over, guys who had been at the ground all day and were a bit bevvied up and lots of others. They were all great and my mobile phone didn't stop ringing. One of the first calls was from Tuffers and there were many others including all the Essex lads, my dad, my sister in Australia – Benu told me that they'd interrupted television and radio programmes in Australia to say that Shane Warne had finally got me out – my brothers, some friends from university and other friends in the game like Dean Headley and Chris Silverwood. It was overwhelming.

Karen ordered us a bottle of champagne and who should then walk in but a large party of Australian players to sit on the very next table! This was extraordinary because the same thing had happened during the winter before the Auckland Test when myself Ronnie Irani and Nick Knight had gone out for a meal to celebrate a certain journalist's birthday and the whole New Zealand team arrived and sat next to us. This time the Aussies were great and all came over and congratulated me. The party included Kasper so I at last got a chance to have a friendly word with him and he spent about ten minutes speaking to Karen, whom he hadn't seen since his Essex days, telling her that Lindsey, his fiancee, would be over later in the summer.

Fatigue soon set in and we went back to the hotel to sleep but not before I asked Karen to wake me when the highlights came on. She did and it was fantastic to hear people like Richie Benaud and Ian Chappell saying complementary things about me. Last year Sunil Gavaskar had been great about my centuries against India and gaining the respect of great players is perhaps my biggest aim in the game. To hear people of their calibre praise you is perhaps the greatest thrill in cricket and their words mean more to me than anything.

Then Karen went to sleep and I sat there wishing I hadn't asked her to wake me because I just couldn't switch off. I dozed but kept waking thinking 'what have I achieved? Did I sound big headed in the press conference? How can I make money out of this? What has my dad told the press?' It was just a whirl and I woke up feeling very tired the next day.

STEVE WAUGH

The game plan for the morning was simple in theory but much harder to put into practice. It required a discipline that few sides can constantly produce. Being in such a poor position, we had no option but to try to keep things as tight as possible and give away as little as we could afford.

Don't you hate it when a plan goes horribly wrong? Well, this one certainly did, although we thought Hussain was fortunate to survive an lbw appeal soon after the start of play. The rest of the session, however, was carnage, with 135 runs being added for the loss of no wickets, which put us completely out of the hunt. Shane Warne bowled as poorly as I've ever seen him bowl in a Test match, although he wasn't helped by the sluggish nature of the pitch, which gave the batsmen the liberty of playing him off the pitch rather than through the air.

I didn't have to look at the scoreboard to know we were in deep trouble. That news came in the form of a cricket ball tossed my way, with the accompanying words from captain Taylor, 'Have a bowl, Tugga.' I was grateful for the opportunity, and pleased I was able to get through 12 overs without any niggles. And I found the edge a couple of times, even though the ball went safely through the slip region.

Both Thorpe and Hussain reached well-deserved centuries, on a wicket that still offered something to the pacemen because of the sometimes unpredictable bounce. The breakthrough was finally achieved, shortly after lunch, when the left-hander mistimed a pull shot to end a partnership worth 288 runs.

As so often happens, the man who has been waiting for a long time (in this case John Crawley) failed to post a score. This, a faint edge to the keeper, was Michael Kasprowicz's first Test wicket and came during a spell where the big Queenslander gave it everything he had. Hussain then went to his double century, hitting Warne for three consecutive fours and receiving a deserved standing ovation from the Edgbaston crowd. Soon after, however, Warne turned one with enough vigour to catch the double centurion's outside edge. Thus ended one of the best knocks I've seen for clean hitting and astute placement.

Mercifully, rain put an end to our suffering about an hour before the scheduled close, at which point we were 331 behind and still four wickets away from bowling England out.

7 June, Day 3, First Test

Australia 118 and 256–1 (Elliott 66, Taylor 108*, Blewett 61*) v England 478–9 declared (Ealham 53*; Kasprowicz 4–113).

I looked at a few papers this morning – some of the headlines were a bit embarrassing and I'm not sure I'll be showing the *Daily Mirror's* England cricket crumpet guide for women to Karen – but everyone was really nice. I obviously looked at the *Daily Telegraph* and *The Times* first and Pring (Derek Pringle) had written a nice article in the *Independent*. The only disappointment was Martin Johnson in the *Telegraph* who didn't really have a nice word to say even though I'd got 200. I thought that was a bit harsh but I wasn't going to let it bother me. When I got to the ground someone had put the *Mirror* article on the wall, not to take the mickey out of me getting high marks for looks but to wind up Stewie for getting the lowest marks, six out of ten! Even then I was trying to focus on batting in case I had to make runs in the second innings and I thought to myself 'I hope I haven't done too much and used up all my runs. Why didn't I score a hundred and save the other for Lord's?' I was also worried that people would now expect too much from me but then I told myself not to be silly and enjoy it while it lasts because there's bound to be a duck round the corner somewhere.

Some people asked me what it was like being a national hero but I'm certainly not thinking in those terms. I'm just pleased I've done something that has pleased the country because I know what it's like, as a football and golf fan, when England win an international or Europe win the Ryder Cup. Hopefully, this is the same for cricket fans. I remember Thorpey telling me last year to keep my feet on the ground when things were going well and not to be too despondent when things are going badly and that's a very important lesson for a professional sportsman. It may sound boring but it's vital.

We expected Australia to make a big fight of it second time around and in a way our bowlers deserve more credit this time than they did for their first innings performance because they stuck at it when things weren't going so well. Our biggest disappointment was that the new ball didn't swing so much this time but Crofty made the breakthrough by getting Matthew Elliott before Taylor and Blewett kept us working hard. Of course Taylor, who was under tremendous pressure, battled to a century and I think that's the closest I've ever got to feeling pleased when a member of the opposition got a hundred. I don't know the bloke that well but I know what it was like when Ath was under pressure and it's not nice. When Taylor got to three figures I ran past him, tapped him on the arse and said well played. I don't know if it meant anything to him but I meant it. A lot of the other guys did the same.

The Aussies had started to bat their way back into the game and suddenly it was a case of maybe they can cause problems for us if we're not careful. So tonight it was a question of regrouping and being patient. It also meant another opportunity for me to have a quiet meal with Karen so Theo recommended an Italian restaurant which we went to. It was very nice and the owner, towards the end of our meal, came over and asked me to sign his visitors' book. A few Aston Villa footballers were there and then I saw some Australian autographs, including Mark Waugh. 'Yes, they were in last night,' the owner said. It took me a while to click but then I remembered Mark was in hospital with stomach problems that day! Karen and I spent the rest of the evening wondering what the pasta might do to us but thankfully we were fine.

STEVE WAUGH

My brother Mark has been feeling off-colour for the past few days, and this morning he finally got a doctor's opinion. The diagnosis wasn't what we were looking for. Suspected appendicitis was the verdict and immediate hospitalisation the treatment, at least until exactly what is wrong with him is determined.

Not before time, we finally achieved a winning session, as we claimed three wickets this morning and then kept England wicketless until the lunch break. Michael Kasprowicz picked up four wickets, after earlier playing two Tests without achieving a breakthrough, and was probably our best bowler. But in truth that status wouldn't have been too hard to achieve, as we had put in one of our worst efforts in a number of years, perhaps even on par with our batting effort on the opening day.

Taylor and Elliott continued on after the lunch break until the score reached 133, which was more than our first innings total, when the Victorian was deceived by a ball from Robert Croft that didn't turn. Taylor, though, continued on – it was great to see our skipper back to something like his best, in what would have been, in all honesty, his last Test innings if he'd failed. His first Test 50 since December 1995 was reached, and such was the look of determination and commitment etched on his face at this point, it seemed a century was a distinct possibility, rather than the remote hope so many of the press contingent had dismissed in the days before the game.

Together with Greg Blewett, Taylor brought us back into the game. Both players looked much more assertive and in command than any of us had in our first dig. It was as if we had woken up today and realised we actually were playing in a Test match, and not just in a warm-up. When Mark reached 99, every Australian player was standing in anticipation, while the Channel 7 and Channel 9 television crews had their cameras hard up against the windows in our rooms, ready for the team's reaction. A quick single was taken, and the boys erupted with genuine pleasure at seeing a comrade come through the toughest struggle of his career. This was a courageous display of inner strength. It was goosebumps all round, but thankfully Tubs settled himself down quicker than the rest of us – he batted through to the close – we were still pumped up some overs after he reached his hundred.

At stumps, the Taylor/Blewett stand had realised 123 runs, leaving us only 104 runs behind with nine wickets still in hand. From a seemingly lost cause, we are now in a position to not just save the game but perhaps even force an unlikely victory. We need to bat all day tomorrow to have a chance.

It was interesting to see how Tubby reacted when he returned to the dressing-room after not so much getting the monkey off his back as shaking King Kong clear. After discarding his protective gear, he simply sat in his chair and then, probably for the first time, realised exactly what he had just achieved. He was very subdued as he accepted the congratulations from his team-mates, not once showing any emotion. It was more of a relief than anything – that seemed to be his feeling.

His performance proved that it is possible to achieve anything if you dig deep enough. There was no way Mark Taylor could have gone into today's innings with any degree of confidence, but he showed that inner strength and mental toughness are the two key ingredients if you want to be a successful run-scorer.

8 June, Day 4, First Test
Australia 118 and 477 (Taylor 129, Blewett 125) lost to England 478–9 declared and 119–1 (Atherton 57*, Stewart 40*) by nine wickets.

For the first hour today the Aussies continued to do well and the tension was mounting a bit. In the end it took an inspired spell from Goughy to get us back on track when, as a batsman, I was starting to think of how many we might be chasing and wondering if we might be on course for another hectic Bulawayo run chase. I thought 'please don't let it come to that.' We finally got down to the last three wickets but our bowlers were getting a bit tired when Ath threw the ball to Ealie, who hadn't bowled all day. I thought 'is he sure that's right?' When Ealie went for a few in his first over I went up to Ath and, trying to be subtle, said 'I know why you've brought Ealie on and I know he's a natural swing bowler, but he's a little stiff and the wicket's a bit slow. Don't you think Caddy or Dev might be a better idea? We don't want to be chasing too many. Remember Headingley 1981.'

I was trying to put myself in Shane Warne's position and was wondering who I'd least like to face but Ath said 'don't worry, I know what I'm doing.' Then, of course, Ealie took three wickets for spit and I went up to the captain and said, 'Brilliant mate, well done!' There was also a nice run out to help us involving Bevan as Gillespie's runner which totally confused Ath. It involved a quick bit of athletic fielding from Goughy, who is usually to be found composing new tunes with the Barmy Army in the field rather than pulling off inspired run outs but when the third umpire was called for Ath thought it must be to decide which one of the two batsmen standing at the same end was out. He'd forgotten that Bevan was there at all. Of course, Goughy loved that when he came back to the dressing room and asked Bumble if he'd been impressed with his quick thinking bit of fielding, so he was obviously pleased with himself.

We were left with 118 to win and had, in theory, 32 overs on Sunday and the whole of Monday to do it. The weather forecast was fine so I didn't think we would be rushing to get them on Sunday. But first Butch and Ath and then Stewie started smacking them everywhere and I turned to Bumble and said, 'Are we going for this tonight?' He said no, just play your natural game but by then the adrenalin was flowing through Ath and Stewie and they were flaying Warne to all parts of the ground. It was exhilarating stuff.

By now I was counting down every run and the dressing room started getting noisy with people packing, patting each other on the back and getting ready for the presentations. I was thinking, 'Shut up, I may have to bat here' but when Stewie hit the winning boundary we just let out an almighty roar and started hugging each other. Stewie, the lovely man, picked up a stump for me and gave it to me as soon as he ran back. I put it straight in my bag before people started pouring champagne over my head and Bob Taylor then came in and said to me 'congratulations, you're the Cornhill Man of the Match'. As we went up the stairs the crowd were phenomenal, singing away and I could see the Australians were absolutely gutted by their expressions. So often the boot has been on the other foot.

Getting the Man of the Match award from Bob Willis was a bit special, especially as he's never been my biggest fan, and to hear him saying it was the best innings he'd seen at Edgbaston put the icing on the cake. There was champagne everywhere, the crowd were singing the Ashes are coming home and we milked the moment. This is what it's all about. It doesn't get any better than this.

When I went downstairs I had to have a cortisone injection in my elbow – I hate needles and had a towel over my head – so that brought me down to earth a bit before Ath said that no-one must go home and we were all going out as a team. We started in the bar at the hotel and went into town, spending some time at a place called the Aussie Bar and ending up back in the hotel. By about 4am there was just me, Ath, fitness advisor Dean Riddle and John Etheridge from the *Sun* left and the drunken conversation, interestingly, got on to the subject of the vice-captaincy.

We were talking about the Ealie bowling conversation and Etheridge said, 'Well Nass, you can say these things, can't you? You are the vice-captain.' I said I wasn't sure that I was because nobody had said anything and Ath said 'That's been bugging you hasn't it?' I said it wasn't bugging me but I wasn't sure whether to advise on the field or not and he said, 'Just do what you've always done. You know we don't have an official vice-captain in the summer and you can presume it's the same as in the winter.' So I think, basically, I'm still vice-captain but we'll have to wait and see what happens if Ath is injured.

STEVE WAUGH

For a while it was all going smoothly. We were decreasing the deficit with increasing momentum, thanks particularly to Greg Blewett, whose century was one of the best displays of strokemaking anyone could ever wish to see. But just when we were looking at further deepening Mike Atherton's anguish, the stand was broken after 194 runs had been added. Taylor played a tired drive at Croft and was caught and bowled. At this point we were just 33 runs behind, with eight wickets still in hand.

Unfortunately for Australia, Blewett followed soon after, bat-padding to silly mid-off, and the balance of the game had been completely turned around once more. Michael Bevan again fell to the short ball, a fact that will be preying on his mind from now on. His struggles in this area must be sorted out quickly, or else they will be ruthlessly exposed – Test cricket is all about sensing a weakness in the opposition and then exploiting it. Mark Waugh, still not feeling well but out of hospital, managed to get an edge to a virtually unplayable lifting delivery from a recharged Darren Gough and was out for 1. We were 399 for five at this point, and back in very serious trouble.

Watching this collapse from the other end was very hard to take, but I knew we needed just one more good partnership to be in a position to make a victory bid. I was beginning to feel at ease at the crease, as I settled in (hopefully) for the long haul. My timing and placement weren't as good as I would have liked, but I could feel myself getting stronger by the minute. With Ian Healy, I took our second-innings score towards 450.

A severe afternoon storm halted proceedings for a short period. Immediately upon the resumption of play, I lost my wicket, playing across the line of a Gough delivery which did little and I was trapped lbw. Just when things seemed as if they were falling into place, I drifted into the 'comfort zone' and paid the price. This game will bite you if you don't give it your utmost respect. A similar fate befell Ian Healy, who appeared to be travelling smoothly until Mark Ealham took a leaf out of Ian Botham's book and lured our keeper into a false stroke at a long hop. The Kent all-rounder then took a further two wickets for no runs, and left his side needing 118 for a morale-boosting victory.

Chasing a target such as this can sometimes present difficulties, if you let potential problems dominate your every move, but England didn't appear ruffled or wary at any stage, even though they lost Mark Butcher early on.

The experience of Stewart and Atherton shone through, with glorious shot-making sending the raucous crowd into delirium as the runs-required figure came down rapidly. Significantly, the winning runs came from a spanking cover drive from Stewart off Shane Warne that epitomised the Englishmen's domination of the game.

Getting off the ground after a home-town victory is always a difficult and dangerous assignment, as Matthew Elliott discovered when he was wrestled to the ground by a spectator looking for any type of souvenir.

It's only a matter of time, while the level of security remains amateurish, before a serious incident occurs and a player or supporter is injured. Once we reached the safety of the pavilion, we were obliged to observe the delighted home team accept their winner's cheque and spray the crowd with champagne, which I guess isn't a completely bad thing – this sight should make everyone extremely determined not to have to see it happen again.

A losing dressing-room is always a very sombre place. But the gloom did lift eventually and the post-mortems began in earnest. For us to come back from what has been a disastrous first month to this Ashes campaign, each player will need to make an honest assessment of their own game and attitude and come up with a plan to turn things around. It has to come from within. Words are cheap unless they are backed up with self-belief and desire.

9 June

I was awoken, at 7am, by a knock on the door telling me that a car from the BBC Breakfast News programme was outside waiting to take me to their studio for an interview. In a drunken haze last night I'd apparently agreed to it! After that it was a case of packing my bags and heading for home. Goochie's got a barbecue tomorrow so I'll be taking my magnum of Man of the Match champagne round there to celebrate with the Essex boys. Apparently there was a loud cheer in the Essex dressing room at the Oval when I got to 200 which interrupted play outside and that means a lot. I want to share this moment with them. My dad, Goochie and Fletch have been the three people responsible for me getting to this stage. It's only one knock, one swallow doesn't make a summer. But I've relished it up to now and after the barbecue it will be history. Then it will be time to look ahead and I'll probably get a bit ratty with anyone if they try to talk to me about it this week. The rest of the season starts here.

STEVE WAUGH

There was nothing unusual about us arriving at the ground and changing into our Australian gear – except that today's scheduled fifth day of the first Test was now a training day, courtesy of the fact that we had lost inside the allotted time. Disappointing as our loss was, we must go forward, learn from our mistakes and build on the positives to come out of the match.

This morning's agenda involved a team discussion on our performance (without going into too much detail) before we broke off into three groups for a 'think tank' session. I found this type of small-group 'practice' enlightening, and a welcome break from the usual routine.

The quick bowlers went out to the outfield, where they had a chat about what happened during the match and came out of their discussion conceding that they strayed away from the basic fundamentals of line and length. The best way of rectifying this situation is quite simple – it involves the use of two cones that are put on a place on the wicket deemed to be the good line and length the bowlers should be aiming for.

The batsmen opted to go to the practice nets where we had a chat about what had transpired during the match and in particular during the disastrous first morning. We came to the conclusion that we were a little underdone in our preparation and, more significantly, that we didn't tough it out enough. It was also noted that it was perhaps also 'just one of those mornings' when we nicked everything. And the Englishmen bowled exceptionally well.

We focused on the positives to come from the Test, especially our much-improved second-innings effort, where we applied ourselves so much better. We now believe that the key to the English attack is to nullify their strike bowler which, if accomplished, leaves them 'flatter' and can therefore alter the tempo of the game. Their 'main man', the bowler Atherton turns to when they need a wicket, is Darren Gough, essentially because he has the ability to 'fire up' the whole side with his enthusiasm and spirit. He is similar to the West Indian quicks in that he 'plays dead' during spells – you think you've got him covered after he delivers a couple of innocuous deliveries. But that is when he is at his most dangerous, and his 'effort' ball (delivered with an extra yard of pace) will often catch you off guard. The way to counteract this is to be aware of his methods and to make sure you play each ball on its merits.

The third group comprised the two wicketkeepers and the two spinners. They talked in more general terms about what had transpired during the match and also discussed ways to try to personally improve for the Lord's Test.

7
BACK TO REALITY
NASSER HUSSAIN

It was nice to see the Essex boys again, both at Goochie's barbecue and at Hove where we were playing Sussex. We had a kick around with a football on the outfield on the first morning of the game and I enjoyed getting back to reality and having a bit of a laugh with close friends. Goochie and Fletch had a quiet word with me and as far as I was concerned Edgbaston was history but there were still plenty of press enquiries and things to deal with.

I had agreed, earlier in the week, to speak to Brough Scott for the *Sunday Telegraph* but really I wanted to look ahead now and just did that as a favour. So, when Andrew Longmore of the *Independent on Sunday* turned up I had to tell him that I was afraid I'd said enough about the double hundred and didn't want to talk about it anymore. It was nothing personal, just a realisation on my part that I mustn't get carried away. Mind you, it was hard to concentrate on the county match, particularly when I got a really nice ovation from the Sussex crowd before going out to bat.

Lord's, though, was just around the corner and there was plenty of conjecture in the press and debate for people to get their teeth into. And, before an unchanged party was announced for the second Test, there were two particular topics which intrigued the cricket world. Amazingly, considering how well we'd done at Edgbaston, both were negative towards England players.

First there was the matter of Fred Titmus, the former England selector, criticising Athers before he broke Peter May's record for leading England, saying that he was the worst England captain since the war. As far as I was concerned this was one of the most ludicrous things I've ever heard. Now, obviously I don't know the ins and outs of every captain England have had, but to say Athers is the worst, to me, sums up the era that people like Fred Titmus belong to.

I just hope that when I finish my career I don't look back, see someone like Stephen Peters captaining Essex and England, and say 'he's the worst they've ever had' and 'it wasn't like that in my day.' It's just not necessary for old players to make comments like that.

Look at, for instance, Ian Chappell and Richie Benaud, two great former players whom I have a lot of respect for. If you do something right they offer nothing but praise but if you do something wrong they tell you, constructively, on television or to your face. There are no comparisons with the past all the time, something that cricket more than any other sport seems obsessed with. To be honest, I just laughed off the Titmus comments and I'm sure Athers has done the same, but no doubt they'll be mentioned in the dressing room when we get to Lord's.

The point is, we should be congratulating Athers and reflecting on how well he has done to still be leading England for a 42nd consecutive Test rather than being so negative. He has always been right for the job since taking over from Goochie during the low of a losing Ashes series in 1993. He's come through some rough times, but you can only ever be as good as your team and when he first took over he immediately planned to identify young players of class and, crucially, sound temperament and stick with them, just as we are doing now. But then he had his hands tied by new people above him and it's sobering to think that this current team could have been together, more or less, for two or three years now. If that was the case then I think our record would have been pretty good over that time.

The other 'storm' to brew up has been comments made by Geoffrey Boycott on television about Dominic Cork, labelling him a prima donna. That's Boycs for you. You know he's always going to have an opinion about what's going on. He's never going to beat about the bush or sit on the fence. Some people in the dressing room hate Boycs while others like him and I must admit that I'm one of the ones who usually thinks he's good value.

The thing is, Boycs actually gets on well with Corkie and I'm surprised he's said these things really. Corkie has hardly played for Derbyshire this season so he can hardly be blamed for their problems and the comments which we really objected to, and ones that Boycs insists have been taken out of context, were those suggesting that we as an England team didn't want Dominic Cork with us in New Zealand last winter. That's daft. Corkie is an integral part of the side when he's fit and he's loved by us all. Okay, he's an extrovert and when things are not going his way perhaps his demeanour on the field can look out of place, but we want people in this side to be completely natural and that's how Dominic Cork is. Ever since I've known him he's behaved like a big kid and he likes the cameras to be on him but you know he's always giving you 100 per cent and you can't expect everyone in a team to be like Graham Gooch or, for that matter, Geoffrey Boycott.

As long as everyone is giving everything to the cause you have to accept different personalities and nobody could ever question Corkie's commitment. It's similar to the way people look at Darren Gough. When things are going his way everyone loves his personality and confidence but when he's having a bad time people expect him to conform. I say, let them be natural because that's how we'll get the best out of them.

8
THE AUSTRALIANS REGROUP

STEVE WAUGH

10 June, Nottingham

With Mark Taylor sitting out tomorrow's fixture, the game against Notts will be my first opportunity to captain Australia in a first-class match. Training this afternoon was a non-compulsory one for the guys playing tomorrow, but compulsory for the reserve players. I went along, and the session proved to be a blessing in disguise for me, because it gave me the opportunity to have two hits – Warney wanted an extra bowl, Stuart MacGill (the NSW Shield leggie) had come along and was happy to keep going, and Ricky Ponting was keen to continue his experimentation with the art of off-spin bowling. This second net went for over 45 minutes and by the time I walked away, I felt like a new player, with my timing, footwork and confidence restored to something that approached what I considered acceptable.

The good thing about a long net session when you're not overly happy with your game, is that it gives you an opportunity to work on a few things and occasionally try something different. I now believe my ordinary early-tour form has been affected by a lack of alertness and sharpness at the crease, which can easily be rectified as long as you recognise it. I picked up the tell-tale signs during this second net, when I became frustrated at being late on the ball on a regular basis and constantly felt rushed in my movements. I tried picking my bat up a little earlier and to put more weight through the front part of my feet instead of through my heels. It's amazing what a split second of extra time can make, by the end of the net I was hitting the ball sweetly. The difference in my batting and confidence between when I went and when I finally came out was both a relief and a reward for the extra work.

Phoning home is always something to look forward to, but at the same time it can be enormously frustrating because one minute you feel reunited, but the next you're back to being separated. Luckily this separation will end next week, as Rosalie and Lynette, in tandem with the in-laws, Phil and Ethel Doughty, will travel to the UK to join up with the squad. Without doubt, the hardest thing for me at the moment is listening to Rosalie either laughing, crying or playing in the background when I'm talking to Lynette, but this is somewhat compensated when

I get a chance to talk to her on the phone. Lynette tells me she recognises the voice and looks around, not knowing where the familiar sound is coming from – for me it's reassuring she hasn't completely forgotten who her dad is.

While I've been away Rosie has started eating a variety of different foods, including broccoli, porridge and tomatoes. And she's sporting two new front teeth. Her crawling has improved too, to the point where she is tearing across the floor in search of any mischief she can find. In a way I feel I'm being cheated of something special, but as always, sacrifices have to be made if you are to achieve the ultimate in your chosen profession.

11 June, Nottingham
Australia vs Nottinghamshire, play abandoned due to rain.
Just what the team didn't need greeted our arrival at Trent Bridge – an ashen sky coupled with consistent drizzly rain that looked to be here for some duration. Consequently, an early lunch was taken, which proved to be the highlight of a very dismal day. After tearing into the baked spuds and grilled salmon main, the apple pie, ice cream and custard went down a treat, especially so as the chances of any exercise being required from me today appeared to be diminishing by the minute.

When the captain and vice captain are summoned to an impromptu meeting with an injured player and the team physio it generally isn't good news. True to form, the meeting was a difficult one for all involved – the news on Bic's troubled lower back is all bad. After a series of extensive tests and injections, it was revealed that the L4–5 level in his lower back are on the verge of developing a stress fracture which would put him out of cricket for between six and 12 months. That area of his back, as it is now, is a potential time bomb. Rest, apparently, is the only cure, which means three months of no bowling, not even strenuous exercise.

To see the anguish and hurt in Bic's eyes as he faced this painful end to his problems is definitely the lowlight of the tour. And it's a real shame for a player who not only has a lot of talent, but is also very influential in helping bond the side and enhance team spirit. It has been decided by everyone concerned that it would be better if Bic left the squad immediately, because for him to keep hanging around the team would be like a slow form of torture for him. Inevitably, he would keep thinking about what could have been.

His imminent departure also leaves a hole in the footy-tipping competition, as he was the man responsible for organising the whole event. But he's probably relieved to be going, as he won't have to cop any more sledging about tipping NSW against Queensland in the rugby league State of Origin series. Heals did, too! These boys are supposed to be staunchly parochial towards their birthplace.

In a dire situation such as Bic's, you have to make a positive come out of the negative. It seems things could have been much worse if the back problems hadn't been diagnosed this early. Now, Bic has the opportunity to be fit and strong for our upcoming domestic and international home season.

It's funny how quickly things can turn around in cricket. Take the examples of Paul Reiffel and Andy Bichel. Just six weeks ago, 'Pistol' received the shock of his life when he wasn't part of the touring squad, and in the heat of the moment he contemplated retirement. Now he's here, having arrived last night after being called over to cover for the injury problems of Bic and Brendon Julian. Bic, on the other hand, has been on the crest of a wave – he made his Test debut and had a prominent role during our one-day success in South Africa. Pistol is in today's team and is also a big chance to play in the Lord's Test, Bic is now considering a holiday in Scotland with his wife before departing back to Oz.

Not only is it frustrating not to be playing due to the weather, it also means that Smithy, our fitness adviser, comes into his own. In seasons gone by, a wet cricket day was seen as a bit of a godsend, as it allowed you the luxury of putting your feet up and relaxing until the captains and umpires deemed it appropriate to start again.

Now it is the signal for hard work, usually via the exercise bikes and a mix of gym-circuit exercises such as sit-ups, push-ups and strength work using light weights.

By the time we were scheduled to have the tea interval, both the Notts captain and I agreed it was time to leave the game until tomorrow, much to the relief of both sides who had been frustrated enough for one day.

12 June, Nottingham

Nottinghamshire 239 (Astle 99; McGrath 4–63) v Australians 51–1.

As I wanted to fire things up a bit and get us going, I decided to have a bowl upon winning the toss. Not that I needed any firing up myself, after what I heard from the groundsman this morning. When Geoff Marsh and I inspected the wicket well before the start of play, we asked the head groundsman. 'Are you going to cut any more grass off the wicket?' His reply was one that you wouldn't normally associate with fair play …

'I'll wait and see who's playing in the home team's side before I make a decision.'

In other words, if we (Notts) include our quicks I'll leave the grass on and if we don't I'll cut the grass off!

Bowling first seemed to have the desired effect on our four-pronged speed attack of McGrath, Kasprowicz, Reiffel and Julian. All bowled with good pace, even if the greenish-looking wicket failed to live up to its devilish appearance. It was, in fact, quite placid and slow-paced. I thought the pick of our bowlers was the ever-improving Kasprowicz, who looks as if he believes he should be here, rather than just being happy to be here. Reiffel, as always, found an immaculate length and troubled all the Notts batsmen as a result, but Julian was again a little inconsistent, with too many 'boundary' balls (as in balls that get hit for four) to go with his customary splattering of unplayable deliveries. McGrath looked a little disjointed in his run-up. It appears to me that he needs a good workout to sort out some minor problems in his action and approach to the crease before he gets back to his best.

The keeping of Adam Gilchrist was the biggest plus for the day. Considering the lack of opportunities and match practice his was a polished display behind the stumps, only further enhancing his reputation as a player who looks well-suited to the additional pressures that a Test-match situation throws up. If he had been born anywhere except in Australia, I believe he would already be a success at the top level.

Overall the team's performance was a big improvement on our recent form. The general lift in our energy output and an increase in intensity combined with a few good laughs to make it an enjoyable day all around.

By virtue of a ridiculously small boundary on one side of the ground, the local fans gained a rare insight into what was happening on the field. This led to Pigeon giving not only the lads some funny moments, but most of the crowd, too. This highly comical turn of events began when a prying spectator, who had perched himself on the top tier of an open-aired seating facility at a point exactly opposite the bowling crease at which Pigeon happened to be bowling, began shouting advice. From his vantage point, this keen student of the game believed that Glenn was continually overstepping the front line without being brought to justice by the umpire. And he let everyone know. As soon as this loudmouth realised he was now the centre of attention, he began screaming out 'No ball' each time a delivery was bowled.

This didn't go unnoticed by Pigeon, who made his own thoughts known by way of a couple of well-known gestures.

The umpire, being only human, was now uncertain as to whether or not he had been caught out by the spectator. So he began studying the crease with renewed interest and indeed found a transgression shortly afterwards. Needless to say our illustrious quick from Narromine began to show some signs of frustration, which was shortly to be compounded when a boundary was struck off the last ball of one of his overs. This shot certainly livened up the small band of spectators who were now giving Pigeon a real going over.

The ensuing conversation between player and spectator had all at the ground thoroughly engaged.

Pigeon was fuming and in the process of pulling on his Aussie sweater in a real huff he was left standing in front of his animated audience with an item of clothing that was on back to front. Not only had all his fellow players spotted this act of folly and begun to laugh hysterically, but so had his tormentors in the crowd. Sensing something was not as it should be, the big tearaway looked down in dismay and instantly ripped the sweater off his body as if it was full of funnelwebs. Down it went to the turf, then up and over the advertising boards seconds later, thanks to a strong looking right-foot place kick.

After such an enjoyable episode, we couldn't let the whole affair die a quick or quiet death. So it was decided to relive the nightmare one more time before the end of play. The opportunity arose shortly after tea, after Glenn had bowled the first ball of an over. As he walked back to his bowling mark, the entire slip cordon quickly turned their jumpers around so that each fieldsman's look mirrored the one Pigeon had modelled earlier. Because he is such a competitor, totally focused on his job, this stunt had to be continued for three balls before it was noticed by our spearhead, who immediately saw the humorous side of the prank and had a good laugh before simply saying, 'Very funny, guys.'

13 June, Nottingham

Nottinghamshire 239 drew with Australia 398–5 (Elliott 127, S Waugh 115, Bevan 75*).

With any hope of a result gone after the loss of the first day, we decided to try to bat out the day. And against yet another sub-standard pace attack which was without the county's top-notch bowlers (who generally rest in games against touring sides), this task wasn't too hard to achieve.

Matthew Elliott once again confirmed he is a class act with an effortless century, displaying all the hallmarks of a man destined for prolonged success at the top level. On the other hand, I felt very disappointed and sorry for Slats and Punter, who both got starts and looked impressive before perishing to their only blemishes at the crease. With so little cricket under their belts, it was a rare chance on tour to impress and push for a Test berth. But the lack of opportunities means they aren't match hardened at the moment and the pressure on them is pretty intense.

They must be thinking, 'I'll never get a chance right now.' The key for them is to be ready and expect the unexpected.

After a scratchy start, I played reasonably well, rediscovering my sense of timing and placement enough to reach my 42nd first-class century and give me a boost in the confidence department.

Bevo cruised into the seventies before rain curtailed his century aspirations, while Gilly made his initial first-class appearance at the crease during this tour, batting for a full 14 minutes in scoring an unbeaten 9. However difficult this situation has been for him to handle, Gilly has remained a positive influence around the side, which doesn't go unnoticed by the team's hierarchy.

Even though we didn't get the victory we were after, the team certainly looks on the way back to something approaching good form. Not surprisingly then, we were able to take a little confidence onto the bus with us, as we headed down the motorway to Leicester for our next fixture, which starts tomorrow.

14 June, London

Australia 220–8 (Ponting 64; Ormond 6–54) v Leicestershire.

After the first Test, only 13 players are required to attend each county fixture. Our game against Leicestershire thus represents my first chance to have three days off. However, before setting off for London I decided to head down to the ground to catch the first session, and to get some 'brownie points' with Smithy by way of half an hour's walking around the Oval.

Not surprisingly, the dull lifeless sky made play impossible in the morning, for much of which a persistent drizzle tumbled down to add to our frustrations. Being in a poorly-equipped dressing room made for only 12 people is certainly not the place to be when your touring squad has 22 members and no play is possible, so, quicker than I had intended, off I went down the M1 to the always exciting city of London.

My reasons for going there are twofold. Lynette, baby Rosalie and in-laws Phil and Ethel are due in at Heathrow tomorrow morning. And an overdue piece of dentistry, in the form of a crown fitting, is to be performed the morning after.

15 June, London

Australia 220–8 declared v Leicestershire 62–4 (Reiffel 3–12).

Due to mixture of excitement and apprehension, my sleep pattern during the night was spasmodic, which was a blessing in disguise as it meant I was well awake when a 7.30am tap on the door signalled the arrival of my family.

It was great to see both my girls, but at the same time their arrival once again underlined the downside to touring life. I have to get to know my daughter again after every period away from home that extends over more than a couple of weeks, which is so disheartening. On this occasion, Rosalie thought she recognised something familiar about me – enough to smile at me – but at the same time I sensed she had some reservations and doubts as to my exact link to her. It was some hours later before I felt we had bonded again, after we'd played some familiar games and mimicked sounds that she knew I had made for her before.

My instant family hadn't travelled all that well, with Lynette and both her parents sporting pretty severe bouts of the flu. And this after the 'bub' had exhibited signs of a nasty virus days before leaving Australia. Today's atrocious weather certainly won't help their cause, so it was early to bed for all in the hope of a change in fortunes tomorrow.

16 June, London

Australia 220–8 declared and 105–3 declared (Taylor 57) defeated Leicestershire 62–4 declared and 179 (Warne 5–42, PR Reiffel 3–49) by 84 runs.

Having needles, fingers, instruments and all sorts of chemicals shoved into your mouth for two-and-a-half hours is, by anyone's standards, a poor way to start the day. But the dentist's chair was my calling and it was here I contemplated what I would like to achieve at Lord's over the next week. To cap off a rather painful stint, the final blow came with the presentation of the bill, which came to a tidy sum of £675.

Back at the hotel, the staff had agreed to let us swap our room for a somewhat larger one, although still some way short of what had been promised. As we were keen to get out of the claustrophobic atmosphere, we ventured down to Hyde Park for a couple of hours of relaxation watching all the events going on around us, in weather that was so much better than yesterday's gloom. There were the paddle boats, families on roller blades, desperate sun seekers topless on the 20-pence-a-session deckchairs and, in the distance, a substantial crowd listening to anyone game enough to mount a soapbox at the famous speaker's corner. This park is such a treasure, as it allows you to feel relaxed and free of the pressures and hassles of life in such a hectic city.

When we returned to the hotel, there was good news on the teletext, which revealed that the guys had just defeated the defending county champions, Leicestershire, thanks to a couple of sporting declarations. It is great to get a victory on board and hopefully it will be the catalyst we've been looking for.

Our new room does provide Rosie with some much needed crawling space. She responded accordingly, scouring the floor in Hoover-like fashion. Hopefully, she'll sleep much sounder tonight than she did last night, when she woke me many times. I guess her time clock is in disarray, a reaction to the long flight from Sydney via Hong Kong.

9
ENGLAND v AUSTRALIA
SECOND CORNHILL TEST MATCH

Lord's, London, 19–23 June

STEVE WAUGH

17 June

Cricketers are by nature a superstitious lot. If you are returning to a ground, you generally want to have the same piece of dressing-room that you have occupied the previous time.

Of course, most of the guys have played at Lord's many times, so we have a number of players who not only know where they will be putting their bags, but where others will be located as well. The newcomers are then left to fill out the remaining spaces. My position, first claimed in 1989, is to the right of the dressing-room balcony, when we are seated looking out towards the wicket. It is a lounge-style seat, big enough to handle two players and stretches the width of two viewing windows. Parked next to me in 1997 is Glenn McGrath, who will no doubt help make this section of the room a messy affair.

When we realised we were to be neighbours for this Test, I said to Glenn, 'Okay Pigeon, you take five wickets and I'll make a hundred.' These feats are, of course, significant milestones for players, but at Lord's they take on a special importance. For it is here that you can be forever immortalised on the honour boards that hang at opposite sides of the dressing-room walls. A century for a batsman means you join the likes of Sir Donald Bradman, while a five-wicket haul places you alongside names such as Dennis Lillee, Malcolm Marshall and Sir Richard Hadlee.

Practice at Lord's is always a well-organised affair, with the local MCC groundstaff providing both teams with a plentiful supply of net bowlers, which has the double bonus of making sure everyone gets a decent hit out while also relieving the workload on the teams' frontline bowlers. The downside to today's practice session was the nature of the practice wickets, which due to persistent rain during the past week had not been prepared adequately. The outcome of all this was that the wickets were extremely slow in pace and low in bounce and bore no resemblance whatsoever to the match wicket that will confront us in two days time. Under these conditions, every player must make the most of what's available. I concentrated on trying to tighten up my defensive technique and getting on to the front foot in a more positive manner. Because of the nature of the wickets, however, by the conclusion of my net, I felt as if nothing much had been achieved. But there was always tomorrow to sharpen up for the Test, even though I'd rather be peaking around now.

On a more positive note, it was great to see so many Aussie faces at the nets today. The influx of tour groups into London has boosted our support noticeably. It's always good to hear that Aussie accent, to see the flags being flung about and to know that you are going to get some rowdy, but good-natured backing.

NASSER HUSSAIN

Lord's is a magnificent venue for Test cricket – once you set foot on the field. You can't beat walking out of the famous pavilion in front of a big Lord's crowd to play in a Test match. But the problems with Lord's occur before the match even begins because it can be the most annoying venue to be an England player.

For a start you arrive to find a whole list of things you cannot do from the moment that you have finally negotiated the traffic problems at the Nursery End and got there in the first place. You must not, for instance, arrive at the Grace Gates, so you head for the Nursery End to find that you are not allowed to do a right turn into the ground. So, after driving up to the roundabout and doubling back on yourself, you're faced with walking, with your kit, right across the ground before you can get to the dressing room.

Then you are told you can't wear shorts on the outfield; you can't play around with a football and you must be properly attired in the nets. When you've negotiated all this to get to the nets you find, as usual, that they're not in the best of condition and, certainly, I've never had a net at Lord's which could be described as being flat.

This year, of course, the bad weather has made them that much worse and the nets today were close to being a pointless exercise. It was like being on a club ground with a damp uneven surface. After the euphoria of Edgbaston all this tends to bring you back down to earth but there have been some good aspects to today. Firstly we arrived to find a good luck fax from Corkie, congratulating us on the first Test win and encouraging us to keep it up. It was signed 'the prima donna', so he obviously took the Boycott business in the right fashion.

The day has also seen huge stick dished out to Ath over the Titmus comments. We've all been asking him what it's like being the worst captain England have had and a few comments like 'we knew you were bad, but we didn't know you were that bad' have been flying about.

Ath joined in too tonight at a big benefit dinner held for him at the Hilton Hotel. He stood up and immediately said, 'I'd like to thank Fred Titmus for not being here'. I think deep down he's hurting about those comments but he won't show it.

18 June

The pre-match team breakfast and meeting was a fairly subdued affair. We've placed the onus on each individual to adhere to the basics and improve on their first Test performance.

The only change to the side from Edgbaston is that Paul Reiffel will come in to replace the injured Jason Gillespie. The inclusion of Pistol will add not only experience but also solidarity to our attack, for he will make it hard for the Poms to score as quickly as they often did in the first Test. This should allow us to build up pressure.

Training was again not as one would have hoped for the day before a Test match, again largely due to the under-prepared practice wickets. But we gained strength from an excellent, intense fielding session – usually a fairly good guide to a confident mood in the camp.

NASSER HUSSAIN

The weather has been so bad that we couldn't even have a net today because the covering wasn't adequate, but the feeling that we don't really belong here lingers. It's as if this is a member's club and the England team are on the outside. I believe even Lord MacLaurin feels this way because I've heard him say that we must try to make Lord's more cricketer friendly and he's head of the England and Wales Cricket Board, so I don't think I'm being unfair in making these comments. We couldn't even do throwdowns on the outfield because that's not allowed, so all we've been reduced to is a few throwdowns on the full at the Nursery End and that's a waste of time. To me, this feels like going back to playing for Ilford on a Saturday.

I also had a medical appointment today. I've been bothered by this tennis elbow problem in my left joint ever since Zimbabwe and I've had all sorts of treatment on it, including that cortisone injection in the aftermath of my 207 at Edgbaston. It just hasn't got any better and I'm getting fed up of taking painkillers before every day's cricket, partly because they're starting to give me stomach cramps and I would like to get it sorted once and for all. Jim Davis, the Essex physio, recommended a specialist in tennis injuries who is based near Lord's so I went to see him today. He says I should have a second cortisone injection followed by a week's rest but I'm not sure I agree with that. The question is, when do I rest? I'll see him again at the end of the Test and we'll take it from there.

19 June, Day 1, Second Test

Play abandoned.

For every Australian cricketer, the chance to play in a Test match at Lord's represents a dream come true. Unfortunately, today it was not to be for any of us, as constant rain tumbled down all day and gave groundstaff their worst nightmare – every time they mopped up some water off the covers, more rain would fall minutes later. By 5pm it was obvious to all that enough was enough and play was called off for the day.

A surprise visitor to our humble abode was the Australian Prime Minister, John Howard, who popped in for a chat and a couple of photo opportunities. As Mr Howard strolled around the room, I noted what each player was doing ...

Warney and Tubs were playing Herb and Bevo at 500 (again!).

BJ was lying on his back, reading a book.

Dizzy was reading a cricket magazine.

Punter and Blewey were working out an order for some new golf clubs.

Gilly was 'juggling' a soccer ball.

Slats was strumming his guitar and singing to himself (thankfully).

Lang was writing his report for the ACB internet site.

Pistol was signing the official team autograph sheets.

Junior was watching the races on the television.

Heals was sorting out his gear, making sure everything was nice and neat.

Hooter was treating Kasper on the bench.

Crommo was sorting out the hospitality and ticket requests for tomorrow.

And Smithy and Swampy were doing an extra boxing routine together. These guys just hate doing nothing!

Where Pigeon was at this moment was anyone's guess.

NASSER HUSSAIN

A very frustrating day. Just never any chance of play. When we arrived at Lord's the first thing that really surprised us was the incredible size of the covering. I've never seen anything like that at headquarters before, they were more like the Brumbrella at Edgbaston. The comment was made by someone that if we were abroad and our opponents were 1–0 up would there be as much covering on the ground as this on a wet day? But, having said that, we could be in a position of strength here if we bowl first and then, if rain came, people would be saying 'why haven't we got bigger covering?', so it's fair enough.

You can hardly go for a wander around Lord's on a rainy day because there are so many people milling around the ground, so you end up just sitting around the dressing room. A card school was set up involving Ealham and Crawley taking on Thorpe and Atherton and every hour or so there'd be rumblings going on because Thorpey wasn't concentrating and Athers would be having a go at him, as Athers is known to do at the card table.

Gough and Croft tend to rule our dressing room in situations like this, kicking a football around or playing jokes on people. You need to be careful and maintain your concentration because you never know when you might be going out to play but there was never much chance today. I found the TV interesting. They were showing an A to Z of the Ashes on the BBC and it was compulsive viewing. There was the sight of Boycs falling over after being bowled by Bob Massie – we all had a good laugh at that – and brilliant matches involving Lillee and Thomson and the fantastic Botham achievements of 1981. Seeing Both hitting Lillee for sixes was inspirational and it made me try to remember where I was when all this was going on.

Lord's being Lord's the food was great, so every now and then bacon butties would be brought in for us and we'd eat them watching the old cricket or the racing from Ascot. Mark Waugh was glued to the racing when I went and had a chat with him and Kasper in their dressing room and I ended up going back to the hotel feeling absolutely knackered having done precisely nothing.

20 June, Day 2, Second Test
England 38–3.

Without doubt, the most lasting memory for me today was the complete hush that swept over Lord's before the first ball of the match. It was one of those special moments that one can only appreciate when you're actually at the ground. Within minutes of that first delivery, Glenn McGrath had their top-order backpeddling with some quality pace bowling. Glenn's displays nowadays are highlighted by his ability to pinpoint a batsman's weakness and then go in after that failing like an anteater attacks a termite mound.

The most talked about incident of the day came immediately after Graham Thorpe came to the crease with the score at 13 for three. He played tentatively at his first ball and edged what at first seemed to be a regulation low catch to Ian Healy. But such was the uneven bounce, the ball 'died' on its way through to the keeper and barely carried. Healy dived forward and came up with the ball in his gloves, together with a quizzical look that suggested he didn't know whether he'd caught the ball before it hit the turf.

I was fielding in the gully and had my doubts as to whether it had carried, as did Greg Blewett at short leg. However, the guys in the slip cordon – Mark Taylor, Mark Waugh and Shane Warne – all thought it was a fair catch.

Heals, to his credit, went to umpire David Shepherd and said, 'I'm not sure, Shep.' The umpires then conferred and gave Thorpe the benefit of the doubt. This incident just proves that at full speed it is often impossible to know exactly what goes on, that things can look very different from different perspectives and vantage points, and that the use of the third TV umpire in these situations is essential.

Making the most of this shaky start, Thorpe, with Nasser Hussain (who seems to be enjoying something of a golden trot as far as playing and missing goes), kept us at bay until even more rain put an end to our aspirations. Even though it was another day of frustration, we have at least set the tone for the Test and let England know we are back and ready for the battles ahead.

NASSER HUSSAIN

The toss was huge today but Ath was undecided as to what to do for the best. His decision was made harder by the state of the wicket because it looked extremely poor. The cracks were more like fourth or fifth day ones and the surface was not the damp, green one you might have expected after all this rain. The authorities point their finger at Edgbaston's surfaces but this one is not going to get very high marks.

So when Ath went out these cracks were staring up at him and he was thinking 'what is this going to be like on the fourth and fifth days if the weather forecast is wrong?' So he was keen to bat but open to suggestions while I thought it was a good idea to bowl. To complicate matters, there was a rumour going around that Australia were, after all, going to play the fit again Jason Gillespie and leave out Michael Bevan which leant more weight to the bowling first option.

I think the clinching factor was a chat Ath had with Ian Botham just as he was going out to toss. 'Both' advised him to bowl and I think he was going to do that before Mark Taylor saved him the trouble by winning again and sending us in. The Gillespie rumour, meanwhile, turned out to be just that. Bevan retained his place.

The final disappointing Lord's factor came when Roger Knight, the MCC secretary, came on the tannoy asking people to watch their behaviour. I can understand people in cricket being wary of the yob element but to us this announcement misjudged the mood of the country. The atmosphere at Edgbaston was tremendous and it really does give you that extra lift when you're playing against top-quality opposition.

Yet here we were basically asking people not to support us loudly and that takes home advantage away from you while also treating the paying spectators like school children. They shell out good money to watch Test cricket and surely their response at Edgbaston was what support is all about. There was little or no drunkenness, little or no bad behaviour and, as far as I could tell, everyone was good humoured. There was a great response to Taylor's century and the crowd contributed hugely to the most enjoyable game most of us have ever played in.

Playing at Edgbaston was like playing in the West Indies. You know you're going to get some friendly abuse and you know there'll be dancing if they take your wicket. It adds to the occasion. Nobody wants Lord's to lose its unique standing in the game but we do need support and the whole downbeat atmosphere of the place might be one reason why England's record is so poor there over the years.

Not that Australia needed any lifting on this occasion. They were very gracious in defeat in Birmingham but we knew they'd come back at us. There were rumours that they'd refused to sign any more bats for beneficiaries, throwing them out of the dressing room and ignoring any other distractions, and they had clearly talked things over and decided that the time had come for them to step up a gear.

You could see they meant business as soon as we started batting today. They'd clearly made a decision to up the aggression from the amount of noise they were

making in the field and it was more like the Australia of old under Allan Border.
Mind you, they'd won the toss and stuck us in on a wicket that was perfect to bowl
on, so if they couldn't get up for that they were never going to be up for anything.

We knew we would have to bat well but we didn't realise quite how much the
wicket would do. It must have been a risk to play on a relaid pitch with huge cracks
in it. Mick Hunt, the groundsman, pressed the cracks before the start, saying they
weren't moving, but they were and it was no surprise to me when I batted again
with England having lost quick wickets. My aim was just to get through before the
rain came again which I managed , on 10 not out, and knew I would have to play
myself in again tomorrow just when I was feeling settled.

21 June, Day 3, Second Test

England 77 (McGrath 8–38, Reiffel 2–17) v Australia 131–2 (Elliott 55*,
Blewett, 45, M Waugh 26*)

Glenn McGrath and Paul Reiffel worked beautifully as a combination when play
began this morning, building on our great start of yesterday. McGrath came
tearing down the slope, angling the ball into the right-handers and away from the
lefties, while Reiffel diligently worked on each batsman, like a dental surgeon
would on decaying teeth. These two bowled unchanged through the morning
session, the only break coming through a 15-minute rain delay, as they cut a
swathe through the English batting order.

Hussain probably battled the hardest of the Englishmen, lasting 108 minutes
for 19 runs, stats which underline the quality of our bowling. It was like playing
back in the under-10s again, with figures you'd normally associate with that level
of cricket being returned. McGrath 8–38, Reiffel 2–17, England all out 77.

The mood in our room was buoyant, as there is definitely now the distinct
possibility of an Australian win. When we entered the rooms, the 'benchies' and
our support staff gave us a huge ovation, and also updated the honour board to
include Glenn's amazing figures. They are the best-ever by an Australian in Test
cricket at Lord's, and we can count ourselves lucky to have been here to see it. A
huge credit must also go to Reiffel, who kept up the constant pressure at the other
end and conceded little more than one run per over.

When we batted, the rain again made the game a stop-start affair, refusing to
allow anyone to settle into a rhythm or to dominate proceedings. Mark Taylor
reverted to his most common form of dismissal, immediately chopping a ball back
onto his stumps, which gave England a ray of hope that their tiny total might be
competitive after all. But at the other end, Matthew Elliott rapidly gained
confidence, stealing quick singles at every opportunity. Greg Blewett, meanwhile,
produced a mixed bag of streaky shots combined with his trademark cover drive
with that extra flourish.

The scoreboard would have looked a lot better for the home side if chances
offered by both batsmen had been accepted. The miss that allowed Greg to escape

AN UP AND DOWN SUMMER
Nasser Hussain

Above: Captain and vice-captain taking a break during training for the fourth Test at Headingley. The Ashes slipped away as we were defeated convincingly.

Below: Thorpey displays the form that makes him such an important member of our side. Here he is seen during his 75 not out in the first one-dayer at Headingley.

Athers is named man of the match after the second one-day international at the Oval in which he scored an unbeaten 113.

Adam Hollioake scored the winning runs in all three one-day internationals. Here he hits out at the Oval for his 53 not out.

The first Test of the summer, at Edgbaston, and another cut for four during my first double hundred in any form of cricket.

Above: The last wicket falls and Australia are all out for a scarcely believable 118 on the first day of the series at Edgbaston. Full marks to our bowlers who really performed well against a strong batting lineup.

Below: A great roar went through the dressing room as Alec Stewart hit the winning runs at Edgbaston. Unfortunately we didn't take our chances after that to win the Ashes.

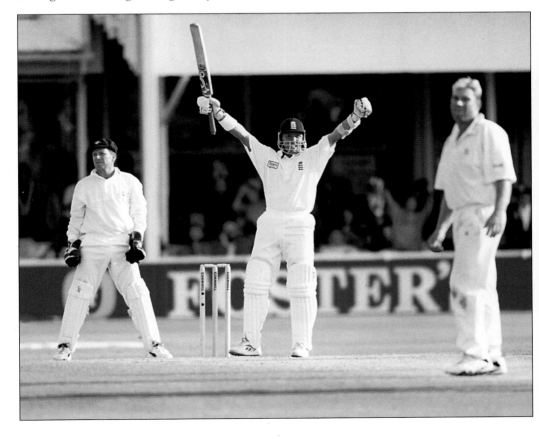

Glenn McGrath, the country boy from Narromine, during his man of the match winning performance at Lord's where he finished with nine for 103.

The pain from Steve Waugh's bruised hand is evident during the first of his two Test centuries at Old Trafford in the Aussies' first Test win of the summer.

Dean Headley is a good friend who made a tremendous impression in his first three Tests. Here he is talking to David Graveney and Mike Atherton before his history making debut at Old Trafford in the Third Test.

A pull shot during my hundred in a losing cause in the fourth Test at Headingley. It was the only one of my five Test hundreds to date scored in the second innings of the match.

'Mr Thorpe, you've just lost us the Ashes.' Poor Thorpey drops Matthew Elliott off the unfortunate debutant Mike Smith at a crucial stage of the Headingley Test. Elliott went on to make 199.

A disappointing end to my century at Headingley. Caught by Gillespie off Warne early on the final morning.

The captain falls to the Healy-McGrath combination in the fifth Test at Trent Bridge, where Athers told me he was considering quitting. Luckily he had second thoughts and will stay on.

Shane dismissed me six times during the series and is seen here bowling me for two at Trent Bridge. But as the man's a genius I won't be losing any sleep over it.

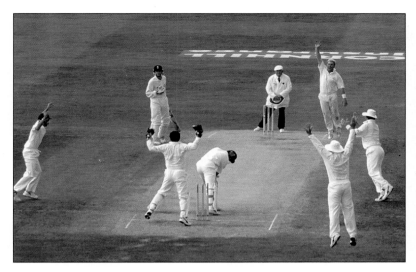

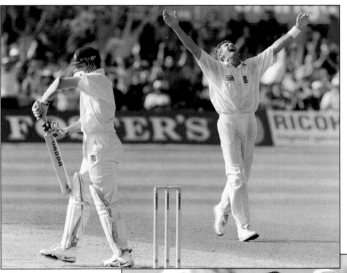

'You come and field over here, said Adam, 'and I'll go on the drive.' Then, next ball, Mick Kasprowicz drove Andy Caddick obligingly to Surrey's captain to set up our dramatic win at the Oval sixth Test. I'd have probably shelled it!

The ball went almost in slow motion off Glenn McGrath's bat and the 'little man' took the catch to win us the sixth Test. Adam, me and Butch lead the congratulations of Thorpey.

A job well done. Tuffers and Caddy, contrasting characters but both committed to the cause, reflect on their match-winning performances at the Oval.

Smiles all round for me, Thorpey and Bumble on the Oval balcony as we await the announcement of the player of the series award – which Thorpey deserved to win.

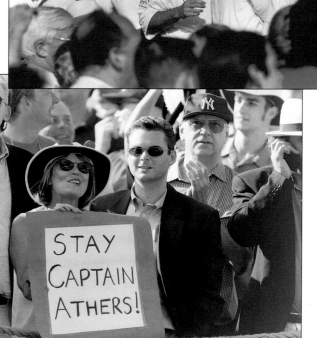

The Oval spectators let Athers know what they think of him after the sixth Test win. We all agreed with them and, thankfully, the captain was persuaded to lead us this winter.

STAY CAPTAIN ATHERS!

was a blunder you wouldn't expect from a schoolboy side. He was beaten for pace while attempting a pull shot, and the ball ballooned off his gloves into the area near second slip Mark Butcher. For some reason Butcher didn't move until it was too late, leaving the ball to lob gently between himself and Graham Thorpe at first slip. The bowler, Andy Caddick, was left to tear his hair out.

Then, after Blewett was eventually dismissed, Mark Waugh should have followed him immediately, but the usually safe hands of Nasser Hussain let England down when Mark teased him with a difficult chance off Robert Croft. The stumps scoreline of 131 for two was reasonably flattering to us, but England failed to convert their chances and may come to rue their slackness.

NASSER HUSSAIN

I felt quite relaxed before I batted today because I knew, with the wicket doing so much, that I might get a ball I could do nothing about, so I just set myself the task of playing straight. McGrath, from the Pavilion End, was proving difficult but I found Paul Reiffel, who had flown in as a replacement for the injured Andy Bichel and gone straight into the side for Gillespie, a little easier. Butch and Ath had fallen to good balls and Stewie, to his cost, had left one that came down the hill and bowled him. Thorpey and I looked to be natural and positive but it was ever so difficult because the ball was doing a lot and the Aussies were bowling in the right places.

I remember being opened up completely once by Reiffel and just had to snigger to myself because I could do nothing about it. Taylor gave Warne a couple of overs and Thorpey cashed in with a couple of boundaries, so pace was clearly going to pose the bigger problems on this occasion. When McGrath and Reiffel came back Thorpey played forward, as you must on a wicket like that, and got out to short leg. He couldn't have done much else to avoid that fate. Then John Crawley was out in similar fashion to the first Test and we were up against it, but I was feeling good.

Ealie and I were going okay when the rain came again and, with Goochie in attendance in the dressing room, there was never any danger of me losing focus during the short break. So I just had a glass of water and waited before we went out again. When we did, people were still sitting down when McGrath came in to bowl the first ball and I was thinking 'shall I pull away here?' To my cost, I didn't. He bowled me a floaty little ball, just a loosener really, and swung it back just a little, something he only usually does towards the end of an innings. It came down the slope and I was stone dead in front. The delay had obviously not done me any favours but that was the story of the week. Delay after delay. I threw my gear around when I got back, because I'd worked so hard and got out to my first lapse in concentration. The innings, meanwhile, was turning into a nightmare for England.

There was a little room at the back of the pavilion where Thorpey and I sat, after we were both out, watching the rest of the innings. We looked at each other and said 'why does it have to be so up and down? One day you're taking part in a record breaking partnership and beating Australia with a day to spare and then this happens.' This turned into 77 all out and now, on television, instead of a list of all the highest partnerships in Ashes series we were looking at a list of all the lowest England scores against Australia. Cricket never seems to be grey, always black or white. At least there weren't that many bad shots. It wasn't as if the England team had been hanging their bats out to dry. But that's not how some people saw it. Robin Marler, the outspoken Sunday Times journalist and now Sussex chairman, apparently said that the wicket had done little and we had just played badly. That annoyed a few people, including I understand those at the top who may have had a quiet word in Mr Marler's ear.

But after all the hype of the first Test and all the personal satisfaction on my part here we were at the other end of the scale. We had to keep our heads up. Ath and Bumble reminded us that it was still a good wicket to bowl on and we were still in the game. Yet what followed was hard to take in.

When you're out for a low score the first few overs of the opposition's reply dictates the course of their innings. As batsmen you wonder how much of it was down to you playing badly, so when you get in the field you hope and pray that the bowlers will prove that there wasn't much more we could have done to avoid the ignominy of double figures. Then all the pressure goes on the bowlers because they know they should perform and so it all boils down to the crucial first 10 overs.

If you can get the opposition 20 for three the self-belief comes flooding back, but if they make a good start you start blaming yourself for your side's low score and heads start to drop. So it was at Lord's today. We got Taylor early – he seems to be the king of the drag on – but then we had a crazy hour or so when I'm afraid we went back to the bad old ways of England sides past. As a team we had been fielding well, but this time we let ourselves down.

22 June, Day 4, Second Test
England 77 v Australia 213–7 (Elliott 112).

Just when we thought we would get another early mark, after another day that again left the groundstaff cursing the Gods, the umpires decided that play would get under way at 5.40pm, with the rule that an extra hour can be added to make up for lost time being brought into play. The dedicated few who had braved (many without cover) the chilly, wet conditions were rewarded with 17.4 overs of action-packed drama.

A chase for quick runs was our only option and it was with these instructions that Mark Waugh and Matthew Elliott returned to the centre. Shane Warne had been promoted to No. 5, with a licence to play shots from ball one, and it wasn't long before he was at the crease, after Mark was caught by Devon Malcolm at third man. This was a grab the bookies would have offered about 20–1 about Big Dev taking, such is his reputation as a fieldsman.

The use of a 'pinch-hitter' such as Shane is a move that rarely comes off, probably because the guy involved suddenly has expectations of himself, whereas when he swings away late in the order he has no such responsibility. Straightaway, Warne went for a big six but only managed to sky a catch. My stay was even shorter – the shortest possible time, in fact – as I was trapped in front by Andy Caddick as I played across the line.

Michael Bevan became the fourth part of the procession, when he was unluckily caught behind, trying to pull, off a bottom edge. Elliott, however, was playing like a genius at the other end, gorging himself on a series of short-pitched offerings from Darren Gough and company, who were trying to either bounce him out or knock him out. That glorious moment for any cricketer finally came for Matty at around 6.50pm, when he pushed Croft into the covers and took off like Donovan Bailey to register his initial Test century.

This is a special moment for any cricketer, but to achieve it at the Home of cricket is as good as the script gets. He finally perished, just before stumps, to the hook shot that he had reaped such rewards from throughout his superb knock. Surely many more hundreds are to follow for this technically gifted batsman.

After the helter-skelter of this 'mini-session', that saw 82 runs scored and five wickets fall, we are still in with an outside chance of victory, though much will depend on our efforts with the new ball after we declare in the morning.

Getting into the Lord's showers is always something to look forward to, with their fire hydrant pressure and heads the size of dinner plates. There are also a couple of extra-long bath tubs available if that's what you desire.

Once showered, we shared a couple of relaxing, congratulatory beers with Herb, before I headed off for the Westbury to grab some Chinese takeaway and contemplate my dismissal.

I've been in a negative frame of mind since the first scheduled day of this Test. I think this can sometimes happen in rain-marred matches, where you can tend to drift a bit and lose focus. When I arrived at the crease today, I felt rushed and not ready for the ball that was about to be bowled to me. This explains my lateness on the delivery. I hope I can use my mistakes here as a lesson for next time. I must begin to work harder, stop whingeing at little things and get stuck into my net practice with renewed vigour and enthusiasm.

NASSER HUSSAIN

I didn't think we were going to play today because whenever there seemed to be a chance of getting out there, the rain would come again. We eventually got on and had a short session in which we didn't do that badly. We took our catches, something of a relief, and Goughy bowled as quickly as I've ever seen him. Alec was back after his back spasm, which forced Crawley into being a surprisingly effective emergency keeper, and we felt a lot more comfortable with ourselves but we have still been left a difficult last day. I had dinner with Ath tonight and he seems in the mood to bat all day Monday. He's proved more than equal to this sort of task in the past.

23 June, Day 5, Second Test

England 77 and 266–4 (Butcher 87, Atherton 77) drew with Australia 213–7 declared.

There was a much smaller crowd at Lord's today than there had been for even the washed-out days, and it was made up predominantly of Aussie supporters. They were there, I presume, in the hope of a stirring victory. Unfortunately, they were denied, primarily by a solid 162-run opening partnership between a dour Mike Atherton and an increasingly confident Mark Butcher. Following in the footsteps of Taylor and Elliott in our second innings at Edgbaston, Atherton and Butcher put together an opening partnership here that surpassed their team's complete total in the first innings.

It might have been different, however, had Mark Taylor at first slip accepted an early chance from Butcher, off Paul Reiffel, that our captain would normally have held blindfolded. But it wasn't to be. Instead the day developed into an exercise in psychological warfare, to see who could milk something positive out of the remaining hours of play.

Both Englishmen were denied centuries. Atherton stepped rather carelessly onto his stumps when a hundred looked a good thing, while Butcher had his defences invaded by a sharply-turning leg break that spun out of the bowlers' footmarks.

Nasser Hussain's dismissal represented many bonus points for us, as he was lured into a big drive by a dipping Warne leg break. The warning here was that if Hussain doesn't treat our leggie with the utmost respect in future he will suffer the consequences – the dismissal must leave negative thoughts in the batsman's mind. Alec Stewart, too, now has plenty of food for thought, after being caught off a wayward hook shot once again. He loves that shot, but it is one that is fraught with danger unless you are in great form and seeing the ball well.

John Crawley and Graham Thorpe played out the remaining time, which was especially important for Crawley, who has scored only two runs in two innings to date in the series. It's amazing what a score such as 29 not out can do for one's confidence and self-belief in such circumstances, and I'm sure the man from Lancashire will sleep a lot more soundly tonight for having scored these precious runs.

The moral victory, if there is such a thing, was ours. Glenn McGrath, deservedly, collected the Man of the Match award, but only just ahead of Matthew Elliott, who will come away from this match as a Test player who not only believes in himself but who expects to succeed at this level.

After such a mixed-up week, the team decided it should get together for a drink and a chat at one of London's trendier restaurants and bars, Quaglinos. As lady luck would have it, behind the bar was an Aussie on a working holiday. He had a lot of trouble locating the cash register throughout the evening, which ended up saving us quite a few pounds before the night was through.

NASSER HUSSAIN

The sun came out after a short shower this morning and the Lord's wicket is always a little easier when it's bright and sunny but we knew we would still have to bat very well because the ball was still seaming all over the place. Something crucial happened to Butch this morning, an incident which could well be the turning point and as pivotal in his career as my 'escape' on a low score during the 1996 Edgbaston Test. He was dropped at slip by Taylor before he had reached double figures and went on to play a large part in our saving the match.

Now I think he would still have played at Old Trafford even if he had scored a duck today and Grav intimated as much, but you have to remember that he was very down and this was a severe test of his mettle. Butch had probably reached the stage where he was quite fatalistic about it all because he had done so badly in this match that things couldn't get any worse and in a perverse way that might have relaxed him. He was still confident on the outside but, if he is anything like me, he would have been really hurting inside before today and feeling that he'd let everyone down. But he does have the inner strength that you need at this level and I think the selectors have recognised that.

To get this in perspective, Butch had only had three innings at the highest level before today after playing for 10 years to reach the top, and the fact is, he was being judged on just three innings against the best side in the world on pitches that were more suited to bowling. The same people, meanwhile, who had been clamouring for his inclusion were now saying he was facing his last chance. Still we like to build people up and then knock them down in this country.

The happy truth is that, after his early piece of luck, Butch played beautifully in partnership with Ath and by the time they were separated the game was virtually safe for us. For me this meant it was another difficult day sitting around with my pads on before the pressure eased and when I did go in we all felt that there was no way we were going to lose.

I must say I'm not at my best in those sort of situations but we had all decided to be positive for the last session and to go for our shots. Stewie is a bit like me – he likes the pressure to be on when he's batting – and he got out hooking here and when it was my turn I got a half volley from Warne first ball which, I'm annoyed to say, I hit straight to cover. Then there were a couple of good balls and then another half volley which I drilled straight to him and he took a good catch. Thank you and good night. A Test duck.

It just summed up the week for me. It had been such hard work and probably the most difficult and least enjoyable Test I've played in but my feelings at the end were still euphoric. We'd come through it and drawn the game. We're still 1–0 up. The weather had helped but it was a save and it was all down to Ath and Butch on the last day. It was nice, also, to see John getting a few before the end, still being positive and emphasising to the Australians that this is a tough England team.

Yes, there were signs in this match that McGrath had hit his straps and that Warne was getting his old zip back, but it's not exactly a huge surprise. They are two of the best bowlers in the world, after all, and the fact that we played so well against them at Edgbaston should not have meant that they should be in any way written off. Any members of the media who did so were always going to be proved premature.

But, then again, our top six are building decent Test records now, with most of us averaging in the forties so it's up to us to combat these guys the way we did at Birmingham, not the way we did here. The game ended with another presentation to Ath, this time by Cornhill, and all of us congratulating Butch. His innings has been such a boost for him. He was quick to congratulate me when he hadn't got many at Edgbaston, so I made sure I returned the compliment today. This England side shares in its triumphs and disappointments. No time for a drink with our opponents. We've all now got to lug our kit back right round the ground, get into our cars and drive to various obscure places for the first round of the NatWest Trophy tomorrow. For me that means meeting up tonight with the Essex boys at Beaconsfield, where we're playing Bucks, but the most urgent thing on my mind is trying to sort out my tennis elbow.

10
A FRUSTRATING
WEEK IN JUNE

STEVE WAUGH

24 June, London

Having a benefit year on the county circuit is always good from a financial point of view, but often the beneficiary's form on the field suffers because of the increased commitments and responsibilities. However, because Devon Malcolm's benefit year coincides with this year's Ashes tour, it has been our turn to do the suffering. This is particularly true of Gilly, who has been targeted by Dev as the man he should approach if he wants anything not nailed down to be signed by the Australian team. It has reached the stage where, whenever Dev knocks on our doors, Gilly sprints for the safety of the toilet. Considering our benevolence, you would have thought Dev might have thrown the odd half-volley our way, especially after we reached the thousand signature mark, but there is about as much chance of that happening as there is of no more autograph requests coming our way from Test cricket's most unorthodox but entertaining batsman.

Thankfully, the event we attended today was to be one of the last of our official functions on the tour. The venue was Australia House, with the purpose being to promote an Ashes exhibition that is being conducted in the building throughout our 1997 tour. Also at the function was the Australian Prime Minister, and those who had not been introduced to him at Lord's now took advantage of the opportunity.

During our visit, I was lucky enough to be presented by Mr Howard with the Variety Club of Australia's award for the cricket personality of the year. This is quite an honour.

As usual, the function went on far too long and to make matters worse the food trays were too hard to track down for our liking. After two hours of small talk, we dashed to the bus, the mood of the team best summed up by a comment that was heard more than once … 'We're outta here!!'

25 June, Oxford

Australia v British Universities, play abandoned.
On most occasions when you play a team like the Combined Universities during a long and arduous tour, the sight of rain tumbling down, together with grey leaden skies, would be a time to rejoice for all. Not so today, as all the squad are keen for

some cricket and many are still searching for that elusive good form. Even more of an incentive to get out there and play is the thought that Smithy is forever hovering around, looking to put into action some fiendish routine sure to leave us praying for the next fine day. That's exactly what happened this morning after Swampy and Tubs returned from the picturesque but rain-sodden ground appropriately named 'The Parks' to inform us that no play looked likely on day one.

At precisely the time the first ball was scheduled to be bowled, we were strewn all over the hotel gym and squash court complex, beginning a circuit of activity that would last for well over 90 minutes.

Each player had to complete at least 20 minutes on a bike or treadmill, followed by a light weights circuit and capped off by some sprints coupled with a tortuous boxing routine. The way things are going with the inclement weather we will soon be stale cricket-wise, but the potential for unearthing a triathlon or boxing star from among the squad appears very promising.

If I had to choose a way to stay fit, I'd definitely choose a boxing routine, as it sharpens up your footwork and co-ordination as well as aiding stamina and enhancing strength. And it's also enjoyable.

The title for the team's worst boxers sits with either Junior, who refuses to don the gloves at all, claiming some sort of previous wrist ailment, or Heals, who it must be said can't really pack a decent punch because of his deformed-looking arthritic fingers that refuse to bend when asked. At the other end of the scale, we have the fast-emerging heavyweight contender, Kasper, whose right hook is assuming Tyson-like proportions (although his lack of nimbleness around the ring appears to be an obvious weakness). Lang, of course, is more than useful, with speed, agility and eyes that glaze over when he starts jabbing those explosive left and rights. But, for mine, the title of best pound-for-pound pugilist goes to Punter. Here is a man who is deceptively powerful and strong – he isn't one to back down and has already had dressing-room dust-ups with the likes of McGrath and come away with the points.

I didn't want to be hotel bound, particularly as the rooms are once again cramped, so I opted for a bit of sightseeing with the family in the city of Oxford. This is certainly one of the most lively places in the UK, with numerous colleges and thousands of students all accommodated in and around the town centre. Some of the other lads went for a round of golf, while others chose the old saviour on a wet day, the haircut.

The most interest however, surrounded the impending birth of the Warnes' first baby, which happened to be due today. Or at least Warney thinks so! The odds are it will be a boy with red hair and a toasted cheese sandwich held in its right hand. Seriously, though, I think Shane is very disappointed he won't be there for the birth and feels a bit helpless as a result. I'm sure it must be a difficult period for him right now, especially so as we've been inactive for the past week or so. This has given him more opportunities to think about what he's missing out on.

Thankfully, Swampy tracked down some indoor nets for those wishing to have a practice session. Under normal circumstances most players prefer not to use the synthetic wickets as they play nothing like a turf pitch and are onerous on the body. For a batsman, they can cause bad habits, largely due to the predictable pace and bounce which leads to poor footwork and technique – you can get away with murder by just using your eyes only. Bowlers dread indoor nets, primarily because they can't go back to their normal run-ups and the stress caused by running on concrete often leads to sore shins and backs. My session was one of getting back to basics, with the main aim to start playing in the 'V' between mid-on and mid-off. I want to use the full face of the bat, combined with a forward movement and a bent front knee, to enable me to keep the ball on the ground. After an extensive session, where Swampy threw balls until his shoulder begged for mercy followed by a full net in which Kasper, Lang and Gilly toiled away, I came away feeling as if I had achieved something. This last point – achieving something positive – is what all players should be looking to get out of a practice session.

We were totally unaware (until we were informed by the local caretaker of this sporting facility) that it was on the adjoining athletic track that Roger Bannister ran the first sub-four-minute mile, back in 1954. When I turned my mind back to that famous footage, I indeed saw the similarities in front of me.

26 June 26, Oxford

Australia v British Universities, play abandoned.
It's beginning to feel like *Groundhog Day* again. We woke to yet another bleak, ashen coloured sky, which was accompanied by steady drizzling rain and an icy cold breeze. This inclement weather meant we found ourselves once again in the hands of our increasingly unpopular fitness adviser.

Smithy must have sensed we were after his blood, because he toned down today's workout to include a racquetball competition ... with the losers going straight to the gym for some extra fitness. The draw for today's play was posted on the notice board and, of course, a competitive edge was quickly added, including prizes for first, second and third.

The prize list read as follows:

First – no gym work for the rest of the tour; second – no gym work for the rest of the week; third – no conversation with Alan Crompton for the rest of the tour.

The only problem with these incentives was that it seemed inevitable that all the semi-finalists would be trying to lose.

27 June, Oxford/Southampton

Australia v British Universities, match abandoned.
It was certainly no surprise to once again find the sky lifeless and crying when I drew back the dark brown curtains that must have been fashionable at one point in time. Consequently, the talk over the breakfast table was of an early departure

to our next destination, Southampton, rather than us hanging around all day in the hope of a session of play. There was, though, much more encouraging news on the baby front, as Warney nervously informed everyone that his wife, Simone, was having a Caesarean section.

Our bowling champion subsequently spent the next couple of hours sitting in the leisure centre, waiting, phone in hand, for the final verdict, like a man condemned to the death chair. As time went on, a crowd began to build as most of the boys, plus Shane's parents, anxiously added their support. Finally, the phone rang and off scurried Warney to receive the news in private while we settled on our last-minute selections. Minutes later it was announced: 'It's a girl! Brooke! She weighs 9lb 6oz and is 56cm long.'

'And she looks like me!!'

It wasn't long before we were choking on our cigars and throwing back the champers, even though it was 10.30am. It's a special moment when one of your team-mates becomes a Dad for the first time.

As is always the case with Warney, the media seemed to know his every move. Within no time at all, the 'snappers' wanted that exclusive photo and the TV cameras wanted that priceless footage. I'm not sure if Warney fully realises what has happened and how much his life will change from now on. No doubt he'll make a good father, and I bet he can't wait to get home to see what his daughter looks like.

After the game against the Combined Universities was officially abandoned, we did set off early to prepare for tomorrow's fixture against Hampshire, a team which contains a good friend of all the squad in Matthew Hayden. When we reached Southampton, I went in search of a haircut, only to be told the earliest anyone could squeeze me in was next Monday. Either there aren't enough hairdressers in town or they all recognised my accent. Whatever, the bonus was that I was able to hit the sheets half an hour earlier than expected and it was there that I stayed for the whole afternoon and into the early evening.

When I did venture downstairs, I found all the lads gathered around the bar area (very unusual, that!). Not only was everyone still toasting Warney's new arrival, they were also celebrating the announcement of Blewey's engagement to Jodie, his girlfriend of 12 months. And Bevo is to become a Dad! The gossip columnists would have given anything to be privy to all this information.

Meanwhile, Lynette, Rosie and the in-laws had headed off to stay with some good friends of ours who we know from my days as a professional in the Lancashire League for Nelson, and who live on the outskirts of Manchester. The team rules demand that during the Tests the wives and girlfriends can stay with the players, but during the county fixtures the team must exist without the family. This gives the team every opportunity to develop a strong team spirit and allows us to get to know each other better.

For me, this line of thought is much harder to accept now that I've become a father. It seems ridiculous that my wife and daughter have to find alternative accommodation, which is often hard to find, when I have a room all to myself. However, in the interest of team unity I'm willing to go along with the rule, especially because, unlike on previous tours, on this trip there has been a concerted effort by management to encourage the families to be part of our Ashes experience.

28 June, Southampton

Hampshire 156 (Kasprowicz 3–33, Warne 3–30) v Australia 157–2 (Elliott 61, Taylor 61*).

Still no sign of the sun, only a dull and menacing sky. However, play began on time and, quite amazingly, the home county won the toss and chose to bat. This is a strategy that means that they'll have to make all the running in the game if they want to win. Normally, a county captain will bowl first and hope that we will eventually give them a total to chase in the fourth innings. This is easier than having to bowl us out to win a game. Such an approach reflects the poor attitude that prevails among many of the counties, as does the fact that most of these teams don't put up their strongest team against us. Playing a touring side should be seen as a challenge for the local team, and a chance for the players to impress the England selectors. Even the incentive of a £9000 cheque for beating us (compared to our meagre £2500 payout for a victory) doesn't seem to inspire our opponents.

So the Hampshire captain, John Stephenson, should be congratulated for his initiative. Unfortunately, his poor judgment of the pitch's condition led to his team's disastrous lunchtime score of 93 for eight. Given that precarious situation, their final tally of 156 was more than we wished for, but the encouraging form of Kasprowicz, Warne, Reiffel and Gillespie was exactly what we needed in the lead-up to the Manchester Test.

Against yet another sub-standard bowling attack, the lads enjoyed an extended 'net session' which left us nicely placed at 157 for two at stumps. Matthew Elliott again showed his invaluable ability to accumulate runs against any opposition, at any time. This is a trait all the great players have – the desire to keep churning out the runs. It's called 'hunger'.

I had another early night, as I tried to speed up my recovery – what was a nasty cold in Oxford has now developed into the flu. However, the room service menu didn't really offer any culinary delights. I settled for the 'vegetarian bake', which in reality was a bowl of mashed potato and raw onions that came with the outrageous price tag of £9.75 (more than $20 in Australia).

29 June, Southampton

Hampshire 156 and 71–2 v Australia 465–8 declared (Taylor 109, M Waugh 173).

The run feast that had begun the previous afternoon continued at a pleasing rate for the sizeable crowd, who saw Mark Taylor score his 36th first-class century and Mark Waugh his 63rd. Both centuries were morale boosters for the guys involved, particularly Junior, who in recent weeks had been surprisingly quiet in the runs department. The ease with which my brother scored his big century will no doubt be a chilling reminder to the English team of his credentials. So far he has looked threatening without going on with the job. I believe his problems have been caused by him going at the ball too hard in his defensive prods, which, because he is already committed, has not allowed him to counter any movement or bounce. Going at the ball with soft hands allows you to adjust and improvise to get out of difficult circumstances – you are more relaxed and in control.

Tubby's hundred was a typically hard-nosed effort, which eventually drained the opposing bowlers to a point where our captain was completely on top of the situation. His long stay at the crease was exactly what he needed before the next Third Test. Batsmen will often say they need more time at the crease to get themselves back into form. There is nothing like batting in a game situation to restore your confidence, and practise your concentration and technique. Net practice is good, but it has its limitations, because the intensity isn't the same as in a match situation.

My brief stay at the crease (for a score of 11) sounds like a failure, but for me it was more of a minor triumph. During the past week or so I've been working on playing straight and making sure I'm looking to get forward at every opportunity, especially early in my innings. For me this is vital, because I know the English bowlers, because of my tendency to play off the back foot, fancy trapping me lbw or bowled early on. If I'm to be successful during the remainder of the tour, I have to find a solution to this challenge that has been thrust upon me.

Of the first six balls faced, I drove confidently at three of them, collecting two runs for each shot. Immediately, I felt reassured and confident.

It's amazing how 'fragile' cricketers can be – even after 12 years at the highest level, doubts which can spread like a cancer still enter my mind. You have to back your own ability, work hard on fine-tuning your technique, and enjoy the challenges that come your way. Easily said, sure, but sometimes hard to achieve, as it is always easier to take the soft option and look for excuses rather than do a hard, honest appraisal. Even though I squandered an ideal chance to get a big score, my gut feeling as I walked back to the pavilion was, 'I'm, back.' I'm looking forward to the next Test.

I must admit to feeling a little sorry for Matt Hayden, who let the second ball he faced from Dizzy go, only to see his off stump cartwheel out of the turf. This was exactly the mode of dismissal that led to Matt losing his way during the recent South African tour. His problems in this area will be another test for him to overcome, and how he recovers will be a good indicator of his mental fibre. I'm confident Matt will be back to play a vital role for Australia in the future, as he has a hunger and desire that very few others possess.

By the end of the day's play, the only thing that stood between us and an early start to our journey to Manchester was the former Test star, Robin Smith, still one of the best players of pace bowling in the world. Smith looked ominous in reaching 31 in a hurry.

30 June, Southampton/Manchester

Hampshire 156 and 176 (R Smith 44; Gillespie 5–33, Kasprowicz 3–69) lost to Australians 465–8 declared by an innings and 133 runs.

As expected, the locals crumbled after the departure of Robin Smith, as Jason Gillespie collected 5–33 off 13 highly impressive overs of pace and swing.

I believe this lad will, by the end of his career, go down as a 'great', alongside his new-ball partner Glenn McGrath. Australia is indeed fortunate to have both these guys at their disposal. My tip for Gillespie is 250-plus Test-match wickets. And while I'm making predictions, on the batting side of things I'll back Ricky Ponting to score 5000-plus Test runs. These two are players of rare calibre and temperament, who both possess a deep desire to not only play at the top level, but also to enjoy it. And, perhaps most important of all, they believe in themselves.

We hit the asphalt just after lunch and arrived in the soccer-mad city of Manchester in the late afternoon, to a typically wet welcome. Lynette and family arrived late in the evening, after spending the day touring the beautiful Lake District, which is located to the north of here.

As always, Rosie appears to have grown up overnight. If there's one thing, above all others, that I miss on tour it has to be her cheeky smile. Just seeing it again made me feel that I'm the luckiest man alive.

11
ENGLAND v AUSTRALIA
THIRD CORNHILL
TEST MATCH

Old Trafford, Manchester, 3–7 July

STEVE WAUGH

1 July

This morning we all realised that a long team meeting wasn't required, especially as the England team hadn't changed a lot (except for the omission of Devon Malcolm, replaced by Test debutant Dean Headley). So we kept the talk to a minimum. But we did decide to target a few opponents for special significance – those who we feel hold the key to England's chances. On the batting side of things, we believe Mike Atherton is the 'stabilising' batsman in their side, the player they look to build their innings around. Taking Atherton's wicket early will give us a significant psychological advantage. Our plan is to bowl six inches outside his off stump on a good length, to try to induce him to spar at the ball in the hope of an edge to the keeper or slips. And we'll occasionally attempt to flick his glove with a short ball down the legside, or even a wider fuller-length ball down the legside which we've seen him glance through to the keeper more than once.

Graham Thorpe is the other batsman we'll target, largely because he can take control of an innings and set the tempo for the rest to follow. We see him as being a bit loose early on, so a concerted effort at immediately bowling in 'the corridor of uncertainty' might lead to his downfall. Thorpe is also a player who must be denied any loose balls, because hitting boundaries is for him a great pressure reliever and something he needs to do. Thorpe isn't a player who likes to slowly build an innings, he likes to get to 20 in a hurry.

Bowling-wise, we have singled out Darren Gough as the focal point. He is the bowler Atherton relies on to get that crucial wicket. If we repel him, however, the spirit in the English side drops noticeably. Gough is a bowler who runs in hard during his first spell, as he desperately tries to take wickets. This, of course, is what England needs. However, he doesn't seem to adapt to situations that need him to tighten up and keep things under control. He lacks a little bit of patience. In such circumstances we can score quickly off him. He remains, though, a bowler to respect, for he can produce a wicket-taking ball and can swing the old ball significantly.

These three players are the dangermen. If they can be kept under wraps, I believe we'll win and win comfortably.

NASSER HUSSAIN

After Essex's NatWest Trophy first round game against Bucks in Beaconsfield, I headed back down the A40 to Lord's for my appointment with the specialist to try to sort out my elbow.

This meant another horrible injection, so I put my head under a pillow for that, and was then advised to sit out the championship match against Derbyshire at Southend. I'll play on the Sunday because I don't like missing too many Essex games, but the forecast was pretty bad so that's another reason why this is the best time to rest the injury. There's no danger of me missing the next Test and it feels odd to sit out an Essex game, but you just need a window of opportunity to sort these things out and when you're playing for England you don't have that many chances in a busy season.

It adds weight, I feel, to the argument for having England players contracted to the ECB. It's the only way to go, especially for bowlers, because to bowl at full pelt all the time for England and your county becomes an impossibility. I can envisage it happening soon and county cricket will be there to get back into nick when you need it.

Anyway, the second cortisone injection seems to have worked and the elbow is feeling about 90 per cent right now. Essex, meanwhile, defeated Derbyshire comfortably so that made me feel a little less guilty about not being there. Now the time has come to head for Old Trafford where I will complete my full 'set' of Test grounds. Old Trafford is a ground on which I've only played three times for Essex over the years and I've never scored many runs there!

There always seems to be a bit of weather around in Manchester and sure enough it was raining when I arrived this morning. Old Trafford is a big, impressive ground and they certainly know how to stage Test matches up here. They look after the players well and as soon as we arrived there was someone around to take our kit up to the dressing room and everything was ready for us.

The only trouble was that they'd had rain for three weeks solid before the game so the nets were under water. Consequently it's been hard to practice in the mud.

This Test sees the arrival of two newcomers in the party, both of whom I know very well. Dean Headley is a very good friend of mine. We shared a house in Cape Town a few winters ago when we were both playing club cricket down there and, the winter after that, I captained Dean on the A tour of Pakistan where we got on very well.

Dean puts the ball in the right area more than most people in county cricket. He's not so much of a swing bowler but he hits the seam and has got a quick bumper. Even when the wicket's flat he seldom gets taken apart because the ball is invariably in the right place at a good pace. I certainly wouldn't be lunging forward at him. He also gets a bit of reverse swing with the old ball so he's got a lot going for him. He should really have played for England before now but every time he's been in the frame and has appeared to be next in line he's got injured so he's been unfortunate.

Dean has, like all of us, got things to work on, like moving the ball away from the right hander more often but that's a small point. He certainly likes bowling and is a bit like Dominic Cork in that he always wants one more over and there's nothing better than that for a captain.

Our other newcomer is a very different character. I've known Mike Smith ('Smudge') since our days together with the Combined Universities side and he was also, briefly because of injury, with us on that A tour of Pakistan. He's always been a good county bowler and has always swung the ball in most conditions. Smudge has always been an honest county pro and his wicket tally must be pretty high now because he's always taken his share and deserves his chance.

The thing with him, though, is that at his pace, which is not much quicker than medium, you won't know whether he will be able to do it at the top until he gets a chance. It's a difficult one for the selectors because if he is going to play it's got to be somewhere where they think it will swing and that's something you can't always tell by looking at a wicket.

Mike is very quiet and you don't really know him until you sit him down and talk to him. He's a bit of an intellectual with a very dry sense of humour and, complete with his glasses when he's not playing, does not look like a fast bowler. He even spends time during the winter acting as a linesman for his football team in Bristol which is an unusual thing to do, especially because it leads to stick from the players.

We had to hang around until 3pm before the rain stopped and then, as the nets were so wet, we had shorter sessions and then fielding practice brought forward from tomorrow, a decision which Goughy had a bit of a moan about but it had to be done as it was so wet.

Dean came up to me to ask my advice after we were finished. The signs are he is going to play ahead of Devon and Smudge, but he is worried about the back injury he has had and the possibility of breaking down during a Test and letting everybody down. I said, 'Look Dean, you're never going to have a better chance than this. Look at that wicket. It's got a bit of grass on it, it's your sort of pitch and we'll be bowling first if we win the toss. If you miss out on this sort of opportunity, someone else may come in in your place, take a stack of wickets and you'll never be seen again. This is your chance.' I reminded him that I'd captained him in Pakistan and that he'd bowled all day there for me whether in pain or not, so I knew he had the heart for the job. My final recommendation was that he should play if selected, with painkillers if necessary, and soon after he went to Bumble to tell him he was fit and raring to go. I'm sure it's the right thing to do.

Tuffers was released from the party again today for the third time and I think he was a bit upset about it this time. The first two times he accepted the situation and was pleased to be involved, but this time he was a little bit 'is this going to happen all summer?' because he's desperately keen to play. I had a chat with him and he said, 'I've got to get in my car and drive to Uxbridge when I would love to stay here' and I just told him to keep his head up and keep on playing. I reminded him that we were never going to play on a Bunsen with Shane Warne around and that with our tail being a bit suspect it's hard to fit Cat in there without making it even weaker.

2 July

The good thing about having a new person such as fitness guru Steve Smith in and around the team is the fresh ideas and enthusiasm that get brought into the equation.

For example, instead of the regulation 'one-lap followed by a stretch' warm-up, day after day, we have found ourselves playing volleyball, touch football, even badminton, which has been combined with a variety of skill work and running. The only downer with Smithy is his love of the dreaded yellow plastic cones, which when placed strategically on the turf mean only one thing ... a combined fitness and 'sharpening-up' session.

Without fail, Pigeon boots these cones as far as he can whenever he gets within striking distance. The downside to this ploy is they always get put back where they'd been and Smithy 'gets off' on the attention we pay to him. He seems to think our complaints mean we are keen and ready to go.

I don't think I've ever done a fitness routine without hearing deep moaning noises from the lads. The loudest gripes usually belong to the Waugh brothers and Warney, but Smithy just keeps telling us that the work will extend our careers, and who are we to doubt their value.

Today's practice featured a 'fielding soccer' game, designed to sharpen our reflexes, which involves members of two teams trying to throw the ball to their team-mates at knee height or under until they reach the goal without dropping the ball. Unfortunately, during the game Gilly suffered a serious injury. He was attempting to take an awkward catch, just as Punter was making a last-ditch diving effort at an interception. Our reserve keeper was left in a vulnerable position, with his top half twisting in the opposite direction to his bottom half, so when Punter landed on Gilly's knee something had to give.

No-one likes to see a fellow player injured, so it was no surprise that we began our pre-Test net session in a subdued mood.

For the second day in a row, I completed training feeling that I had prepared as best I could for the upcoming match. This is something Swampy has constantly stressed that we should be aiming for at every practice during the tour, and an objective I always try to achieve. It's an attitude that I think caught a journalist by surprise afterwards, too. He asked me, somewhat casually, 'Is this Test match a vital one?'

I don't think he was ready for my reply, which was without hesitation, 'This Test is the most important one of our careers.'

I believe if we have this attitude then we will be hungry and ready to seize the initiative when the moment presents itself. And anyway, you never know which Test is going to be your last, so you owe it to yourself to play as if you mightn't get another opportunity.

NASSER HUSSAIN

Woke up to a shock this morning when I found one of the interviews I am doing with the Daily Mail after each Test this season in today's paper. My understanding was that the interviews would appear at the end of each Test, not the day before when the pressure on you can only be made worse by you being in the media spotlight. What made today's piece worse was that the headline said, 'It's payback time for Warne' and I thought, 'Hang on a minute, I've never said anything like that.' Then I realised the whole of the first paragraph was complete fabrication, basically alluding to what I was going to do to Shane Warne when all I'd said was that I was going to try to be positive. Luckily not many of the Aussies seem to have read it, but Stewie did and he took the mickey out of me over it.

You don't need distractions like this before a Test. I was keen to do paper interviews this season as an extension of this book and everything up until now has been fine, but the last thing you need to read is 'PAYBACK TIME FOR SHANE WARNE'. Talk about setting yourself up for a fall. It might have been different if it had been 'Payback time for Joe Bloggs' but we are talking Shane Warne here. I had a word with Brian Scovell, who is conducting the interviews, but he told me the material had been changed by his office after he had filed it. I must make sure any copy is faxed to me for my clearance in the future.

The nets were a little better today and now people started walking around and having a look at the wicket. Up to now it's been covered most of the time and the groundsman, Pete Marron, has kept it covered today even though the sun has come out because he wants it to stay damp and green. The grass here is very fine and when the sun gets on it the ends dry up very quickly which is obviously not what we want.

When it was finally unveiled about 2pm it was very green but very bare at the ends which is a bit of a worry. We want to bowl first but, looking at those ends, we are a bit sceptical about them drying up so there was quite a bit of chat about it. We also had a long talk about Lord's over a cup of tea and a sandwich. It's vital we remain upbeat. Bumble, typically of him, accentuated the positive and said that if it hadn't rained at Lord's we could have batted on and set them a target and that's the way we have to feel.

3 July, Day 1, Third Test

Australia 224–7 (Elliott 40, S Waugh 102*, Reiffel 26*).

As I was walking up the steps to our dressing-rooms on arriving at the ground this morning, I had mixed feelings about the day ahead. One moment, I was full of doubts. I didn't want to fail again, as I had at Lord's, and I kept thinking about the poor state of this Test wicket. But then I was telling myself to see our situation as just another challenge, to be positive, confront the situation head on, back my technique and mental strength. I thought about Bob Simpson scoring his epic 311 here in 1964 and realised that anything is possible if you really want it. Fortunately, it was the idea of creating a small piece of history that was my lasting thought as I settled into our cramped home for the next five days.

It was a cold, overcast morning, further encouraging the abundant grass cover on the moist-looking Test wicket. Losing here will virtually guarantee England the series. Having said that, part of our game plan is not to worry about long-term objectives such as the series result, but rather concentrating on winning the next session of cricket we play and then each subsequent one. That approach will ensure that our overall objective will be achieved.

At about 10.25am, 35 minutes before the scheduled starting time, Mark Taylor, as usual, returned to the dressing-room to put on his playing gear and don the Australian blazer in preparation for the 10.30 toss. It was at this point that he turned to me and dropped a bombshell. 'Tugga,' he said, 'I think I'm gonna have a bat if we win the toss today.'

I couldn't believe it. However, there was a method to his madness. Tubs believed the wicket looked similar to the pitch of 1993, which turned out to be hard work for batsmen on the first day but after that got even more difficult as it turned quite appreciably. The only problem I could see with his strategy was that we needed to survive the first day to be in a position to let our spinners take control of the game. Mark's was a gutsy decision that very few would have agreed with. But it is a move that confirms that we are playing for a win and encourages our opponents to be more aggressive in their attitude. Soon after, the toss was once again ours and we were getting ready to take on the under-prepared track.

Following in the footsteps of his famous grandfather, the legendary West Indian batsman of the 1930s and '40s, George Headley, and father, a West Indian Test batsman in the early 1970s, Ron Headley, Kent's opening bowler Dean Headley became the first example of three generations from the same family all playing Test cricket. He certainly wasn't out of place, settling into a nice rhythm from the start as he moved the ball off the wicket at good pace and created enormous problems for our left-handed opening combination. In tandem with Darren Gough, Andy Caddick and Mark Ealham, Headley gave us the fight of our lives as he we struggled to reach the lunch break without losing a grip on the Test.

Taylor, Greg Blewett and Mark Waugh all fell early on to edges, as the ball darted about alarmingly. On such a wicket, where the sideways movement is often extravagant, the ball that gets results is more than likely the one that doesn't deviate much. This is because you start to look for 'gremlins' in the wicket, which leads to a loss of concentration and focus on the next delivery. A tentative prod at the ball, with your feet going nowhere, is the usual end result and that's exactly how our top three perished.

Watching the ball constantly dominate the bat can be very unsettling from the pavilion. I found myself again having to fight hard to exorcise the demons that wanted to take control. When the moment of truth arrived, I took a deep breath and heard the boys wish me well. Out the door I went.

I think it's important to get out in the middle as quickly as possible, to let your opposition know they're in for a battle. Positive body language definitely helps. It was a bonus to get off the mark first ball – there is something significant about seeing runs next to your name and not that big '0'. But it was a real battle early on, with the ball beating the bat a few times and a close lbw appeal going in my favour. Ever gradually, though, I managed to find the middle a few times and began to relax.

Making matters even worse for the batsmen was the fact that one of the sightscreens wasn't big enough to cover the full height of Andy Caddick's arm when he delivered the ball, which, of course, gave him a significant advantage. A lunchtime score of 78–3 was, in the conditions, a pretty even opening session and it left the next two hours as potentially the most important session of the whole Test, perhaps even the series.

As the afternoon wore on I began to grow in confidence. I realised that the English attack had 'lost' their game plan and had got carried away with the extra bounce at their disposal. The short stuff came thick and fast, but from my perspective it was a godsend as it meant the bowlers were exerting a lot of energy but not putting the ball in the danger zone on a good length.

With the score on 85, Matthew Elliott went to a faint edge that, after studying the super-slow-motion replay, probably wasn't an edge at all (but in 'real-life' speed the ump's decision did appear to be the correct one). Michael Bevan copped a real going over with the short stuff, before obliging Alec Stewart, and when Ian Healy (after a stand of 37) and Shane Warne fell we were in dire straits at 160–7.

By now, though, I felt in control of the situation. I had benefited from time I'd spent in the middle and from the attack that was feeding me plenty of half volleys in between the bouncers, which allowed me to not get stagnated but rather to keep the score rolling along at a good pace. We badly needed a partnership, and our saviour was found in Paul Reiffel, a guy whose batting has often been underrated. He is a sweet timer of the ball and his placement is generally very good, but at times he can be a shaky starter. Today, however, he looked the goods from ball one and together we clawed our way towards a reasonable position. But it wasn't all smooth sailing and had Stewart held onto a steepling Headley delivery that found the edge of Reiffel's blade we would most probably have been all out for under 200.

In the last hour of play we turned down three offers from the umpires to go off for bad light, mainly because we felt the runs were coming as easily as they had at any time during the day. The final opportunity to take the light presented the toughest dilemma. There were three overs left in the day, the quicks were still bowling and I was well into the nineties. On the scoreboard there are five lights which are used to help the umpires judge the quality of the light. If no lights are on the batting conditions are perfect. If three lights are on, the umps will confer. Now, all five lights were shining brightly.

I took the unusual step of asking Mike Atherton who was going to bowl. Realising the quicks would mean an end to the day and being hungry for an eighth wicket the England captain replied, 'Croft and Ealham will see out the day.' Knowing this, Pistol and I elected to bat on.

With one over remaining I was within four runs of a century. Croft prepared to run in. In this situation, it is difficult not to premeditate any shots, as you want your 100. Of much greater importance, of course, was that I had to be there at the close of play, so I put the hundred to the back of my mind. Croft moved into bowl …

I have never been more appreciative to see a short ball come my way. I rocked back and clouted it through cover point to bring up one of my proudest moments as a cricketer.

In the dressing-room, a great reception awaited me, with plenty of backslapping and handshaking. But the first thing I needed to do was get some ice on my right hand, which had taken a beating today from all the deliveries that hit the splice of my bat. Then it was off to do the rounds of the media – three separate TV interviews on top of the media conference.

It was a huge relief for me to score a century today – it was a crucial innings in difficult circumstances and I had successfully fought some self-doubts that had crept into my mind, almost to the point where I doubted my ability. You can imagine what a relief it was to be finally able to venture back to the hotel to see my immediate family. They, like me, are ecstatic with the outcome of today's events.

NASSER HUSSAIN

The Old Trafford pitch can change session by session but, looking at it this morning, I was sure the Aussies would bowl first if they won the toss. It was so damp and there was so much grass on it. So there we were, sat at the window of the pavilion as Athers went out for the toss. As the coin goes up everyone is a bit nervous, wondering what we're going to do, and as the coin came down Tony Lewis went up to Taylor, so I was sure we would be batting. Then Athers signalled we would be having a bowl. It was very surprising and very brave of Taylor but when you've got Warne in your side, the forecast is good and you see the ends are bare I suppose you're just playing your trump card.

When we first went out there the ball was moving about so much I was convinced he had made a mistake. Dean was given the new ball and the onus was now on him to make the most of it in helpful conditions. He could easily have been afflicted by nerves or got carried away, but he used it brilliantly. Before his first over I went up to him and said, 'Good luck mate, you're good enough.' And how he proved it. You just knew as he ran up that he would do well. I think it was right to give him the new ball because on this wicket first up you want to get them coming forward and Dean bowls that half a yard further up than Caddy who, on this occasion, was relegated to first change. When the wicket is flatter Caddy will come into it more because he'll be harder to drive but this was Dean's day. I knew he wouldn't let anyone down and would play through any pain he was suffering. He likes the big occasion. Led by Dean, we bowled extremely well up until tea, having them 160 for seven at our best stage.

We really should have rolled them over for 170 or 180 but showers hit us after tea and perhaps we lost our concentration a bit. At one stage it looked as though we wouldn't be coming out for any more play but we did and they made us pay. In the third over after tea, with the wicket actually seeming to quicken up, Dean got Reiffel to nick one to Stewie and he missed it. We had all come up a bit because one earlier had dropped short of Butch but now they were flying through and Stewie was caught a bit off guard. That probably cost us 50 runs.

We also felt Steve Waugh was very close to lbw to Caddick early on and if we had got that one things could have been different, but as it was Waugh and Reiffel put together an extremely valuable stand for the eighth wicket and we had failed to separate them by the close.

4 July, Day 2, Third Test
Australia 235 (Waugh 108, Reiffel 31; Headley 4–72) v England 161–8 (Butcher 51; Warne 5–47).

Reaching a total in excess of 250 proved too tough an ask for us this morning. I was first to go, managing to chop an inswinging half volley from Darren Gough onto my stumps. It was a lazy shot, and disappointing considering how hard I'd fought yesterday to survive and prosper. Still, the partnership of 70 between Paul Reiffel and myself was an invaluable one for the team and one that I believe could be the difference between winning and losing.

Reiffel and Jason Gillespie went shortly after, leaving Glenn McGrath to dwell on yet another century nipped in the bud. We thought our total of 235 was at least very competitive and this was further confirmed when Mike Atherton gave himself every opportunity to cash in on the lunchtime fare by perishing just before the interval.

The remainder of the day was dominated by the genius of Shane Warne, who visibly grew in confidence as he saw the ball gripping and ripping on a surface that was ideally suited to his skill. From a comfortable 74 for one, England capitulated to a disastrous 123 for eight before an unlikely alliance of Andy Caddick and Mark Ealham came together to add 38 runs by the close of play.

Watching Shane bowl was immensely enjoyable for us all, but without doubt the highlight of the day was the freakish leg-side stumping Ian Healy produced off

Michael Bevan's bowling to rid us of Mark Butcher. Bevan is a spinner who bowls the ball at almost medium pace, which obviously makes life difficult for the keeper, who hasn't much time to move around while he's standing up to the stumps. Healy, who had his vision impaired by the batsman in front of him, took a wide half volley that had been speared down the leg-side, and swung round and dislodged the bails in one motion. It was quite extraordinary. To glove such a delivery and at the same time know instinctively that the batsman has overbalanced requires a skill very few possess.

Butcher's dismissal provided the impetus that got us on a roll, to a point where the English batsmen didn't know how they were going to survive, let alone score runs. We're now in the 'driving seat', with every chance to square the series. Warney's haul of five wickets puts him equal with Richie Benaud on 248 Test wickets for his career, while Heals' great stumping was his 100th victim in 25 Tests against England.

NASSER HUSSAIN

A bad start for Thorpey this morning, as he was fined £100 by the England management for wearing his cap at breakfast in the hotel – which just shows that the England heirarchy are determined that we look the right way and say the right things.

We got their last three wickets very quickly this morning, just what we needed, and when we replied we made a solid start. But then, inexplicably, we suffered a dramatic collapse. I am already hearing people saying we should have been more positive against Warne but I'm not sure about that. Perhaps we should have been more positive against the seamers because it was quite flat then, the sun was out and a roller had been on the pitch, but when Warne came on it was that much harder to force the pace.

Again I was out after a break, very frustrating. Warne hadn't been turning that many before tea, apart from those turning out of the rough, and just seemed to be concentrating on top spinners. Bumble had a chat with me at tea and I told him that we were going to have to work hard because Warne was just starting to get it right. He had slipped in a few flippers which he hadn't done at Edgbaston and there was also the occasional googly and Bumble said, 'Yes, but he hasn't turned any off the straight, has he?' Then, as if to order, in the first over after tea, he turned one a long way and caught me by surprise. If I'd been prepared for that much turn I would have tried to be further forward but I went with it and it turned out to be a ball I should have left. It's easy to say in hindsight but that's why he's such a good bowler. You think you know what he's doing and then he'll turn one that much more. John got out the same way as me and suddenly we were in big trouble, not helped by some brilliant wicket-keeping from Healy. He had pulled off a fantastic stumping to dismiss Butch and now, with the wicket misbehaving and Warne getting his variations going, the bloke did not put a foot wrong.

It had looked so good earlier and we were hoping for a lead of a hundred. We wanted to dictate the course of the game and see how they reacted to batting under pressure but it all went horribly wrong and we finished the second day on 161 for eight, some way behind. It's difficult to explain it. When Warne is bowling like that there are not too many things you can do. Use your feet? Definitely not. When he's turning it that much, no-one can use their feet, I don't care who they are, because the percentages are not in your favour. The sweep is an option and one that I tried to employ as it is a shot I like but one I didn't use much at Edgbaston. This time he came a bit straighter at me, which I expected, so I decided to sweep and it worked while I was there. It's an ongoing challenge against the best in the world.

5 July, Day 3, Third Test

Australia 235 and 262–6 (M Waugh 55, S Waugh 82*, Healy 47, Warne 33*) v England 162 (Warne 6–48, McGrath 3–40).

The last two English wickets fell for the addition of only one run, which left us with the opportunity for the batsmen to go out and win the Test match. By making England chase anything over 300, we will set up a position where they would have to defy history for us to lose side – few teams manage more than 300 to win a Test match. Because of the nature of the wicket, and the way it's going to turn, getting anything more than 150 batting last will be very, very difficult.

Unfortunately, our second innings began poorly when Taylor was out for half his first-innings score, and Blewett fell in highly-controversial circumstances. Judging from the replays, Greg has every right to question whether or not Nasser Hussain caught him cleanly at first slip off Robert Croft. It appeared to most people that some turf preceded contact between flesh and leather, but the England vice-captain came up from the ground claiming a vital wicket. This certainly left a nasty taste in our mouths, especially after Ian Healy's sporting gesture at Lord's when no-one, including the umpires, knew for sure whether the ball had carried or not. The debate after stumps had been drawn over this dismissal focused on whether the third umpire should be used to rule on catches that even the fieldsman involved can't be 100 per cent certain about.

Dean Headley, meanwhile, continued his love affair with our left-handers, disposing of Elliott with a ball that left the batsman off the wicket. We were 39 for three and the match was wide open once more.

Elliott's was a dreaded dismissal for me, as I was in the cubicle having a 'nervous one' when I heard the roar of the crowd and knew I was required out in the middle. Fortunately, I got off to a dream start, finding the gaps and timing the ball nicely from the jump, a legacy of my time in the middle in the first innings.

At lunch, Mark Waugh and I were set to produce a big partnership. We were both in the twenties and had enjoyed the benefit of playing ourselves in on a wicket that was never going to get any better for batting. But after putting on 92,

Mark was deceived by a fine change of pace from the always thinking Ealham. In the meantime, I had been struggling with my hand problem at the other end. By now it was restricting my shot making and the power I was able to get on the ball. At the fall of Mark's wicket, I called for an ice pack to ease the swelling and to relieve the soreness a little. However, the pain gradually worsened to a point where I couldn't force the ball through the field at all. I was basically defending one-handed, as I tried to minimise the pain that was going through my thumb joint and the space between thumb and forefinger.

When Michael Bevan came to the crease, it looked as if his mind was tortured. He failed to come to terms with a barrage of short balls aimed at his body, before popping up a catch to the gully. I really did feel sorry for him, as he looked like he'd hit rock bottom as he walked away. The only consolation is that now there's only one way to go and that is up, but in between a lot of hard work and soul-searching must transpire.

I needed a partner to keep things moving, as I wasn't about to set the game alight with dashing strokeplay. This time it was Ian Healy and then Shane Warne who put their hand ups. Healy hit a crucial 47, while Warne played his shots from the very first ball he faced. But he was a little fortunate. If Blewett had been unlucky earlier in the innings, then Warne probably made up for this when he was given not out to an appeal for a catch close in. The umpire thought the ball had been jammed into the ground, but that super-slow-motion replay revealed the umpire had erred (from my vantage point at the bowler's end, however, it was virtually impossible to tell what the correct answer was).

By the conclusion of play, I had battled to an unbeaten 82, while Warne had made it look easy on his way to 33 not out. Our lead was 335. For England, Headley was again the pick of the bowlers. Croft claimed a couple of poles, but didn't turn the ball as one would have expected him to have done in the conditions.

My hand wasn't a pretty sight when I pulled it from the glove to give Errol a closer look after play. It was nearly twice its normal size, with a deep bruise dominating the area in distress. After ice treatment, the joint was wrapped and bound to try to stop any further bleeding and to reduce the existing inflammation.

NASSER HUSSAIN

To be realistic, we now know we're up against it. The footholes are now huge, it's a bit of a beach and Warne will be bowling with us batting last. But as the wicket is so dry it is also aiding reverse swing and we made a good start when the Aussies batted again until an incident which is sure to be discussed and analysed for some time. And it involved me.

It was basically one of those things that happen but they quite often seem to happen to me. There I was looking for a quiet day in the field before concentrating on scoring runs in the second innings and, before I knew it, there I was at slip, standing fairly deep for Crofty because a lot of their batsman flash at the ball, when Greg Blewett ran down the wicket, so he's now an extra yard away from me, and nicked it. Now some people say the fielder should always know if the ball has carried but there are times when he genuinely does not and this was one of them. I went for the ball and I thought I'd got two fingers underneath it before it hit my palm and I then caught it with my other hand.

I'd say I was about 80 per cent sure I'd caught it but Blewett stood there, looking at me, and I said to him, 'I think I caught it.' Not 'I've caught that'. I was not completely sure but I thought I had. At times like that you need confirmation from those around you and without fail the others came up to me and said, 'Well done, you caught that, great catch.' They included Goughy at backward point, Butch in front and Stewie alongside me, so I got a variety of opinions on it.

I then saw the umpires conferring and it went through my mind to go up to them, but then I thought, 'What do I say?' I thought to myself if I go up there and say 'I think I caught it but I'm not sure' then they'll give him not out because they'll say there was an element of doubt. But if then it comes up on the big screen and it was out I'll look a complete idiot and would have to face the prospect of explaining to Bumble why I had denied England a catch at a crucial stage of an Ashes Test.

So I was in a complete no-win situation. I know it will be compared to the Ian Healy incident at Lord's when he admitted he wasn't sure he had taken a catch cleanly but that was different. He thought he had caught it, but then people around him said they weren't sure so he told the umpires that. But everyone was telling me it was okay and each time it has subsequently been shown on television it has still not been completely clear and each time John Crawley has come up to me and said 'I don't know what the fuss is about. You caught that.' I just wish they could go to the third umpire in situations like that because it helps me out, it helps Blewett out and there seems no reason as to why technology can't be used in those situations.

I'm a batsman and I know how Blewett feels. There's no way I would cheat him or anyone else out. I know how much a Test innings means to any batsman. If it had gone to the third umpire there would have been no incident, no problem between me and Blewett and the game would have gone on. Fine. Blewett's happy, the Aussies are happy and the crowd are happy. It could be time consuming to keep on referring to the third umpire but the game's played so hard now and there's so much talk about these sort of things that it has to be done. The drivel talked about these type of incidents is just as time consuming as referring a disputed catch to the television replays.

Of course, it bothered me after it happened so I wanted to have a look at the replays when I came off. They must have shown it about 30 times on television and I still wasn't sure either way. Half of the people were saying it looked as if it bounced and the other half were saying it looked as though I got my fingers under it. The only thing I'm sure about is that the fielder, me, was in the worst position to tell when it happened. My head was up as I lunged forward and I couldn't tell where my hands were in relation to the ground. You know if it's clear cut because you hear two noises but on this occasion I didn't. It's a worry but at least I know now, looking at the replays, that it wasn't clear cut either way.

I also knew I would get some stick from the Aussies about it, that's inevitable, but I didn't expect to get it while I was still in the field! But that's what happened when Warne came out to bat. He was soon turning round to me, calling me a cheat and predictable stuff like that. I could understand them being upset about it and I don't mind verbals, it's part of the game and it fires you up. I'll just try to put it to the back of my mind and I was pleased to bump into Tony Greig in the car park after play. He told me not to worry and that the third umpire has to be used in those situations. I agree.

Meanwhile we were back in the game when they were 132 for five but that man Steve Waugh had other ideas. He was absolutely magnificent, just as he was in the first innings and at a time too when he was suffering from bat jarring and we were expecting him to give his wicket away at any minute.

Of course, Steve has a great reputation and I've seen him get runs on flat wickets but to score this many runs on a wicket like this was phenomenal. The bloke just hates giving his wicket away and sets an example to us all. He's not always the prettiest of cricketers but he's the type you've got to watch and learn from. He gets runs and that's all that counts and if anybody was going to play the match winning innings for Australia when they had their backs to the wall it was going to be Steve Waugh. He's done it too many times for it to be a fluke.

Karen came over from Southport tonight and we went for a curry in Rusholme. The owner recognised me and, as he was serving up the popadums, said: 'There was no way you took that catch cleanly. You should have owned up.' It didn't exactly add to my enjoyment of my chicken tikka masala!

6 July, Day 4, Third Test

Australia 235 and 395–8 declared (Waugh 116, Warne 53, Reiffel 45; Headley 4–104) v England 162 and 130–5 (Crawley 53*).

I wasn't feeling too nervous as I tucked into a bowl of honey snacks this morning … until I read in the paper that if I managed to score another 18 more runs today I would become only the third Australian in Ashes history to score two hundreds in the same match. The two Australians to achieve this feat were both left-handers, Warren Bardsley and Arthur Morris, with the last double being achieved by Morris back in 1946–47. Now I was a fraction nervous about the prospect of becoming part of such an elite group. The hand had pulled up reasonably well, with a distinct reduction in the swelling, but the sharp pain in the joints remained, as I stretched out in the hotel's indoor swimming pool.

Warne and I got off to the perfect start, hitting 20 runs from the first three overs to set the tone for the day, and to further put England out of the game. Shane completed his second Test half-century, but just when a 100 seemed a possibility, the way he was striking the ball, he fell 47 short of that landmark.

Whenever a player gets to 99 he immediately tenses up – you're so close to that elusive milestone that you don't want to stuff it up now. On this occasion, going from 97 to 98 to 99 was torturous, especially as I kept recalling how I'd been robbed of three runs earlier in the innings when the umpire had given leg byes instead of runs. My second hundred was finally secured with a push through mid-wicket off Robert Croft. The elation was not as intense as in the first innings, but the satisfaction was the same, especially considering the handicap I'd played through.

Headley put paid to my aspirations of a big hundred when he produced a near unplayable lifter that steepled off a good length and 'gloved' me through to the keeper. The good news to come out of this event was that it confirmed that the wicket was still playing a few tricks. But Reiffel and Gillespie made the pitch look benign, scoring freely in an unbeaten ninth-wicket stand of 62 before Mark Taylor declared 20 minutes after lunch, leaving England the option of surviving a minimum of 141 overs for a draw or scoring an imposing 469 runs to win.

England got off to a solid start before Gillespie started the rot, sending back Atherton with one that beat him for pace and trapped him in front, not long after the English captain had sent a hook shot into the full-house crowd. Stewart became Warne's 250th Test scalp shortly after, and he was closely followed by Hussain and Butcher.

Butcher was again beaten for pace, top-edging a hook to Glenn McGrath at fine leg, who came sprinting in to take a fine one-handed catch (even though he attempted to gather it in both hands). Glenn's fielding has improved out of sight on this tour with his ground fielding being exceptional. There was, though, one notable exception to earlier on our trip – an 'air swing' off a top-edged sweep that, to everyone's amusement, spun wickedly past his outstretched arm at deep backward square.

The prize scalp of Thorpe went to Warne, who out-thought him with a wrong'un that claimed the edge and plunged the home side further into the abyss at 84 for five. Restoring some local pride was John Crawley, who feasted himself on Bevan's mixed bag of goodies. Generally, it was the gift full tosses that the batsman hit to the advertising boards, but in between Crawley had to be watchful of that unplayable ball Bevan has the ability to produce.

The afternoon session was marred by spectator interference, which seemed to be some sort of protest against the home side's poor showing. The pitch invasions were numerous and tiresome, with play continually held up while the intruders frolicked around the outfield. One notable exception was the 'kamikaze kid' who raced out and dived full length into the stumps, in an imaginary tackle that may well have even stopped the All Blacks' Jonah Lomu. When play was possible, Ealham and Crawley added 46 before we left the field in search of a cold one and to have a chat about the day.

NASSER HUSSAIN

We were now in big trouble but we had knocked their last three first innings wickets over quickly on Friday morning and now we had to try and do it again. But it did not work out that way. Waugh went on to his second century of the match and Warney came in and played well, as did the rest of the tail. We thought they would declare at lunch but it's typical of the Australian mentality to completely batter you when you're down and make sure you're completely out of the game before they call it a day.

As a batsman it does make things a little more difficult when they delay the moment of truth but you're professional enough to keep your mind focused on the task in hand because you know you've got to bat at some point during the day. It doesn't matter when it is. We knew the pitch was not too bad by now and that the main threat, again, would be Warne. Athers and Butch got us off to a good start when we eventually got out there but we always knew we were up against it. The game had gone perfectly for them and for us to bat for five sessions was a monumental task. We needed two of us to get stuck in like me and Thorpey did at Edgbaston but while we are all capable of playing the big innings only John Crawley came anywhere near it on this occasion.

Ath was out, then it was my turn to face the challenge. There was a bit of sledging going on and they were saying things like, 'Let's get him for Blewett' but that just made me more determined and didn't affect the way I batted at all. I was determined to fight and show them that I wasn't affected by it and I dearly wanted to be there at the close so that I could stick two fingers up at them. We'd have done the same to them, to be fair, and the abuse wasn't that bad. Nothing too personal, all part of the game. I just wanted to show them that it didn't upset me.

But I got an lbw that I wasn't exactly ecstatic about. I had made one run. When I got back to the dressing room David Gower was saying on television that I could easily have been given out lbw on 82 at Edgbaston so these things level themselves out. I know that's true but it's not a great consolation at the time. We had lost five wickets by the end of play and, to all intents and purposes, it seemed like game over.

7 July, Day 5, Third Test

Australia 235 and 395–8 declared defeated England 162 and 200 (Crawley 83; McGrath 4–46, Gillespie 3–31, Warne 3–63) by 268 runs.

The mood was jovial and confident as we limbered up in the rooms this morning. There was no rain in sight and only five wickets separated us from a comprehensive victory. When play began it wasn't Shane Warne, but the thoroughly professional Glenn McGrath who claimed four of the five wickets to fall. Warne again bowled superbly, but without the wheel of good fortune turning in his favour.

John Crawley could consider himself to be a bit unlucky, when he dislodged a bail while fending off a short ball, but the rest of the batsmen were simply not good enough on the day. Robert Croft, in particular, looked a mess at the crease. He seemed ready to be pummelled by the short ball, as he knows his technique isn't going to cope with the onslaught. Some hard work awaits him in the nets during the off season.

The winning margin was a whopping 268 runs, one that will give the English squad plenty to think about in the future Tests. The celebrations afterwards were moderate by our normal standards, because we know there is a long way to go. The journey has just begun.

Again, I was summoned to the press conference by the media, along with Tubs. I was covered in beer, champagne and red wine, and sat shivering with cold while every question was directed at Mark. What a waste that press conference was for me. Then it was time for that sweetest of all times, the team song, which was again sung with such gusto and pride one was immediately covered in goosebumps.

NASSER HUSSAIN

Our biggest hope today was that John would get a century and we would make the Aussies fight for victory as much as possible. Even though John's a good player he was under a little pressure and with Warne bowling out of the rough it wasn't easy out there. As it turned out John trod on his stumps – something of a Lancashire habit as Athers did the same at Lord's – and fell 17 short of his hundred. I suppose it's something of a curiosity that two Test batsmen could get out hit wicket in consecutive Tests but it has much to do with the fact that the Aussies are short of a length bowlers who mainly bowl back foot balls so you are going back a long way to them. Also, we've left the wickets fairly green so the wicket ends are a little bit slippery. Basically, John was unlucky and it was a great shame for him because a century against Australia is worth having in whatever circumstances it comes.

After John went it was then just a matter of time and when it was all over we had to hold our hands up and accept that we hadn't played well. There is no point sulking or complaining about things. We had opportunities to win the game. If we'd bowled them out for 60 fewer in the first innings we'd have had a chance and if we'd batted better throughout we'd have had a chance. It's the first time for quite a few matches that our top six have lost us a Test and we've got to accept that we should have got 350 in the first innings and if we'd done that we wouldn't have been in a mess second time round. We have to take responsibility. This is Test cricket and Test cricket is difficult. This is also Australia and if anyone thought, after the one-dayers and the first Test, that we would win the series comfortably then they were always going to be sadly mistaken. Spectators and press have got to remember that we have lost to these boys by wide margins the last few series and this summer so far has been a big improvement on that. But we've got to learn from this. It's half-time. It's 1-1 and we'd have settled for that at this stage at the start of the summer. It's a three-match series now and we have to win it.

It's a hard season but I've now got a bit of time off so I'm going back to the nets to work hard. I may even play a second team game before Essex's match at Northampton to try to get some runs under my belt. Fact is, double century or not, I haven't done enough in this series yet. I want to beat Australia and I want to get on the winter tour to the West Indies. I need to get at least one more hundred this series and I want to average 40 for the summer. I want to do all these things but, most of all, I want to beat this lot and if I can contribute another hundred in a winning England cause in the three matches to come then I'll be pretty happy.

All that was left at Old Trafford now was the presentations and we found ourselves in the position so many England sides playing Australia in the recent past have found themselves. Having to watch visiting celebrations. The Aussies went ballistic on the balcony and their dressing room was awash with champagne. It meant a lot to them. I went and shook most of their hands. There were no problems. The Aussies are superb in defeat and they are superb in victory. I also wondered whether I should approach Greg Blewett but he still seemed a bit heated about what happened so I decided not to. I might try to see him at Headingley or it might be better just to forget about it.

In the meantime I contented myself with speaking to their coach, Geoff Marsh. I said, 'Look, in my opinion I thought I'd caught it. I don't want this to cause a problem between the sides. Sledging doesn't bother me but I don't want you boys really thinking I'm a cheat.' He said, 'That's fair enough, Nasser.' He then advised me to have a word with Mark Taylor to tell him the same but this was right at the end of the game and Taylor was doing stacks of interviews so I didn't really have the opportunity.

I left Old Trafford with music blaring out from the Old Trafford dressing rooms. The Aussies had some rock band on really loud so Bumble retaliated by turning Oasis up full blast in ours to show them we were not despondent. It all created quite a racket. In Bumble's words we had to stare them in the face and show them we were up for the fight. Then, without exception, we all wished the Kent boys all the best in the Benson & Hedges Cup final to take the piss out of the Surrey boys and went our separate ways. I got lost in Manchester and got home about 7pm. It summed up the week.

12
BREAK FOR THE BORDER

STEVE WAUGH

8 July, Newcastle

Australia 290–7 (Julian 106) defeated Minor Counties 281–9 (Cockbain 82; Slater 1–7, Langer 1–19) by nine runs.

Whoever pencilled this match into our itinerary has obviously never been part of a winning side before. To have to front up to this politically correct fixture against the Minor Counties XI the day after a Test win and after two-and-a-half hours on the motorway is so ridiculous it defies logic. All we could do was take the attitude of 'Oh well, we're here now and we have a job to do'. Today was captain's day for me, as Tubs was having a breather (something which I probably should have had as well, considering the state of the painfully swollen joint between my right thumb and index finger). In fact, I have assumed the captaincy role for this leg of the tour while Tubs linked up with the captains of all the Test-playing nations for a meeting in London to discuss various issues and concerns of the players.

This type of match isn't popular with the players for a number of reasons. One, the opposition is nothing like what we face at international level. Two, while such a fixture is okay at the start of a tour, when we are still finding our feet, by the tour's half-way mark tough opposition is required so we can fine-tune our game. And, three, it is assumed that we will win in convincing fashion – if we don't the doomsday clouds come from all around, usually in the form of headline-seeking journalists.

Fortunately for us, we had no such problems. This was thanks largely to the prodigious hitting of BJ, who, after we batted first, looked as if he was playing with his brothers in the backyard on his way to 106 off just 89 balls.

On a personal note, I may have created a record as skipper today by claiming no wickets, not facing a ball and taking no catches. Obviously the captaincy brings out the best in my game!

With most of the families joining us on this section of the tour, it made a pleasant change to get out of the hotel atmosphere and enjoy a barbecue in the fresh air. It was something we should do more often, as it bonds not only the players but the families, too – if you can keep everyone happy you are well on the road to success. To cap off the night, the Blewetts were surprised with an engagement cake, but hopefully what then happened isn't an omen because it was soaked by a thunderstorm that arrived unexpectedly.

9 July, Edinburgh

The Waugh family looked a bit shabby as we loaded our ever-growing luggage into our Toyota sponsored van. Once again, we had endured an interrupted sleep due to the absence of an air conditioner combined with the ridiculous central heating that made conditions so hot and humid it was hard to breathe.

Rosie didn't enjoy the sweltering temperatures. It's becoming increasingly noticeable that she is not coping well with the constantly changing routine, with different hotels, long car trips and noisy rooms. She isn't able to shake the slight bout of flu she's been carrying around, and I'm beginning to think that she's better off at home with Lynette, even though I love having them touring with me.

The two-and-a-half-hour trip was made worthwhile by the sight of the Dalmahoy Hotel, which is set among a pristine looking golf course on the outskirts of Edinburgh. While most of the lads ventured out onto the course, I took Rosie to the nearby leisure centre for a swim. This is an activity she seems to have a real liking for. Perhaps she'll be a future Olympic champion, although I fancy she'll be a tennis or squash player because her birthday coincides with two Australian greats, Heather McKay and Evonne Cawley.

10 July, Edinburgh

My first task today as captain was to front up at a press conference which was staged to try to help promote our upcoming fixture and cricket in general in Scotland. In general, it was quite an enjoyable hour-long interrogation, but one question did stand out. It came from somewhere near the back of the room, from a middle-aged man who appeared to know what he was talking about. That was until he quizzed me on Shane Warne. He inquired, 'What is wrong with Shane Warne, he doesn't seem to turn them any more. Has he lost it?'

Considering Warney had claimed nine wickets in the third Test only last week and bowled numerous unplayable deliveries that spun at times viciously, I couldn't quite believe what I had heard. My response was brief and enjoyed by all except the bloke who asked the question.

'Don't you own a TV?' I asked. 'Didn't you watch the last Test?'

Amid the growing laughter, he admitted that he had been on holiday in France and missed the action. I'm sure he now regrets his lack of preparation for today.

If I get a free day on tour, I love nothing more than to visit the local zoo. I find it relaxing, therapeutic and as far away as possible from anything related to cricket. And having Rosie with me means such a venture is now doubly enjoyable, for every animal she sees and every smell she senses are new to her. To see the gorgeous, ever-curious look on her face is something that rivals anything I can achieve on the sporting field.

With the sun not setting here until around 10pm, you can squeeze a lot into one day. The extra daylight tonight provided the opportunity for me to visit the hotel complex's driving range, in preparation for our journey tomorrow to golf's equivalent of Lord's – St Andrews. However, judging from the resting spot of my 50 practice balls, I'm a good thing to make it three hundreds in a week, with the duck hook and pushed drive two shots certain to feature prominently after I get on the first tee in the morning.

11 July, Edinburgh

At about the same time the team bus was heading for golf's Mecca, both Warney and Gilly were about to board a jumbo that was heading back to Australia. The diagnosis on Gilly's left knee was a severely stretched medial ligament, which requires rest and then much strengthening work in order for him to enjoy a complete recovery. It was such a shame to see him leave, as he was a very popular team member and a guy destined for higher honours (which I'm sure will still come so long as he treats this setback as a test of character and not something that will permanently damage his career). Victorian keeper Darren Berry has been called up as his replacement. Warney, by contrast, was going home because of some good news. The tour hierarchy had allowed him to spend a couple of days back in Oz, so he can see his new-born baby in the flesh.

This is an initiative that is new in cricket circles, but I'm glad he's going home because he'll have a chance to bond with his daughter and see her in the flesh, rather than having to make do with the couple of photos that have been sent over. I just hope the Australian press give him a couple of days peace with his family.

Arriving at St Andrews is heaven for golf freaks. Every second shop sells everything to do with the game and there is a whole chain of links courses in the close vicinity. Among our squad, Punter and Blewey were particularly excited about the prospect of today's round – especially Ricky, who already has two sub–70 rounds to his name this tour, one of them on the Belfry's championship course.

First stop was a guided tour of the renowned St Andrews clubhouse. The only catch was the need for a jacket and tie, which quite a few of the lads had forgotten to bring along. However, the boys somehow managed to scrounge together the necessary items to enable them to make the tour. BJ was quite a sight, dressed in a vertically-striped tie nestled atop a horizontally-striped shirt and finished off with a diagonally-striped jacket. Next to that outfit, the highlight of the clubhouse tour was seeing the oldest ever painting depicting the game of golf, which hung unobtrusively in the members' sitting room with a value of over £2 million attached to it.

The only downer for the day was that we weren't playing the historic 'Old Course' but the 'New Course' (which was first played on in 1895). Having played the Old Course in 1989, this wasn't the huge disappointment for me that it was for some others. The surprise packet of the day was Justin Langer, whose group took out the team prize ahead of the more fancied combinations. Blewey had a shocker by his standards, shooting in the high 80s. Late into the evening, he was still shaking his head in disbelief as he struggled to come to terms with 'taking the gas on the big occasion', as he put it. Punter was steady, carding a 77, which sounds impressive until you discover just how good this guy strikes the ball.

Smithy, meanwhile, was confirming my theory that if someone hasn't any co-ordination at ball sports they take up fitness work to cover their deficiencies. His score was of epic proportions, 137 strokes in all. Knowing Smithy, he would have enjoyed every one of them, if only because of all the walking he did to retrieve his wayward balls.

To cap off a great day, most of the team sneaked out into the Old Course just before dusk to play the famous 17th hole – the Road Hole. The sceptics said it wasn't possible, but these rebels succeeded in doing so before any of the course marshals spotted their efforts. Like Lord's, there is strict protocol and rules here that must be obeyed by all, especially the law that requires you to be on the first tee 10 minutes before your scheduled starting time. Tragic stories have been told of overseas visitors arriving for their game only marginally late, and being given their marching orders. This would be an extremely severe blow, as you have to book 18 months ahead just to swing a club on the course.

12 July, Edinburgh

Australia 278–9 (Slater 95, Langer 46; Sheridan 5–65) v Scotland 95–6 (Kasprowicz 3–28) no result.

An unexpected full house came to the impressive Grange Cricket Club for the eagerly awaited clash between the Australians and the latest team to qualify for cricket's 1999 World Cup. The success of the Scots at the recent World Cup qualifying tournament in Malaysia has increased the profile of the sport here ten-fold, to the extent the story of their success kicked soccer off the newspaper back pages, if only for one day.

Going out to toss was, inevitably, a major event, with cameras from Sky Television and various local stations, plus journalists from the print media, joining George Salmond, the local captain, and myself as the coin went up. The toss even had to be re-enacted for one cameraman, who happened to miss this momentous event the first time around.

The unwritten rule in these types of games is that we bat first, to set a big total and give the crowd value for money. This is exactly what occurred, even though Salmond called correctly on a placid looking strip that seemed ideally suited to batting. Slats then came out guns blazing and gave the opposing bowlers a lesson in how not to bowl to a player capable of executing the most ferocious pull shots known to man. After 15 overs, it looked as if a team total of 400 might be attainable, but this notion fell by the wayside when Slats fell five runs short of a century. Lang and Punter were the only other Australian batsmen to do themselves justice, as the middle to late-order handed the left arm orthodox spinner, Keith Sheridan, a gift 'five-for' and a guaranteed place in Scotland's cricket folklore.

My stint at the crease was a waste of time, as I was barely able to hold the bat, due to the stiffness and pain in my right thumb joints. The medicos tell me this is a problem that needs up to six or seven weeks rest to fully correct – a gap in the schedule that is impossible to find in a whole year, let alone on this tour.

Playing for a Test spot should always lead to excellence, and it was once again Kasper who put his hand up. He produced a decisive spell of quality outswing bowling that left the Bravehearts in dire straits after their first 10 overs at the crease. Dizzy was also impressive, but BJ's wretched run of luck continued. An infected ingrown toenail threw his approach off balance and led to a wayward spell that has probably condemned him to last place on the bowling queue.

Late in the day, just before the match was abandoned because of a torrential downpour, the cricket became a sideshow to the main event – a tandem streaking act. The male intruder was apprehended almost immediately, but his female counterpart somehow escaped the wrath of the security guards to frolic merrily across the outfield, much to the delight of the capacity crowd and some unnamed observers on the playing field.

The whole day was a great success for what has been until recently a 'remote' cricket outpost. If the game is to prosper into the next century it is the cricketers of these embryonic nations who must be fostered, to ensure the continued expansion of the game. We appreciated the opportunity to have a chat with the opposition after the game – not just because they're good fellas, but especially because they are eager to acquire as much cricket knowledge as they can so they can try to reach a competitive level during the 1999 World Cup.

After the post-match festivities, Slats, Heals, Kasper and I set off down the motorway for Birmingham – a minimum four hours – so we would be there for the start of the British Grand Prix at Silverstone tomorrow. One of Heals' sponsors, Foster's, are a major contributor to the Formula One events and when four guest spots became available to the team, the names of the petrol heads in the squad went into a hat. I was one of the lucky ones.

I've always wanted to see exactly how quick these cars go and what skills the drivers need to be successful. There's something about a major sporting event that always stirs my imagination. Maybe it's the thrill of the unknown outcome, or perhaps the aura and mystique that surround the spectacle. For me, I think it's the chance to observe the very best in action that makes these occasions special.

13 July, Silverstone

Following Slats's instructions, we set off at 7.30am in search of a remote airfield on the outskirts of Silverstone. From there we were to be airlifted, via helicopter, to the race track. This, we had been told, was a very good move, as the circuit is inevitably surrounded by many kilometres of gridlocked traffic on the morning of the Grand Prix. However, we missed our designated lift-off time, which meant we didn't arrive until an hour later than we had hoped and therefore didn't get to enjoy a proposed tour down pit straight.

The race itself was highly entertaining, extremely loud and a very worthwhile experience. The only downer for me was that watching the race was somewhat repetitious in nature, because you can see only one section of the track. For Slats, this wasn't a concern. He was in revhead heaven. We certainly got the impression, though, that a lot of people come to this sport for the social life in the marquees and the 'celebrity spotting' opportunities rather than the sport itself. The Aussie boys were as guilty as anyone in this regard, as we enthusiastically pointed out, among others, Pierce Brosnan and Melinda Messenger (the 'Page 3' girl).

The power of the sport almost cost us dearly as we headed for London afterwards. Kasper's execution of a roundabout exit all but came to grief, due to what might be described as his 'overexuberance' at the wheel. Thankfully we all arrived at the Heathrow Excelsior Hotel in one piece, and set about preparing for tomorrow's one-day game at John Paul Getty's private estate.

14 July, Ibstone
Australia 267–5 declared (Elliott 95, Bevan 54) drew with JP Getty's Invitation XI 237–4 (R Smith 57, Crowe 115; Bevan 4–85).

Being a tour selector can have some advantages, particularly in these 'goodwill' fixtures where the off-field hospitality more than rivals the on-field action. Consequently, my duties today were strictly family orientated. Lynette and Rosalie had driven down from Scotland by themselves to be part of the festivities.

John Paul Getty's love of cricket has a rather unusual, perhaps even unique, origin. During a stint at a clinic for alcohol rehabilitation, Mr Getty (who is, of course, one of the world's wealthiest men) was introduced to the Rolling Stones' Mick Jagger – a man whose love of the game is legendary. Jagger suggested the billionaire recluse give cricket a try, and the rest is history. Soon, JPG was the owner of *Wisden*, the English equivalent of the Bible, and he had also donated a couple of million pounds to the MCC to help finance the renovations at Lord's.

In fact, Mr Getty fell for the game so badly that he built his own ground at his private retreat, which is situated about an hour's drive from London. The winding narrow road which leads to his magnificent property offers no clue as to the majesty of this ground. Then, suddenly, it's there in front of you – a beautifully manicured outfield, scoreboard complete with thatched roof, a traditional quaint clubhouse with 'bat-and-ball' railings, and ample space for spectators to laze about on the lush hillsides which surround the playing surface. Throughout the day, a Queen's regiment band played tunes in the background, while an ice cream vendor handed out free cones to anyone who felt the urge. This highly enjoyable day also included a guided tour of Mr Getty's personal library, which has an estimated value of more than £15 million and features historic items such as the first-ever atlas of the world and scrolls that were written by monks in the 11th century. Among the celebrity guests in attendance were Mick Jagger and Marianne Faithful, but for me the highlight was meeting Mr Getty himself.

Out in the middle, Matt Elliott continued his love affair with English bowling attacks and further enhanced his rapidly growing status in the process, but without question the innings of the day came from New Zealand's best-ever batsman, Martin Crowe, who caressed his way to a superb 115. Martin is retired now, yet he made his ton using one of my bats, which he had never picked up until five minutes before he walked to the crease.

As late as we dared, the Waughs hit the bitumen to journey to Manchester. I have four days off, which we will be spending with our old friends from the Nelson CC. I must say I'm looking forward to spending some worthwhile private time with my family, who have faithfully followed the team around the country, always supporting me but never being able to enjoy a steady routine because of the constant changing of hotel rooms and endless hours on the road. Rosie is missing her own bed and doesn't like not having enough room to move – I'm pretty sure she and Lynette will leave for home earlier than we originally intended. Asking them to continue this process is not fair on them when they can't get a decent night's sleep.

In the meantime, I'm going to have four days off from writing this diary. In my absence, Justin Langer will keep you up to date.

15 July, Cardiff

Last night, we left the Wormsley CC for a three-hour journey to Cardiff, where we are to play Glamorgan tomorrow. As you can imagine, most of the guys were pretty tired after the day's play and spent the trip watching the film *A Few Good Men*, playing cards or sleeping.

Although Heals didn't play yesterday, he had spent the day playing with his kids, socialising with the crowd and going for a five-kilometre run with Smithy, Kasper and Swampy. So he was as worn out as the rest of us by the time we boarded the coach.

At 11.30pm, we reached the Copthorne Hotel in Cardiff and everyone eagerly went straight into the reception desk, checked in and were comfortably asleep in their hotel beds … dreaming about runs, wickets and run outs. Everyone that is, except Heals, who had fallen asleep at the back of the coach and, unbeknown to his team-mates, had been left asleep in his seat!

As is standard practice Huey, the driver, parked the coach, locked it up and went to his room for a well-earned sleep. However, as luck would have it, he had left something behind in the coach and went to retrieve it about an hour after we had checked in. While searching for his toothbrush in the luggage compartment, Huey made enough noise to wake Heals, who was still locked inside. Who knows,

Heals may still be there now if Huey hadn't gone back to the coach well after midnight last night.

Warney arrived back in the UK this morning, smitten with his little girl, Brooke Victoria. It is great to have him back on the tour – not only for his bowling, but also for his presence around the team. Most people would be suffering from jet-lag by now, but this didn't stop Warney getting out onto the golf course this afternoon. I am not sure what he loves most – his two girls, Simone and Brooke, his cricket, his cards or his golf. I wouldn't like to ask him!

Until tomorrow, Justin Langer.

16 July, Cardiff

Australia 369–4 declared (Taylor 71, Blewett 54, Ponting 126*, Langer 50*) v Glamorgan 30–0.

The singing and 'abdominal' sensation, Peter Andre, is staying here at the Copthorne Hotel. Talk about groupies! There are beautiful, young women everywhere, trying to catch a glimpse of their heart-throb hero. We cricketers have decided that we must be in the wrong business, judging by the following of young female admirers who melt at the mere thought of catching a glimpse of their Aussie star. Even though Peter talks with an English accent, he still claims to be a 'proud Australian'. The biggest surprise for me was that he is one of the few men in the world that I am taller than ... that is, besides Steve Smith, of course!

Today turned out to be a good, solid, batting practice exercise for the team. All the guys spent time in the middle and enjoyed batting on a very flat wicket at the Sophia Gardens cricket ground, home of the Glamorgan County Cricket Club.

Ricky Ponting batted superbly. His feet have been moving well for the last couple of weeks and it's no surprise that he finally cashed in with a big undefeated century. He is a determined young man, who works very hard to ensure that he makes the most of his wealth of natural ability. Others with unlimited, natural ability often fall into the trap of relying solely on the gifts they were given by their parents. I don't think Punter will ever go to his grave, or come to the end of his career, wondering if he could have done more with his ability or talent. He is a hungry young cricketer who I am sure will play a lot of very good cricket in the next decade.

Until tomorrow, Justin Langer.

17 July, Cardiff

Australia 369–4 declared and 100–5 (Reiffel 35*) v Glamorgan 254 (James 91; Reiffel 5–60).

Fifteen wickets and 300 runs in a day's cricket isn't bad going for a match which seemed last night to be destined for a mundane finish. If you had predicted after yesterday's play that The Sophia Gardens wicket would start playing tricks today, I would have considered you to be an Aussie Rules commentator, rather than a cricket expert.

The wicket started to get a little uneven after lunch, and Pistol showed why he is such an important part of the Australian bowling attack by cleaning up the Glamorgan tail and helping himself to five wickets. Bevo bowled as well as he has all tour and had the Glamorgan batsmen playing all around his wrong'uns and top spinners. When he's bowling well, Bevo is a very difficult package, who presents the batsmen with challenges they very rarely have to face on a day-to-day basis. India's Anil Kumble is considered to be one of the world's best bowlers, and Bevo is in the same mould. They can be more than a handful.

Cricket can be such a frustrating game! As if in slow motion, I watched the ball roll off my thigh pad and dribble towards my leg stump so slowly that I could almost see the seam of the 10-over old ball ticking over towards its target. In a desperate attempt to stop the ball from dismantling my left bail, I tried a series of 'Maradona-like' moves, but because of my ordinary soccer skills I failed to stop the metal from reaching the magnet. Call it unlucky, but at the end of the day the scorebook says, 'Langer bowled 10.'

Life goes on! A win for the good guys tomorrow will ease my frustration.

Until tomorrow, Justin Langer.

18 July, London

Australia 369–4 declared and 217–7 declared (Reiffel 56) drew with Glamorgan 254 and 211–3 (James 79, Maynard 45*).

I am writing this on the morning of the game with Middlesex. Last night, the team was announced for the three-dayer at Lord's and I wasn't in the XI. When the combination was read out, I was sitting on the coach next to Slats. He's been left out, too, so we are both feeling pretty down in the dumps at present.

I guess the hardest thing about this 'dream tour' of England is that for every game six players have to sit on the sidelines. Unfortunately for those six guys, it means that time has to be spent off the ground simply thinking about the game rather than playing it. Believe me, this is hard to come to terms with, especially when you love playing the game as much as I do.

First thing this morning, it was the time of the tour when our green, gold-and-red-striped blazers were worn with our cleanest whites and polished shoes and shown off in public for the official Ashes team photograph. As usual, there is no such thing as a 'simple' team shot. Among other things, the same recurring problems of player placement, staring into the glare, a photographer who wishes he was a clown, too much sunlight, too much cloud … It happens every time! We posed in front of Tower Bridge, with Japanese tourists taking as many snaps of the team as was the official photographer. I wonder if they know what they were taking photos of? Eventually, after 15 to 20 minutes of waiting for the perfect light, the photographer, who reminded us of Dudley Moore in *Arthur*, decided it was time to 'click' away and the job was done.

Receiving the photograph at the end of the tour will be a moment to be cherished by all the players. In years to come, we can show our grandchildren and anyone else who is interested exactly who played in the successful 1997 Ashes Tour. It was a shame, though, that Adam Gilchrist and Andy Bichel weren't with us this morning.

They have as much right to be in this photo as the rest of us.

Regards, Justin Langer.

19 July, London

Middlesex 305 (Ramprakash 76, Gatting 85; McGrath 4–61) v Australia.

I hope Lang hasn't shown me up too much over the past four days. For me, it is back to the Westbury Hotel … and goodbye once again to Lynette, Rosie and the in-laws (who we picked up yesterday at Manchester airport after they had enjoyed a 10-day adventure around Ireland). As I have explained earlier, the Australian squad's policy is that wives and girlfriends can stay with us during Tests, but during our matches against the counties the team must bunk together and the girls have to find their own accommodation. This generally works okay, but in London a hotel bed can be hard to find at short notice and they are always outrageously expensive (upwards of £150 per night).

After our team photo was taken, we headed to Lord's to face Middlesex. If there's one game against a county that every member of an Australian Ashes team wants to play it's this one. Firstly, the game is played at the Home of Cricket. Secondly, the lunches are the best in the country. And, thirdly, Middlesex always put out a competitive XI, which ensures we receive good match practice before a Test match.

As always, Lord's was in immaculate condition. In fact, the wicket looked to be a much better one than the Test-match strip. Middlesex's captain is Mark Ramprakash, English cricket's biggest underachiever at Test level but county cricket's best batsman, and he won the toss and wisely decided to give his batsmen first use of the wicket.

By close of play it was Middlesex's two most experienced and classy batsmen who had cashed in on the ideal conditions. The ever-expanding Mike Gatting, now, of course, a Test selector, contributed an inspiring 85, which was made more impressive by the way he handled Warney (as well as anyone has done all summer), while 'Ramps' once again put his name in front of the English selectors by compiling a textbook 76.

Perhaps Warney held back a bit today. I'm sure 'Gatt' would have been looking for a chink in his armour or a few pointers that might help his lads in the upcoming Test. At the other end, Pigeon again showed us that he now has that rare ability to take wickets even when he's not at his best. This, for us, is a huge advantage because 'positive-body-language-intimidating' types don't come around all that often.

Tonight, for the first time, the whole of my travelling family went out for dinner as one. Rosie, of course, isn't accustomed to eating out, especially Italian, and she barely made it through her vegies before deciding she'd had enough. As a consequence, we all took turns showing her the sights around Marble Arch, while the others completed their meals. Rosie really is growing up quickly over here. She interacts extraordinarily well with people and kids she's never met, appearing to bond with them immediately. I'm so glad she's over here – I would have missed out on so much of her growing up if she had stayed at home.

I can imagine what it would have been like if we had been reunited at Sydney Airport in late August after I'd been away for four months. It would have been like two strangers, introducing themselves to each other.

20 July, London
Middlesex 305 v Australia 351–6 (Elliott 83, M Waugh 100*, S Waugh 57).
It was a refreshing change to be able to play with the sun beating down on our backs. I think the sunshine acted like an instant source of power for all the boys and we batted as an Australian side should – aggressively, positively and creatively. The day was capped off superbly by a Mark Waugh single off the penultimate ball of the day, which left him unbeaten on triple figures. This was a confidence-restoring innings. Others to enjoy themselves were Herb, who scored 83, and yours truly, with 57. In fact, all bar Tubs and Punter gorged ourselves on the local attack, while no-one missed out on the banoffe pie and ice cream at the lunch break.

For Angus Fraser, of Middlesex and English renown, this was his last throw of the dice in the hope of a Test recall, but it wasn't to be. This highly-respected professional ended up wicketless and close to a sidecar (100 runs) at the end of the day. However, he had a much better time of it afterwards, when a wine-tasting benefit function was held in his honour at the ground.

21 July, London
Middlesex 305 and 201–6 (Gatting 47, K Brown 48*; Warne 3–55) drew with Australia 432–7 declared (M Waugh 142*).
Junior continued his pillage of the Middlesex attack into the second hour of the morning, before Tubs decided to let our quicks loose on the county's top order. Mark's unbeaten knock will hopefully be the turning point for him as far as Test scores go, as this has been a disappointing tour for him, run-wise, to date. He is a real confidence player who thrives on striking the ball well. If the runs aren't coming as naturally as he'd want, his confidence level falls significantly.

Our victory bid was thwarted by Mike Gatting, who looked set for back-to-back fifties until I was called on to make a rare bowling appearance and sent him packing with a useful off cutter which broke my tour duck with the ball.

The Poms have included the uncapped Gloucestershire bowler Mike Smith in their squad for the next Test. In my opinion, this is a move that won't improve their chances, even if he's the 'form' bowler in the county championship. While Smith does have the ability to swing the ball, he looks to me to be a metre short of the pace needed to trouble top-class players. Time will tell if I'm right, and there have been many players picked in the past who have elevated their games to levels not many thought they would. Mark Taylor is a prime example. Back in the '80s, Tubs was seen by many as being a steady cricketer with not quite enough shots or talent to make the step up from Shield to Test cricket. But once he got the chance, he confounded those who doubted his credentials.

In Phil and Ethel, Lynette and I had ready-made babysitters, so tonight the two of us headed off to see the *Phantom Of The Opera*. It was my fourth and Lynette's third visit, but it was still a buzz to see the curtain lift up and the performance begin, especially as the star of the show is the Australian, Peter Cousens, and another of the performers is a lad from Panania, in Sydney's Western Suburbs, where we were brought up. It was a superb show, and to cap off the evening, we enjoyed a backstage chat with the cast, who, judging by their inquisitive questioning, are all cricket mad.

13
THE END OF AN ERA

NASSER HUSSAIN

It was time for me to regroup as well as England. I returned to an Essex side in good shape and in contention for three trophies after a Stuart Law-inspired NatWest Trophy second round victory over Worcestershire. We still, as a team, have the odd bad day but I think we've got a great chance in the NatWest with the draw taking us to Nottingham in the next round.

We are desperate to get to the final to make up for the crushing disappointment of last year and our collapse to 57 all out against Lancashire. We've got a lot to prove after that. This is very much an exciting time for the 'new' Essex with Test-class players like Law, Ronnie Irani and Mark Ilott in our team. We are very lucky to have them day-in day-out. Ronnie, in particular, is unfortunate not to be involved in the Ashes series because he's been putting in outstanding performances without there seeming to be any way back into the England team for him at the moment. Most watchers, meanwhile, must look at Stuart Law and wonder how on earth the Australians could leave him out of their touring party.

It can be hard going back to county matches after a Test but fortunately there are people in the Essex dressing room who realise how tough an Ashes series can be and how demoralising it is after a defeat. Graham Gooch, of course, was the master of coming back to Essex and scoring runs after a Test match. It is very important that you still do your bit for your county when you're a regular England player and for me it's a question of trying to get the balance right between rest and practice to keep enough in the tank.

The selectors have taken the unprecedented step of naming the same party for Headingley already with others on the fringe of things joining us for another team building session run by Will Carling's company, Insights, prior to us arriving in Leeds. I think this is a good psychological move. The selectors are saying these are still the best players, so why keep two or three of them on the edge of their seats waiting to see if they have been retained? The message to us all is 'You had a bad game, now put it right.' It's an act of faith that we must repay.

I watched a bit of the Benson and Hedges Cup final on television and it was very encouraging from an English point of view to see Ben Hollioake play so brilliantly for Surrey. It won't be long before he's pushing to be included as a Test all-rounder, yet they are now talking of him going to play for England Under-19s against Zimbabwe which I find unbelievable. He's got to be, at worst, playing county cricket now but I think Surrey must look at themselves a bit before they moan too much about losing him to the Under-19s. They have left him out of their championship team at times this year and when he has played he's sometimes batted as low as No 8, but this bloke can clearly bat and he needs to be in the top order for the good of himself and England. He looks a real talent.

I had a difficult decision to make the day before Essex's match against Northampton. There was a second team game that I felt it might be an idea to play in just to get another innings under my belt. I've been hitting the ball well but not going on to play a big innings so I asked Fletch what he thought. He said to me 'just make a cricketing decision, you'll know what's right' and then it was a question of deciding whether I should have a day in the garden with Karen – chances to do that are few and far between – and rest or play. I played in the end, got 40 odd against the MCC Young Professionals at Chelmsford and went on to score runs at Northampton, so it proved a worthwhile exercise in getting the ball rolling.

Northampton, however, will be remembered for more than me getting in the runs again and us losing narrowly on the last day. For this was when Graham Gooch decided to announce his retirement from cricket. It really was the end of an era.

Goochie's decision took me by surprise but I suppose the writing was on the wall. A few weeks ago, when I was on my way back from the Edgbaston Test, Prich (Paul Prichard, the Essex captain) rang me to say that Goochie had approached him and told him he was thinking of packing it all in because he wasn't scoring runs and was holding Robbo (Darren Robinson) back. Prich wanted to know my opinion so I said, 'He's going through one of those phases when he's down which, even though he's a great run scorer, he has a tendency to do, so it's worth saying to him, 'Don't be silly, you're going to go out and score 200 soon and Robbo's turn will come.' But I also said that I was sure Goochie had given it a lot of thought and that if he's really serious about it then you should go with what he says. He's a proud man and if he genuinely believes that he's holding Darren Robinson back you have to listen to him. In any case, the next time I turned up for an Essex game Goochie was there so clearly, between him and Prich, they had decided for him to carry on.

Yet by Northampton his form had still not improved even though he had never really looked out of nick – for instance, he hit the first ball at Northampton for six – and each time I have played with him, when he's begun his innings, I have thought 'this is it, he's on the way back, he's going to get a hundred today.' Then somehow he's got himself out. I did not know, though, what he was about to say when, during our run chase on the last day at Northampton after we were both out, he said 'come on Nass, let's go and have an ice cream and walk round the ground.'

After buying me a 99 we discussed many things, like the England set-up and what sort of team I felt we should be putting out against the Aussies. Goochie is very good at gathering opinions from people and I just thought this was another instance of that. Then, out of the blue, he said 'I've got to tell you that next week's game against Worcestershire will be my last for Essex.' It was almost a double take and it took me a few seconds to appreciate the importance of what he was telling me. I didn't know whether to say well done or bad luck. Basically, I wanted to say well done on a great career, this is a big moment. But I also wanted to say bad luck because deep down I knew how much it would have meant to him to finish on a high note. So I didn't know what to say. It just didn't click at all that I'd played my last match with Goochie because I was going to be at Headingley while he made his final appearance.

I would love to have said – and I'm not very good with Goochie because he's such a legend – 'Thanks, mate. All the things I've done for England have been down to you and Fletch and I owe a hell of a lot to you.' I would have loved to have blurted it all out, but I barely said anything apart from telling him that things will never be quite the same again and that he will leave an enormous gap. So I must sit down in the next couple of weeks and write him a card just to say thanks for everything. He was the first person to pick me for England and while we've had our fall-outs and he's disciplined me a couple of times, that's all water under the bridge now and we've ended up mates. Although Goochie is a very private man he's also a very proud man and a big team man and I think he'd like us to give him a fitting farewell. I think, as a normal bloke from Leytonstone, he would like his feats to be recognised and for people to tell him that what he's achieved has been fantastic. I'll be very disappointed with Essex if they just give him a little tankard in a small ceremony in a marquee at the end of the season. They should have some sort of gala dinner or major evening as a tribute to what Graham Gooch has done for Essex County Cricket Club.

So while I was trying to take it all in Goochie told me not to tell anyone about what he had just said. I presumed he was going to tell Prich and Fletch, but it didn't quite work out like that. I subsequently realised that I was the first cricket person he'd told. He'd clearly been agonising over it and even now I would bet money that he would have scored a big hundred at some point between now and the end of the season if he had carried on. That's all he needed to keep him going.

Goochie didn't say a word in the dressing room after the match to give any clues that he was packing it in. He just told us he was on his way up to Headingley to have a look at the Test wicket because a lot of fuss was being made about it up there. I just said 'See you up there'. That night it was difficult to keep the secret because Robbo had a chat with me in the bar about how frustrated he was getting. It was tempting to say 'Don't worry, you've got a regular place from next week' but I couldn't because I'd promised Goochie I wouldn't. Next morning, when I came down to breakfast at the hotel, someone asked if I'd seen the *News of the World* and there was Goochie's announcement tucked away inside.

Everyone was in a bit of a state of shock but I owned up to the fact that he'd told me the day before but sworn me to secrecy. There was no point feigning surprise. I don't think anyone expected him to carry on beyond this season but there was still surprise that he went when he did. Now there was a realisation that we had a gaping hole to fill. Fletch, apparently, had received quite a few calls at home on Saturday night from the press asking him if it was true that Goochie had retired because a lot of media people had seen the first edition of the *News of the World*, but Fletch denied it because he genuinely knew nothing about it. All he wanted to do was have a quiet night watching the golf on the television. I'm sure Goochie meant to tell him in advance.

Of course I'm disappointed that I won't be at Chelmsford for Goochie's last match but I wouldn't have it any other way because I'm playing for England. The word 'great' is overused in sport but Goochie is a great, no question and I think he made the right decision to choose his moment to go. I suppose the ideal time would have been at the end of last season after he had scored all those centuries, but as everyone knows he played on this year for his dad until he had just hit the wall. It's amazing how long he has gone on for. I'm 29 and I'm finding it hard to come back to county cricket at the end of a Test so for Goochie to produce the goods so often for his team after all he achieved for England took huge willpower and self-discipline. To get up at Northampton, Derby or Leicester and score hundred after hundred after each Test is truly immense and he doesn't owe anything to anyone involved with Essex or England.

So I felt it was a bit ludicrous of Peter Edwards (the Essex secretary-general manager) to say he was disappointed he didn't know about it before it was in the paper. It's basically nothing to do with him. It was a very personal decision and maybe Goochie should have told Prich and Fletch in advance, but after all he's done he didn't have to tell Edwards earlier.

What next for Graham Gooch? Well, he's as keen to contribute as ever but he's never been a great believer in managers or management. I think he would like to be more of a specialist batting coach while carrying on as a selector and I'm sure within a year or two he will have a full-time role somewhere in the national set-up. It's hard to see him getting a job at Essex because Fletch and Butch (Alan Butcher) are doing such good coaching jobs, but it's hard to picture him at another county. If he does become a coach somewhere else I think it will have to be close to home, maybe like Surrey, where he knows people well and where he'll be within easy reach of his daughters. I know that Grav and Bumble feel he's doing a tremendous job as a selector and for the rest of this season he's going to be working at all levels with Essex. If we go on to win something this year it will mainly be for the lads who won it because most of them have not won anything yet but in the back of our minds, if we win the championship or the NatWest, I'm sure someone on the balcony will dedicate it to Goochie and that will be right.

14
ENGLAND v AUSTRALIA
FOURTH CORNHILL TEST MATCH

Headingley, Leeds, 24–28 July

NASSER HUSSAIN

21 July

I travelled up from Northampton to our base in Yorkshire late last night with Ashley Cowan following me up the motorway to meet up for our get together ahead of the fourth Test. When we arrived we found Ath, Goochie and Grav in the bar and had a quick drink with them before, realising it was already midnight, heading for bed. The itinerary started early this morning so it is going to be a busy couple of days. Much has been made of the merits or otherwise of these 'team bonding' sessions but I can honestly say it was very useful at the start of the season when we previously got together to concentrate our minds on the task in hand and I'm sure this will be viewed the same.

There is much discussion on the bus to Harrogate for our team tasks about the merits of Ben Hollioake playing for the Under-19s. Stewie appears to be in favour which I guess is not that surprising as his dad is the ECB development man, while Butch and Ben himself seem to be leading the arguments against.

When we arrive we are split up into teams and it's a huge relief to me to see Caddy in our side. He's known as 'Ceefax' because he knows everything and it meant that me, Adam Hollioake, Crofty and Ashley, the other team members, didn't really have to solve much at all. Every time we were set anything it was a case of 'over to you Caddy' and we walked the competition. We had to do things like be guided blindfolded through a golf course by our partners and then picking numbers out of a hat which decided which golf club you would have to use next, so you were faced with the possibility of teeing off with a putter or putting with a driver.

One disappointment was that there was none of the Lions rugby team, recently triumphant against the odds in South Africa, present to tell us how they overcame the might of the Springboks. I know Bumble was particularly disappointed about that because he hoped they would be able to make it. Instead we had to make do with a new video featuring various personalities, including some Lions, Rob Andrew and Alex Ferguson, giving us good luck messages and urging us to beat the Aussies. At the risk of using a cliché, at the end of the day these things have to come from within. The video and other stuff helps, but really it's down to you to do it on a Thursday.

We all had fat tests tonight before a team dinner with our percentage body fat assessed by a dietician. Crofty and Ealie came out with glum faces clutching lists of do's and don'ts as to what they could and couldn't eat. They felt they were picked on a bit – then proceeded to eat five-course dinners!

STEVE WAUGH

Dropping a player from the Test XI is always a gut-wrenching experience, not only for the unfortunate player but also for the selectors involved. I'm sure Bevo must have known it was coming and, in a funny kind of a way, he'll be relieved to know he now has a chance to sit on the sidelines, re-group and gather his thoughts so that he can come back a stronger player and person. Once we'd made up our minds that Ricky Ponting would come into the starting side, Swampy, Tubs and I sat with Bevo, and talked to him about his game and his ambitions. He knows what he has to do to come back and, for the sake of Australian cricket, let's hope he does so – he has a rare talent that has yet to be tapped at Test level.

This morning, before we headed north to Leeds, we set off for a rare treat – a visit to Buckingham Palace. There were definitely a few nerves among the boys as we entered the gates at the Palace, driving slowly past the hordes of tourists who were waiting to watch the changing of the guard. The boys certainly looked the part, dressed in our official tour blazers. And we were keen to make a good impression, especially as it was well over 20 years since an Australian side had been invited to have morning tea with the Queen.

We were escorted to one of the official meeting rooms, the 'Bow Room', at which time tea, orange juice and biscuits were made available. Some 15 minutes later we were told to assemble in a semi-circle, for a meeting with the Queen. I've never seen Mark Taylor so anxious and on edge, so I tried to comfort him by saying, 'Geez Tub, I hope you don't forget anyone's name.' He just smiled and said, 'Thanks a lot, Tugga.' as he tried to dry his sweaty palms on his trouser leg.

When the big moment finally arrived, it was like watching a movie – except we were in it. Her Majesty walked into the room, followed by Prince Andrew. Both were looking formal, yet relaxed. Tubby did the introductions, at which time the royal hand was extended and met with a 'Maam' or a 'Your Majesty'. Heals, standing directly next to me, on my left, was like a schoolboy up in front of the headmistress for the first time. He presented the Queen with a painting by his six-year-old daughter, Emma, drawn especially for the Queen's Birthday. She seemed genuinely pleased to accept the gift.

Pleasantries exchanged, it was time to throw off our formal hats and have an informal chat with the Queen and Prince Andrew. Speaking to her was like chatting with one's grandmother; at least she reminded me of my father's mother, not only by her looks but also by her chatty disposition. Much of our conversation is a blur for me, as I was slightly overwhelmed by actually having this special opportunity.

The most unusual question of the day – and perhaps the tour – came from Kasper, who asked the Queen, 'Did you watch the Military Tattoo versus the Gladiators on television last night?' 'Yes I did,' she replied. Kasper pressed further with this follow-up question, 'Was it your idea to go on the Gladiators?', which drew a response, 'We didn't do too well did we?' Trying to cover for her team, the Queen showed the lads a couple of moves that led to their downfall, at one stage putting her right foot forward and showing the technique used.

This was a meeting to remember. We all came away very impressed by both members of the Royal Family and their comforting natures, which made us feel more at ease than we had originally expected.

Cricket-wise, I feel as if I'm approaching something like peak form. Everything is hitting near the middle of the blade and I can't see any reason why I shouldn't finish the tour off strongly. My only concern is the swelling and continual sharp pain that is emanating from in and around my right thumb joint. Hooter has tried to combat this by devising a pad that can fit inside my glove and take some of the impact. I only hope that by the end of the Test I've got one sore and swollen thumb, because that will mean I've scored a few runs.

23 July

I rang the ground at Chelmsford this morning to wish Goochie all the best in his last game but could only get through to Danny Law. I told Danny to ask Graham if I could have his last bat for my benefit!

We all had a long chat with Lord MacLaurin this morning and he wanted to know how we felt the summer had gone and our views on the winter tour to the West Indies. It wasn't so much cricketing things but how he could help us with little things like travelling. Some of the boys, for instance, had been playing at Canterbury on Sunday and had not got up to Yorkshire before midnight so there was talk as to whether we should have a coach or drivers to bring us to Tests. Bumble felt it was a good idea to travel by coach to the ground once you'd arrived at the hotel but the possible problem with that is that players have their own superstitions and I, for instance, like to arrive at the ground by 8.30am whereas Goughie prefers to come in about an hour later so it would be difficult to organise a coach which left at a suitable time for everyone. Maybe we could have two.

Lots of small things were discussed which may not seem important but which all go towards making you feel part of a slick set-up and Lord MacLaurin is a very good listener. Stewie asked why only two of the four tickets allocated to each player for each day's Test cricket included lunch and tea and the subject of the attendance of wives and girlfriends in the West Indies was also discussed. It was confirmed that they would be allowed to come this time but then it was a question of when was the best time. Basically, it's all going to be much more lenient and it seems as though they can come out to Barbados and Antigua towards the end while there may be special dispensation for people like Karen who's a teacher and may only be able to get out at other times.

The fact that Test match money hadn't been increased for a while was also touched upon and Lord MacLaurin told us he'd be looking into that. He also asked what we would like to see in his blueprint for the future of the game and he gave us the impression there will be a lot less cricket and that he was hoping that England players would be a lot more accountable to the ECB than the counties. We shall see.

I mentioned the fact that net facilities are not up to scratch at many grounds and someone else asked if big NatWest games would still be scheduled for the day after Tests finished and he said that wouldn't happen again. He wouldn't, however, tell us exactly what was in his plan because he said he had to tell other people first.

By this time it was clear that quite a storm was brewing over the decision of the ground authorities to switch the pitch for this Test last weekend. All of us felt it was a lot of fuss over nothing. All summer we've looked at the pitch before each game and felt that it would do a bit and this one is no exception. They've all been pretty different to previous summers but we've felt all along that damp green pitches were the best bet for us against Australia and this is of that ilk. If the pitch is dry we'll have Shane Warne against us and if it's doing a bit we'll have three top-quality seamers against us so it's going to be hard either way. A late switch of surfaces didn't really seem to be a good enough reason for Alan Crompton, the Australian manager, to make a complaint about David Graveney's involvement.

Even if the England Chairman of Selectors was the man who said the pitch should be switched, why is that a problem? I just can't imagine us being in Australia and Bob Bennett making a similar complaint. It would then, I'm sure, be a case of 'f*** off Pommie, what's it got to do with you?' and we've got to take the same attitude. We've got to tell visiting teams 'this is what we are going to play on whether you like it or not' and I can't see why it matters whether the chairman of selectors or the ECB pitches inspector took the decision to change it. We do seem to bend over backwards to help our opponents at times. The pitch is 22 yards long, you put stumps in it and you play on it. They're the best side in the world and they should back themselves to play on anything we put in front of them. To be fair I don't think the players complained, but their management just seemed to get a bee in their bonnet about it for some reason.

This game is going to be the toughest test yet for the 'new' England. This is an Australian side who are now playing well but we retain confidence in ourselves and the strides we are making as a team.

STEVE WAUGH

It's not unusual to see wickets tailored to suit the home side's needs. In fact we'd been stitched up last October in New Delhi by a wicket that looked five days old before the Test started. That pitch was dry, cracked and close to falling apart, but, most significantly, ready-made for India's three-pronged spin attack.

You couldn't really compare the late change of wicket here to that situation, because at Headingley the Test wicket has been swapped for another to try to stop one of our bowlers from gaining an advantage. We have heard that the English chairman of selectors, David Graveney (formerly a left-arm orthodox spinner at county cricket level), checked out the intended wicket and was very concerned about how dry it was and its lack of grass cover. Obviously, such a wicket would suit Shane Warne down to a tee. Graveney decided that a change of wicket was necessary, to give his selected team a better chance of success. A new wicket was chosen, and prepared to the best quality possible in the three days the groundsman had to work on it. This is fair enough if the groundsman believes he has misjudged the timing of his pitch preparation, in regards to watering or rolling the surface, but for a chairman of selectors to throw his hat into the ring was unacceptable.

Our management have formally objected to Graveney's involvement in the switch, via a letter from team manager Alan Crompton. The whole episode has led to denials from everyone who has had a finger pointed at them, but one brief conversation leads me to believe our information is correct. Walking over to have a look at the new, decidedly green, well-covered pitch, I crossed paths with Graveney, who said to me, 'You should have seen the other one they'd prepared. I could have turned it square on that!'

It was a sleepless night all round for the Waugh family, owing to Rosie's reaction to the impatient eyeteeth which are forcing their way through her gums. She must have woken five or six times, and each time Lynette got up so that I could get enough sleep to prepare for the upcoming Test match. This is just another example of the sacrifices she's made and makes for the sake of my career and for which I am truly grateful.

Yesterday at practice, following a schedule agreed upon by both coaches, Geoff Marsh and David Lloyd, we stepped into the nets before the Poms. Today, they had the first option, which gave us the chance to watch the conclusion of their hit-out. It appeared that the English session was noticeably quieter and flatter than ones we'd watched in the past on this tour, while we are looking sharp and focused. We can all feel the momentum shifting in our favour.

Tonight's team meeting was, I believe, the best of the tour so far. It was brief, uncomplicated, informative and motivational. We are now entering the crucial phase of the tour, when all the hard work we've done should hold us in good stead. We've designated the remaining four-and-a-half weeks as a 'mini-tour', to which we must devote our full attention – there is no time to contemplate returning home or for our desire and commitment to finish off the job to slacken. Swampy has given us the challenge of performing better than our opposite number in this match, which means I am 'taking on' the talented but inconsistent Graham Thorpe. This type of motivational element is something that Swampy encourages and believes in, and one that has, in my opinion, been of benefit to all on tour to varying degrees.

The meeting was enhanced by some inspirational footage of our two most recent Test successes at Headingley (1989 and 1993), intertwined with footage of The Don and other Aussie greats. I must say I feel relaxed, knowing that my previous two Tests here have both produced unbeaten 150s. Here's hoping I can make it three in a row!

24 July, Day 1, Fourth Test

England 106–3 (Atherton 34 *) v Australia.

We were faced with a poser this morning over the toss. Yes, the wicket is damp but traditionally batting last at Headingley is fraught, so do we put them in or not? Ath planned to bat because he wanted us to make at least 250 and back ourselves to dismiss them for 300 or fewer, giving us the opportunity to set them a difficult last innings target. In the end, then, it was hardly worth tossing because Taylor planned to put us in and so he did, giving us, I felt, the worst of the conditions today that we are going to see in the match.

The big team decision was whether to play Mike Smith or Caddy in our attack. I think it was a split decision and it was certainly a tough one. We knew that if it swung then Smithy was the man, but if it didn't you wanted someone big to hit the deck. The selectors knew that and gambled on Smithy, sending Caddy back to play for Somerset. Outwardly he didn't seem up or down about it but I'm sure inside he's hurting. Caddy has a reputation for being a loner and I suppose there's the nagging feeling in your mind that if people thought he was mentally strong they would never have sent him away when faced with a wicket like today's. He has, after all, had a pretty decent series so far. It's the need to have a Steve Waugh mentality I suppose but then we all wish we had one of those. Caddy is more of a team man these days so I'm sure he'll be back.

So in we went to bat and down came the rain. These days are the worst. You wish it would either chuck it down and be done with it or clear up and let us get on with it. But I made my mind up that I would be batting so that I would be ready for it when it came. Butch and Ath gave us a good start but Butch was unlucky after hitting the ball straight at Blewett's midriff and Stewie chipped one up – he seems to be getting out in funny ways at the moment.

So in I went and Ath said to me 'we're going to have to get stuck in here' and it was certainly a two-paced strip, some hitting the splice and others keeping low. But we fought well and I've got a couple of bruises to prove it where the ball hit me. We reached 100 for two and I had about nine balls to survive until the close when McGrath bowled me a good one, it's opened me up a bit, I've nicked it and Taylor has pulled off a good slip catch. I was distraught. There's a huge difference between 100 for two and 100 for three. We'd have had a good day if I'd still been there with Ath on Friday morning but as it was the game is in the balance now.

I knew that tomorrow the sun might be out and the wicket might be a bit easier. It would be flat for a couple of days and then, with the cracks opening up already, it was likely to be uneven on the fourth and fifth days. So I sat in the dressing room for half an hour after the others had gone, thinking how I could have been there first thing in the morning, cashing in while the bowlers got loose. I looked at the replay and felt it was a pretty good ball, so I wasn't too disappointed with my shot. There had been a few chirps from Warne in the field about the Blewett business but I think really that's all been forgotten now.

I had a drink with Dean Headley and Ian Chappell in the hotel bar tonight and my admiration of Chappell is increasing. He was very forthcoming with his advice. Dean, the nightwatchman, told me he would score more than I managed in the morning and for once that's a bet I wouldn't mind losing.

STEVE WAUGH

After the pre-match conjecture over the late change of wicket, the pitch turned out to be one with more than average grass covering, but still less grassy than the over-sporting one we had encountered in the Test at Old Trafford.

Mark Taylor continued his golden streak with the toss, but this time wasn't as bold with his choice, choosing to send the opposition in on what looked to be a bowler-friendly wicket. But on a day that was continually interrupted by the vagaries of Yorkshire's weather, England clawed their way to 106 for the loss of three wickets in front of a crowd that were desperate to get vocal but had very little to get excited about.

This was a frustrating day all round. Our attack bowled too short, as can often happen when the wicket is expected to suit the quickies. They were aware we expected them to get the breakthrough and consequently pushed too hard for success. This was certainly the case for Glenn McGrath, who would have hoped to have had three or four scalps on his belt, but instead had to settle for just one and an 'economy' rate of over three runs per over – a rare statistic for this miserly master. Paul Reiffel, though, was again a model of consistency, making the batsmen earn every run as he probed away looking for a chink in their techniques.

For England, Atherton showed his undeniable value to his team in difficult situations and conditions by riding out the initial storm before settling in for the long haul. He was looking a little apprehensive, but was still good enough to put the loose ball away.

Mark Butcher looked the most comfortable we'd seen him, before he clipped one off his toes only to see Greg Blewett take a freakish catch (or fortunate catch, depending on which side of the fence you're sitting) at short leg. Not long after,

Greg gobbled up a spooned catch off the handle of Alec Stewart's blade, to even out the difficulty of the two snares, but soon after he discovered the perils of his position. Nasser Hussain forced a certain boundary straight into our short leg's visor, to remind him of the suicidal tendencies that one needs to be successful in such a despised position. David Boon turned fielding in this spot into an art form; I'm not sure if Blewey wants to make it a long-term position.

The Gods must have been smiling upon us when Hussain perished after the clock had forged past 7pm – a time normally associated with dinner being served on the table, not with having to fend off a McGrath 'throatseeker'.

I rated today as an even contest, with neither side doing enough to take an advantage into the second day's play. By the time we got back to the hotel room, it was 'nighty night' to Rosie and off down the road in search of some Chinese takeaway for Lynette and me.

25 July, Day 2, Fourth Test
England 172 (Atherton 41, Gillespie 7–37) v Australia 258–4 (Elliott 134*, Ponting 86*).

I was sat on the physio's table this morning, having treatment for a slight hamstring problem, watching Dean and Ath make a good start and I thought 'this is brilliant'. I knew from the A tour of Pakistan that Dean could do the nightwatchman's job so I put his name forward here and at one stage it looked as though he'd win his bet against me. But then he made the cardinal mistake of not having a look at the new bowler when he first came on to see if he was moving the ball away and Gillespie got him with his first ball. I suppose I would never have heard the last of it if he had actually got more than me!

Then, suddenly and spectacularly, our wheels came off. They bowled well on a helpful wicket but there were a few unusual dismissals in there. Creepy fell after hitting Blewett's boot at short leg before he caught it and John felt you could not be absolutely sure it hadn't touched the ground first. So he considered it was a bit harsh of the umpire to give it out straight away and got stuck into Blewett when he came in off the field, calling him a cheat. The tables were turned! I sat there enjoying the fact that my accuser was now the one being accused. I had a little smirk to myself, thinking 'now you know what it feels like'.

But, if Crawley was unlucky or not, we were all out for 172. We were dismissed far too quickly to be competitive, exactly what we didn't want to happen. The wicket was easing, the sun was out and we were in trouble.

When we came out the ball didn't swing for Smithy but we still made inroads before the big Thorpe dropped catch came along. I had just moved out of slip to go in that little perch at short midwicket, because Elliott was hitting Smithy there a lot, when Elliott edged one, almost in slow motion, and it flicked Thorpey's hand and dropped beyond his despairing dive and fell to the ground. It all happened so slowly that I was almost running up to Thorpey to congratulate him before he dropped it.

There was a deadly silence. From the very next ball Steve Waugh got out so they were 50 for four and could have been 50 for five. Ricky Ponting, brought in for Michael Bevan, was new to the crease and he would have been joined by Healy who only knows one way to play and gives you a chance by being so positive. So we would have been very much in the game. It was a huge catch to drop.

Thorpey's my mate, he's a good slip catcher and this is the first one like this I can remember him dropping for England so I won't crucify him. I field there and I know there's no such thing as an easy slip catch. You can stand there all day and then when they get a nick you're expected to catch it. If you drop one everyone knows about it. Thorpey was devastated and his mood got worse and worse as Elliott went on and on and on. Ponting, meanwhile, was playing beautifully at the other end and this could well be the partnership that turns the match.

Thorpey's head got lower and lower while we tried to cheer him up and I know that he would have been thinking that he'd let everyone down. Smudge dropped a hard catch towards the end of the day to complete our misery. It's a long way back from here.

STEVE WAUGH

Today Jason Gillespie conjured up what will be remembered as one of the greatest spells of express bowling ever seen in these parts. First to go was the nightwatchman Dean Headley, snapped up by the 'lightning' reflexes of yours truly in the gully. What followed was almost procession-like in the way the English batting order came and went, all blown away by what Ian Healy later described as 'the quickest spell of bowling I've ever kept to'.

Gillespie had it all. Those huge strides and that loping run came together at the crease for a back-straining coiled delivery and release. This is all accompanied by a monumental follow-through that sees his head almost come into contact with the turf while his bowling hand extends to behind his left ear. It's a graceful yet brutal action that can produce genuine pace and a lethal late outswinger. Headingley looked as if a typhoon had made its presence felt, with casualties everywhere – Headley 22, Thorpe 15, Crawley 2, Croft 6, Gough 0, Smith 0. Mark Ealham survived the onslaught, but came away with a bloodied brow after trying to pull a good-length ball from Paul Reiffel, only to top edge it into his helmet grill. The shot Mike Smith played to register a duck on his Test debut was one he won't want to invite friends around to sit and watch on the video. It can best be described as a timid-looking attempt to swat the ball away.

Only Mark Butcher and John Crawley could consider themselves a little hard done by. This was particularly so in the case of Crawley, who was caught at short leg after a firm leg-side shot cannoned off Greg Blewett's boot up into the air for Greg to complete a freakish dismissal that turned the tables well and truly in our favour. England were 163 for six before Crawley's demise. Nine runs later they were all out.

A golden opportunity was ours to take advantage of, after rolling over England for around 150 short of what they would have expected after the first day. However, it appeared we were heading down the same treacherous path when we lost four wickets for 50. But Matthew Elliott and Ricky Ponting then took control.

Our top-order collapse had begun when local hero Darren Gough sent the crowd into a frenzy by getting a shortish ball to brush the glove of a retreating Mark Taylor before our captain had scored. Blewett went soon after, driving late at an outswinger, while the Waugh boys spooned catches that resulted from a lack of pace in the wicket and a lack of soft hands by the batsmen. To be caught at bat-pad off a 'nothing special' type of ball is a waste, and if I could have kicked my own backside I would have given it a real going over. A centimetre or two either way of fieldsman Crawley and I was safe, but in all honesty I deserved the fate that befell me. Wasting good form is a crime and I was guilty of it here.

Our precarious position of 50 for four would have been worse had Thorpe not grassed a sitter off Elliott's blade from Mike Smith's bowling the ball before I departed. Perhaps Thorpe was snoozing at slip, because it certainly didn't seem likely there was going to be a chance coming his way. Smith looked nervous and unsure, but I felt he was handled poorly considering he is a new-ball swing bowler. He should have been given an opportunity to show off his skills and excellent recent form without having to wait too long for his chance. By the time he did get that opportunity, the ball had lost its shine, the breeze was against his natural swing and he was running up the hill and into the wind. For his sake, tomorrow had better see a marked improvement or else he'd better begin to savour every moment of what will be his only Test appearance.

At the close, we had taken control of the game. Ponting and Elliott's superb partnership is already worth 208 runs, with the prospect of many more tomorrow. Both players looked class acts today, displaying excellent techniques, fine judgment and a natural talent to seize opportunities at the appropriate times. Both are fine exponents of the hook and pull shots, a fact obviously unknown to our opponents, who must have sensed a weakness in there or had been given dud mail by their spies. Strangely, Mark Ealham was again underbowled, and must be wondering what he's done wrong. Whenever he's been used he's performed very well and has never let his side down.

26 July, Day 3, Fourth Test
England 172 v Australia 373–5 (Elliott 164*, Ponting 127).

Athers tried to have a laugh with Thorpey this morning. Christopher Martin-Jenkins in the *Daily Telegraph* had written how Douglas Jardine once turned to a fielder who had dropped an important catch against Australia and said 'don't worry, you've just cost us the Ashes.' So Ath announced to the dressing room 'Don't worry Mr Thorpe, you've just cost us the Ashes.' I'm not sure Thorpey saw the funny side of it but we all thought it was hilarious.

The new ball started doing things today, even with our short attack – that was the one thing, with hindsight, which has done for us, the lack of height in our attack apart from Dean – and our batsmen started looking at each other saying 'oh my God, this is uneven now.' We knew that our plan to be level or thereabouts with them at the end of the first innings had gone and all we could hope to do was bowl them out as quickly as possible while knowing that we would be batting to try to save the match again. That makes a huge difference. When you're batting to win a game, like at Edgbaston, your whole mental approach is positive but when you're batting for a day and a half to save a game you're never quite sure how you should be playing. You want to be positive and natural but then you think 'if I get caught at slip chasing a wide one I'm going to look like an idiot.' We got a couple of wickets early on but the forecast was bad today and sure enough the rain came to leave us fretting in the dressing room.

The rain was heavy now so there was little chance of our going back on and it gave me an opportunity to look around Headingley. I enjoy this ground. The crowd are always totally behind you and they are very keen on their cricket. The only problem is the rugby league dressing rooms which are like dungeons and you have to go upstairs and sit outside on the small balcony to watch the game. But you are looked after pretty well.

There were also a couple of incidents involving the stewards and surreal talk of a man dressed as a carrot being seriously injured for going onto the pitch which is a bit stupid. You could see it happening. In the old days if someone ran on they would be put in an armlock and marched off but now there seems to be a competition between the 'bouncers' to see who can tackle a streaker the hardest. I'm convinced someone's going to break his neck if this carries on. People run on, completely out of their trees with no clothes on, not knowing what's going on and some big rugby idiot tries to kill them.

One streaker a day used to be a laugh and you would stand there wondering how far he'd get before the steward caught him and, while I agree that the numbers of them we've seen at Old Trafford and Headingley this year have been an irritant, there must be a better solution than being so heavy handed. My answer would be to march them out to the nearest main road, leave them there stark naked and say 'now get home mate.' Let's see how many people do it again after that. I don't care how drunk you are, you'll soon sober up if you walk through the middle of Leeds on a Friday night with no clothes on.

STEVE WAUGH

Disappointingly, today was to be a day of frustration, with more action happening in the next-door gymnasium of the local Leeds Rhinos Super League team and on the card tables than out in the middle. There was, however, enough time to see Ricky Ponting bring up a masterly 'beyond his years' century before he was dismissed for a memorable 127. This was the only wicket to fall during the whole day.

In many ways, Ricky's century reminded me of my first Test century, scored some eight years ago on the same ground. It was a hundred full of attacking shots, scored off a relatively low number of balls and one that helped set the side up for victory. At the other end, Matthew Elliott continued his marathon – crushing every attempt the Poms could muster to dismiss him, while at the same time growing stronger as each ball passed.

I wouldn't like to be in Graham Thorpe's shoes right now. Every run Elliott scores must be like a dagger through his heart, with the tally being 135 runs since that fateful chance was put down. At the end of the day's play, we had moved on to373 for five. We are the only ones with any hope of a win, which may end up being the psychological advantage that will guide us to victory.

27 July, Day 4, Fourth Test

England 172 and 212–4 (Hussain 101*, Crawley 48*) v Australia 501–9 declared (Elliott 199, Reiffel 54*; Gough 5–149).

All the Aussies came in and played well this morning while our fielding was average again which was disappointing. We just seemed to be waiting for the declaration which you should never do. You should always be trying to bowl a side out because that sets the right impetus for your batting. If you dismiss a team invariably you bat well because you're in the right frame of mind and that's why Australia tend to bat on for a long time in these situations. They just grind you down.

We went in for lunch unsure of what they were going to do until about 20 minutes before the resumption when Taylor put his head round the door and said 'Ath, you can have a bat again.' Every team leaves it quite late before informing the opposition what they plan to do to keep them guessing. Twenty minutes is about right because you need a bit of time to get the roller on and for the openers to prepare themselves.

So it was lunch on the fourth day on an up and down wicket with a good forecast and we know we've got to bat for four and a half sessions. Again we got off to a positive start and again Butch looked good before getting out. He seems to have a game plan but he hasn't had much luck so far and we haven't really found out too much about him. It will be nice to see him on a flat wicket. Ath got a good ball that bounced on him and as we passed near the pavilion he said to me 'come on, let's fight these f***ers.' For someone who had just got out it was a big gesture and showed how determined the captain was that we shouldn't capitulate. So I said the same thing to myself.

There was also the added incentive of an article I'd read in the *Independent* by Henry Blofeld after the first innings which went something like: 'This English side has again flattered to deceive and we are going to have to do something about this batting line-up.' He went on to say that I may have got 200 at Edgbaston but that 'perhaps he's the sort of player who is not as good as we think he is.' I thought 'Okay, fine. I haven't scored many runs for two Tests so I must be crap.' Those sort of things keep you going when things are tough. But what gets me is that you never hear that sort of thing from the Aussies. For instance, if you asked any of their press guys what sort of summer Steve Waugh has had I'll bet they'll be positive about him but the truth is he's done absolutely nothing apart from having a great game at Old Trafford. If he was English they'd be crucifying him. Look at Greg Blewett. He got a hundred at Edgbaston but nothing since then and I don't hear anyone questioning him. Everyone talks about Ponting being brilliant and, don't get me wrong, he's a very fine player but this was his first Test hundred and if he was English people would be saying he still has much to prove. Meanwhile, our guys who are constantly having to justify their places – people like Ath and Stewie – have stacks of Test hundreds and average 40 each over a long period of time. They can't be that bad.

The point I'm trying to make is that we still don't back our guys enough and recognise that we do have good Test players. Instead we just seem obsessed with comparing our blokes with people who have inferior Test records but if they're Australian they must be the best thing since sliced bread. Why couldn't Blofeld have said that Hussain is good, but he's had a couple of bad Tests on bad wickets? That's what the Aussies are saying about Mark Waugh, who has yet to score a hundred in this series. No-one is saying he's not as good as we all thought. So I'm doubly determined to have at least one more good score in this series.

While I was waiting to bat I had decided to learn from watching Steve Waugh when he starts an innings. The big thing about him is how he takes singles early on and rotates the strike, so making sure he can have a good look at the bowling from the non-striker's end before he gets his eye in. I decided to use this, so I dropped my second ball down and took a single. Now I knew that Bevan was quick but I didn't realise how quick Ponting was. If he'd hit with his throw I was gone but, having had a lot of experience fielding in that position short on the off side myself I know how hard it is to hit the stumps from there.

But it was a poor run. I was only trying to learn from the legend Waugh but I nearly blew it. As it was the throw went for four overthrows and I was away with a five! Sometimes on a good wicket you have to check yourself to make sure you don't play too many shots and end up giving it away and by the same token you can't allow yourself to go into your shell and be too circumspect on bad wickets. You want to be positive and appreciate that Headingley is a fast scoring ground and I'd decided that if someone bowled me a bad ball, whoever it was, it was going for four. When Alec got out to a ball that shot along the ground it just reinforced my decision to go for it. I said bad luck to him as he passed me because you could see he was down. It's true that when things are not going your way they just get worse and worse.

Now I made up my mind to forget the scoreboard and just played for a while. It was a question of shutting the match situation out and treating it like any other Test innings. Bloody important.

When Thorpey came in he got a couple that went up and down and said, in a determined way, 'it's fun out here isn't it?' He's a fighter and even though he'd been low he fought here before getting a nick.

John came in and played the anchor role while I went for my shots and you know in your own mind when you're getting back into form after a leanish spell. Today was the day. I just knew that, unless I got a really good one, I was going to get runs. I still felt that way when I got a few on the fingers and the ribs and I was bruised all over by the end of it and aching like hell.

I didn't think in terms of saving the game, simply that if John and I were together at the end of the day then we'd have a chance and the best way for us to still be there was to play my natural game. Before I knew it I looked up and I'd got 50 and it crossed my mind that I had to prove the double hundred was no fluke. Then I just rattled along.

When I looked up again I was in the nineties, not a question of being stuck in the seventies for ages like I was in Bulawayo, but Shane was bowling really well. I was determined to get to the hundred before the close and Shane knew that and set a negative field. I was on 95 for a while and survived a loud shout for lbw off Shane. Apart from the fact that I'd touched it and it was going down the legside it wasn't a bad shout! I don't know why Healy got so excited behind the stumps but luckily Merv Kitchen wasn't swayed by him. Then Warne bowled me a low full toss which I swept for three and was ready to face McGrath on 98.

He had two men out so I knew he was going to pitch it short, which is not a bad policy to stop someone scoring. I was determined the century had to come in this over. McGrath had been getting stuck into me verbally from the start and it got worse after they had an appeal for a catch behind off John turned down. That's when McGrath got particularly angry, having a go at John and calling me a cheating this and a f***ing that. The normal sort of verbals. I honestly don't mind it, particularly when it comes from McGrath because he usually bowls better when he's quiet. You don't mind winding him up because he starts bowling too short whereas when he's in a good frame of mind he bowls a length.

McGrath and Warne are easily the two noisiest bowlers in their side while Steve Waugh says quite a bit in the field. They're the biggest sledgers. Healy's a typical wicket-keeper, slimey, very chirpy but Gillespie and Reiffel, like Kasprowicz earlier on this summer, don't say a word to you.

When the century came it was pretty satisfying. One ball every over was playing up so this was a more gutsy, in adversity type of innings than Edgbaston. It was also the first of my five Test hundreds to be scored in the second innings, so I don't know what that suggests. But, again, Edgbaston was a match-winning effort whereas I always knew this wouldn't be so that stifles the satisfaction somewhat. Pointing my bat around the ground was just a natural reaction. The Western Terrace had given me a lot of support so I wanted to salute them as they hadn't had a lot to cheer in this match. Then I just pointed my bat to the dressing room where all the boys had come out to clap, including Goochie, but that just happened to be in the same place as a television camera so it looked as though I was saluting the viewers too.

The most pleasing thing was that so many Aussies came up to congratulate me as I walked off soon afterwards. Warne, Blewett, Steve Waugh and Elliott all said well played to me. All the people who had earlier been giving me so much stick. That's how the Aussies are and that's how I like it. They call you all the names under the sun but when you do well against them they seem totally genuine in their appreciation of what you have done. To get respect from these people is what it's all about.

STEVE WAUGH

The papers this morning gave England little chance of survival. They predicted the worst, showing no faith whatsoever in the home team's ability to fight back. On the field, Elliott continued where he'd left off, in complete control as he picked up the tempo whenever he wanted. His level head and hunger for more runs drove him onwards towards the revered double hundred club. Following his effort at Lord's, once again he managed to score more himself than England did in their first innings. But just when the team was ready to acknowledge a magnificent 200, a searing Gough yorker ripped his stumps apart.

Paul Reiffel again underlined his value to the side with a cameo of real class, timing his way to an undefeated 54 off 72 balls. And he was capably supported by the batting bunny, Glenn McGrath, who outscored Messrs Taylor, Blewett, M Waugh, S Waugh, Warne and Gillespie with an impressive knock of 20 not out. McGrath and Reiffel added an unbeaten 40 for the last wicket before a declaration was made during the lunch break.

For the third successive Ashes tour, Australia had compiled more than 500 at Headingley, dispelling the myth that the square is a batsman's nightmare and a seamer's paradise. Even more remarkable is the fact that each of the top seven in the Australian batting order have scored their maiden Test hundred against England. In fact, if you add Michael Slater into the equation, every member of the Australian squad who has hit a Test hundred has hit their first against the Poms. This is a bit of a damning statistic for the county and Test bowlers doing the rounds in this country. For McGrath, his innings was notable in that it was only the third time in his Test career that he'd reached double figures, which, realistically, is like most batsmen scoring a century.

A sizeable first-innings lead allowed us the luxury of setting attacking fields and making aggressive bowling changes that we might not have tried if the match was more evenly poised. Sensing the moment, McGrath sprinted in down the hill with added zest and duly removed both Butcher and the tormented England captain before the crowd had settled back into their seats after the lunch break.

The wicket of Butcher was a beautiful piece of bowling. We have been regularly aggrieved to see the ball pass the outside edge of the Surrey left-hander's blade. But we've noticed that Butcher continually plays the same line, which means that if the ball moves off the wicket, or goes across him from a right-handed bowler's normal angle from over the wicket, he will too often play and miss. Bowling around the wicket negates that angle, while making the batsman wary of leaving balls just around the off stump. In other words, Butcher now had less room for an error in judgment, and it was this new angle that led to his downfall. He again played the same tried and trusted defensive prod, only to see the ball catch the edge instead of flying harmlessly through to the keeper.

Alec Stewart was the victim of a low shooter that sneaked under his guard, but if he is brutally honest he'll admit he should have been on the front foot and not stuck to the crease, in batting's 'no-man's land'. The vital wicket of Thorpe was taken by another swift Gillespie 'Exocet', before Hussain and Crawley began an excellent backs-to-the-wall counterattack. From a precarious 89 for four, the home team reached a respectable 212 for four by the close of play, but hopefully the not out batsmen have only delayed our victory celebrations. For England to escape with an honourable draw they will have to not lose a wicket for a session, the same feat they achieved late this afternoon with considerable skill and courage.

28 July, Day 5, Fourth Test

England 172 and 268 (Hussain 105, Crawley 72; Reiffel 5–49) lost to Australia 501–9 declared) by an innings and 61 runs.

I received a lot of nice phone calls again last night but I think a few people got carried away by our position. All John and I had done was give us an outside chance of survival but people were saying to me, mainly because it's Headingley I suppose, that we could make history here. It was always, to be realistic, a forlorn hope.

Once again, as usual when I get runs for England, I couldn't sleep last night. I may have to start taking sleeping tablets. I used to be like this when I scored runs for Essex but now it only happens when I play for England. All the adrenalin is still flowing and I keep thinking about the innings with all sorts of things swirling about my head. I must have only slept about an hour in total, first watching late golf, then Sky News at five, then I read a book and eventually it was time to get up.

Before play this morning I knew the new ball wasn't very far away and that really meant, with our tail barely scoring a run all summer, that they were about 40 minutes away from winning the match if they could get me and Creepy out. Bumble told us to start again and see what we could achieve but the only way we were going to save the game was by getting our noses in front so runs were very much part of the equation as far as I was concerned. It was always unlikely that we could bat all day so we needed to score well while we were there, perhaps leaving them with 100 to get in 15 or 20 overs and thus giving ourselves a chance of the draw.

So I felt I had to go for it before the new ball because that's when the best scoring opportunities would be there but my problem was that I chose to hit a ball from Shane that dipped on me at the last moment and was a little bit more of a top spinner than a leg spinner. Once he'd brought the man in at silly point I was always going to have a drive at him but I just succeeded in hitting it to mid off.

I was disappointed because I was the one they needed but I didn't question my tactics. I had to be positive and Shane wasn't as big a threat on that wicket as the new ball, so he was the one to attack. It's all percentages and a case of weighing things up. This time it didn't work out because instead of hitting it in a gap I hit it straight to a fielder. Dismissed by Warne again? Yes, that was disappointing but there's always more of a chance of that happening when you get a big score because he'll be bowling and it will take someone as classy as him to get you. I'm not too fussed who gets me if I've got a hundred.

I sat around for an hour or two afterwards thinking that we had a slim chance while I was there but that I had got myself out and sure enough when the new ball came we went down like a pack of cards. Then I had to watch the Aussies celebrating again. Their champagne corks were popping and we had to shake their hands and wish them all the best again. Then, as everybody packed their bags away, I sat quietly for a few moments of reflection with Creepy and Thorpey. I lit up a fag even though I don't smoke and just sat there looking into the distance and discussing how we could get better, what we needed to do, what sort of wickets we needed to play on and should we change our tactics.

This is the first time I've been in a losing England side in consecutive matches since I returned to the side and it leaves you very low. It makes you think 'we can't go back to the old days, we can't go back to being thrashed by Australia and chopping and changing all over the place.' Everything you do in those sort of situations seems to be a backward move and you just go from bad to worse. All of us desperately want the new regime to work and we don't want to go back to the drawing board. I happen to think a lot of good has been achieved this summer but we mustn't spoil that now.

We want to do well for Ath, Bumble, Lord MacLaurin and everyone who has supported us. But, of course, you mainly want to do well for yourself and your team-mates and I thought the days of turning up for Test matches expecting to lose had gone. We've got to make sure that's still the case. Even if we don't win the Ashes we've got to fight like hell at Trent Bridge and the Oval and get back to the point where the Aussies need to be at their best to beat us. The biggest change since Edgbaston has been Australia playing to their enormous potential with virtually everyone hitting form. They needed an injury to Andy Bichel to get Paul Reiffel over here and that's worked in their favour. They're now a better side with Ponting replacing Bevan and our batting has slipped too on the bowler friendly wickets that we're producing.

I think the wicket policy has been justified. We have to play them on wickets

A QUALITY TEAM PERFORMANCE
Steve Waugh

David Leatherdale of Worcestershire wouldn't normally get a bowl in a Chinese restaurant. But he can start filling up his scrapbook with the newspaper reports of his miraculous deeds after taking five wickets against us.

Fitness trainer Steve Smith, the human equivalent of an energiser battery, puts captain Taylor through his punching paces during our stay in Oxford.

Darren Gough appeals for my wicket during the first one-day international at Headingley. He was without luck on this occasion.

Left: Two Australian fans enjoy the rare early season sunshine at the Oval during the second one-day international.

Right: There is nothing I can do to stop Mike Atherton saving the rain-ruined second Test at Lord's in partnership with Mark Butcher.

Below: Michael Bevan had a disappointing summer, but scored an unbeaten century in the one-dayer at the Oval with this sort of fluency.

Left: The looks on the faces of me and Tubby Taylor on the balcony at Lord's tell the story of our 3–0 defeat in the one-day internationals.

Below: I go on the attack during our match against Gloucestershire at Bristol at the end of May.

Below: Shane Warne takes a breather as we are forced into fitness activity before the first Test at Edgbaston.

Left: My fellow diary writer Nasser Hussain on his way to an impressive 207 in the first Test at Edgbaston.

Below: One of these ducks amply sums up my performance in the second Test at Lord's, a match we could have won but for the weather.

Left: The third Test, Old Trafford, Manchester. The satisfaction of two centuries in an Ashes Test was immense. Here I am during the first of them.

We await the third umpire's verdict on Ian Healy's brilliant leg-side stumping of Mark Butcher at Old Trafford in the England first innings. He was out.

Some Poms form the Rolf Harris fan club at Old Trafford to give the home side a much needed cheer.

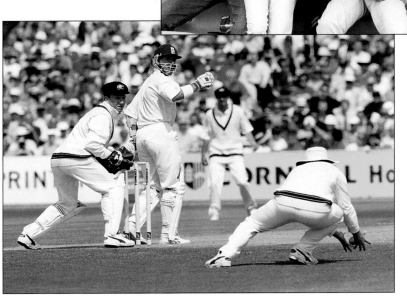

Alec Stewart, still without a Test century against Australia, edges to Mark Taylor during the third Test.

I take a break on the famous bridge at the 18th hole of the Old Course during my round at St Andrew's before we played Scotland.

The great Shane Warne in animated fashion during the fourth Test at Headingley.

Victory is secured at Headingley to give us a 2–1 lead in the series and the dressing room celebrations begin.

Right: Fishing in Northern Ireland during a break before the final Test. Unfortunately, along with most members of our party, I failed to catch a thing.

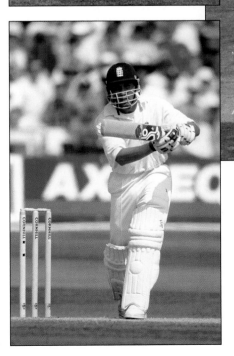

Left: Jason 'Dizzy' Gillespie. Refused to acknowledge the presence on his dining table of raw tuna in a pepper based sauce at the Café de Paris. 'Absolute crap' was his verdict.

Above: Ian Healy, the man of the match at Trent Bridge, completes another fine piece of work, this time to catch Alec Stewart in the fifth Test for 87.

Left: England should look after Ben Hollioake, a refreshing presence in their side, at just 19, for the fifth Test at Trent Bridge.

Glenn McGrath dismisses Mike Atherton, a regular sight during the series, in the second innings at Headingley to put us on the road to victory.

What it's all about. The most important tour on the calendar ends with mission accomplished and Mark Taylor displaying the legendary Ashes urn.

that do a bit and are green and slow. But where I have disagreed with Ath is that once we have settled on these sort of wickets we really shouldn't consider batting first, as we have done. We've got to back our bowlers to bowl them out in a day and then back our batsmen to bat well when the wicket's at its best. If we play well in that type of scenario then the Warne factor doesn't come into it and we don't have to worry about batting last against him. We just have to gamble on sticking them in if Ath ever wins the toss in this series.

There was no real team inquest as such. A lot of people had to rush off to NatWest quarter-finals. Also, now we've got a dietician and others like that on board, we're discouraged from drinking alcohol at the end of a game in the dressing room. I can see the point and I'm all in favour of greater professionalism and attention to diet but there are times, if you win or lose, when you should all savour the moment as a team in the dressing room with a beer or, alternatively, sit there as a team, staring into space and getting things out of your system.

That's what the Aussies did at Edgbaston. They sat in their whites talking about it and having a drink and they do the same when they win. We just always seem to have to hit the road. There's no contemplation after five days hard work.

STEVE WAUGH

All was in readiness for later celebrations as I sat in a chatty and animated dressing-room minutes before we were due out onto the field this morning. A bottle of Southern Comfort was on the nearby afternoon tea table, my John Williamson and Cold Chisel CDs were ready for the call and I'd even remembered to have a couple of towels handy, to protect my gear when the champers and beer began to flow. I think deep down we all expected only one outcome from the day, but at the same time we knew we had to make it happen, not sit back and expect someone else to do it for us.

Hussain's departure to a loose shot early on signalled the beginning of the end. Mark Ealham then fell to a superb reflex catch by Mark Waugh that said to all of us – let's go for the jugular, it's our day. The brittle lower half of England's batting order was being found wanting in the commitment department again, and once their only ray of hope, John Crawley, was out there was no stopping us.

Except for the luncheon adjournment. This came with England nine-down and was a huge blessing in disguise, as it enabled us to fully prepare for the mandatory dressing-room debacle that was to follow. Robert Croft obviously had plans to get on that motorway for the long drive back to Wales as soon as possible, for he played a 'shot' to the first ball after the break that was more likely to catch a fish than repel a cricket ball. We now led the series 2–1.

Making our celebrations just that little bit extra special was the presence of the Canberra Raiders Super League team, who had come to the ground to support us dressed in shorts, singlets and outrageously coloured wigs. It was a fabulous couple of hours sharing the victory with football greats such as Mal Meninga,

Laurie Daley and Ricky Stuart and a time we will cherish and long remember. Not satisfied with the festivities at the ground, we kicked on to the bar area of our hotel, where family, friends and Raiders gathered for a long night.

It was here in the relative safety of the bar area that I not only contemplated but executed one of the most foolhardy acts ever witnessed. Feeling that added strength and invincibility that one gets from alcohol, I challenged Big Mal to take myself, Junior and a couple more of my braver team-mates on. His objective was to try to run through us and score an imaginary try between the two guest sofas situated some two metres behind us. A Foster's can was in Mal's hand, as the 'footy', but all I saw were two hairy 'oak trees' pumping in unison at good pace heading straight for me. (Mal Meninga, as everyone knows, is a very big man.) With pride and reputation at stake, I went in head first, full of tenacity but mainly hope, only to be sent catapulting through the air after a bone-shattering confrontation.

We dusted ourselves off, shook hands, and headed for the bar for a beer and chat. It wasn't until a couple of hours later that turning sideways began to present problems and I realised that I might be spending tomorrow morning searching around town for a neck brace. Later on, I was minding my own business as I heading for the men's room, when the nightmare resurfaced. Big Mal was in my face again, this time catching me off guard in a crunching tackle, pick-up and pile-driver. Of course, I did the manly thing and attempted a reply, with hitman Healy in support, but I was further humiliated.

All in all, it was a night to savour. I feel privileged to have been injured by one of the best of all time.

Do we need changes for Trent Bridge? Well, I don't think that any of the top six deserve to be dropped. Hussain, Thorpe and Crawley certainly don't. Atherton has a proven Test record and Stewart may be out of nick but last year he was the leading batsman in Test cricket. Butcher? Maybe, but he looks better each innings he plays and all he needs is a big score and away he goes. On the bowling side I'd probably keep Smith in the squad but would be unlikely to play him. I'd bring back Malcolm for the Oval, but probably not Trent Bridge and Caddick would certainly return now while we should keep a close eye on Cowan.

The personnel is basically right but we need to get runs in the first innings and set the agenda. We're just playing catch up far too early in the game. You can talk about the batting order but Alec is best in the top three because he's not so good starting off against spin. I'm not fussed whether I go in at three or four but I certainly wouldn't want to go any lower. The difficult one is whether to move John and Alec because there's a hell of a difference between three and six. Maybe on reflection I'd bring in one new batsman and one new bowler to give us fresh impetus and give all of us a kick up the arse and remind us that our places are not guaranteed. I certainly, though, wouldn't discard anyone who was left out. Maybe a swashbuckler like a Hollioake should come in as the all-rounder but then again Ealie hasn't done much wrong.

We just need to show we're still moving in the right direction. If we lose 4–1 now people will question the new regime and it will set us back two or three steps at least. We've got to build like the Aussies did in the mid-eighties by backing players of quality and they didn't get it right in one series. It takes time.

I think we're on the right road but I can understand that a lot of questions will be asked if we end up losing three or four in a row. We cannot let it happen.

It was only when I set off for Nottingham and tomorrow's big cup game that I pondered on the fact that my record is looking pretty good now. At the start of last season I hadn't played Test cricket for three years and I wondered if I would ever get a chance of a good run in the side. Now, 14 months later, I have five hundreds, two of them against the best side in the world and one of them a double in a winning Ashes Test. I've worked hard for it but it's going well personally and I must maintain it and never feel that I've done enough. There is still a lot of work ahead for me.

15
SPILLS AND THRILLS

NASSER HUSSAIN

It is ludicrous to go straight into a big NatWest Trophy game the day after a Test has finished. I left Headingley at around 3pm on the Monday and didn't get to Nottingham until about five. The first task was getting all my gear washed which I managed to do by the time the Essex boys started arriving at the Royal Moat House by about 7pm.

The contrast in our moods said everything you need to know about the need for change in this regard to our game. The Essex boys were all raring to go when I met up with them, all up for their big quarter-final and intent on proving a point in the NatWest after what happened to us in last year's final. Meanwhile, I was thinking, 'God, I could do with a week off.' But it was a frame of mind I could not afford to be in. This was very important. But I still felt as though I had switched on to auto pilot by the time I got to Trent Bridge for the early start the next day.

Thankfully, my team-mates have been brilliant all summer. They fully understand my position and know you can't just force your body to do things when it has had enough. So if it looked as though I was going through the motions when we embarked on our fielding practice with Fletch, I was confident it would be okay with the boys.

The fact is, I've got a bit of a hamstring injury and I'm bruised and battered. My tennis elbow refuses to go away and I got a Test hundred two days before, so I'm knackered. And 60-overs a side makes for a very long day. It's just madness and whoever puts our fixture list together is insane. Thankfully, I understand they're putting this right next year but it's not before time.

Then, what happens when we go out to field first against Notts in our biggest game of the season? I drop three catches, that's what. Now I could make a hundred excuses and say that it must have been due to my state of mind and body after the Test. I was very tired and not mentally right. I've got sore fingers and Nottingham is not the best sighting ground. All those things are true but I'm not the first England player who has had to play in a big game so soon after a Test and I consider myself one of the best fielders around, so dropping three catches was just not acceptable.

Two of them were hard but I would expect to take all of them. In those sort of situations you drop one and immediately hope you get another chance soon after to atone for it. But then you drop another and you start to hope the ball doesn't come your way again. When the third one went down I was hating every minute of being there. It was the last thing I needed. I just wanted a game where I could field, score my runs, win and then bugger off.

But dropping three catches before lunch, then seeing the familiar faces of Essex supporters in the crowd as I came off and how much it meant to them; then seeing the other players looking at me made me think 'I've cost Essex the NatWest. What have I done?' Television was there and I knew they'd be talking about me and I'd already decided to take all the blame for our defeat in my *Southend Evening Echo* column. It was a nightmare and I was very low at lunch. I didn't eat anything and I didn't talk to anybody.

I just sat in a corner of the dressing room until Fletch came up to me and said 'Come on, pick yourself up.' I didn't say anything so his voice got a bit sterner and he added 'Look Nass, you can still win us this game.' I wasn't convinced until what I feel was the turning point in my fortunes and probably those of the team occurred. Soon after lunch I ran out Nathan Astle, the man who had stopped us winning the first Test in Auckland last January and now the Notts overseas player, with a direct hit and it immediately lifted me no end.

At first I thought umpire Vanburn Holder was going to turn it down without calling for the third umpire – to be honest I think he forgot the facility was there – so I gave him a little reminder by making the square signal with my hands because I knew Astle was gone. Thankfully he called for it, Astle was out and that went some way towards us restricting them to 288 for five when it could have been worse.

Then I had to focus on my batting and the knowledge of the drops made me concentrate that much more on the task in hand even though the red light was on the fuel tank, as Goochie might say, and I was fast running out of gas. I was determined to see the job through after Stuart Law and Prich had given us a tremendous start because even if I'd scored a hundred and we'd lost I wouldn't have redeemed myself because the defeat would still have been down to me dropping three catches, two of them to reprieve Paul Johnson who went on to get a hundred.

We're a positive side and the game plan was for everyone to go for their shots around me but we may have been a bit too positive at times because we lost wickets at bad stages. So I was relieved when Ashley Cowan came in to join me at a crucial moment and smacked a few runs to help me through. It may have appeared that Ashley was being a bit reckless at times during his cameo but I had told him to play his natural game and go for his shots because it's pointless telling Ashley to block. He can't do it.

There was a crucial moment when Johnson seemed to have caught Ashley but immediately signalled that he hadn't taken it cleanly – that had to happen with me at the crease after the Blewett affair, didn't it? I just put my head down and looked away! But we won the game with 10 balls to spare and I ended up unbeaten on 89. David Gower gave me the Man of the Match award and I pretended to drop it while the boys all threw things at me during the BBC interview. We headed back to Chicago's in Chelmsford for a bit of a celebration and I was one mightily relieved Essex player.

16
OUT WEST

STEVE WAUGH

29 July, Taunton

The trip was only made bearable by the good reading to be found in today's sport sections. And when we arrived, Swampy proved he is human after all, by taking pity on the squad and ordering an afternoon off, much to everyone's joy and obvious relief. Further good news arrived in the form of a palatial room, complete with double bed, in the Castle Hotel, a famous old castle which dates back to the early 16th century and has been converted into modern accommodation. Meanwhile, Lynette and family bunked themselves in at the less salubrious 'Travel Inn', which is located a couple of kilometres down the road.

This will be the last leg of their journey. Originally, Lynette and Rosie were planning on seeing out the tour, but because of the stresses of travelling that can't be overcome, we've agreed that they should go home early – even though it will be hard to be so far apart again. Thankfully, Rosie's first birthday is in two days time, so at least we can finish their travels together on a high note.

30 July, Taunton

Days off on tour are precious and one was upon us today. Most of the single lads on tour opted for a round of golf, while the couples either hit the pavement in search of a bargain or indulged in a spot of sightseeing. For the travelling Griswalds (aka Waughs), we headed off to the historic city of Bath, which is no more than an hour from our current location. Inevitably we missed a couple of vital turnoffs and added a significant amount of travel time to the excursion, but at least the countryside was pleasantly relaxing and the weather invitingly warm. An enjoyable day was had by all, especially by Lynette who uncannily tracked down a shop that stocked miniature collectibles and doll's house items that just happened to be the ones she'd been looking for without luck in recent times. Activities such as today are invaluable on a cricket tour, because they not only get you out of the hotel and into the fresh air, they also get you away from the team.

This is important – we virtually live out of each other's pockets all year round and constantly socialise together. In some ways, it's an environment where the 'real world' almost doesn't exist.

31 July, Taunton

To head off the threat of complacency in the camp, the team split up into two groups at training this morning. With Tubs enjoying some R&R, I looked after the batting group, while the bowlers were in coach Marsh's capable hands. During the batting group's chat, we emphasised the need to finish the tour off strongly. In recent times, the team's ordinary performances in the last Test of a series that has already been decided have been as a direct result of the batsmen under-achieving. The fact that we batsmen have taken this responsibility is in itself a breakthrough, because it would be easy to blame outside factors or even the bowlers. Taking further the approach we first adopted in the lead-up to the fourth Test, starting from tomorrow we have decided to knuckle down and treat the last four first-class games of the tour, including the last two Tests, as a separate entity to all that has occurred to date.

Unfortunately the practice wickets today, like so many we have put up with on tour, were not up to standard. These were very well grassed and offered the local net bowlers a lot of movement both vertically and horizontally, which is fine if you are seeing the ball well but destructive if you are struggling with your form.

Being captain for this fixture against my former county (I played two seasons with Somerset, in 1987 and 1988) gives the game an extra edge for me. From a team point of view, it would be great to keep the momentum going and achieve a third victory over a county team on this tour.

With the captaincy comes the added responsibility of dealing with the media and today was no exception, with local and international crews all jostling for an interview after practice. The only problem for me today was the lack of time I had available for the cameras and the journos, because I had a young lady's first birthday party to organise. Interviews over, I dashed into nearest Marks and Spencer department store, and thus began a mad scramble in the food section, shopping basket under one arm while the other scooped items off the shelves at impressive speed. Already in my hotel suite were drinks, balloons, streamers, courtesy of the hotel's concierge who had gone searching on my behalf. And, of course, there was a birthday cake …

Amazingly, it all went like clockwork. All I needed now was the birthday girl and the guests. Soon after, Rosie's eyes lit up like beacons when she crawled past the door to be mesmerised by the sea of balloons. She somehow sensed that all that was in front of her was because of her. Seeing her smile was all the thanks I needed and made me realise how lucky I was to have her with me on her first birthday.

For Lynette and I, this was a perfect last day together as a family. It was desperately difficult to bid a final farewell as they left for their own hotel. The last six weeks have been a whole new experience for both of us, with Rosie putting a whole new complexion on touring life. Fortunately, Phil and Ethel have been a tremendous help as always, but still it's been tough for everyone to adjust to family life on the road with a touring team.

1 August, Taunton

Somerset 284 (Parsons 71, Turner 58; Warne 5–57) v Australia 182–4 (S Waugh 51*).
Today's crowd was one of the biggest seen at Taunton since Bradman's 1938
Australians played here, proving again that there's nothing better for the English
game than an Ashes tour. Not only do the television rights, ticket sales and
sponsorship bring in 'telephone numbers' for the ECB, the counties clean up, too,
through the large attendances, then those players enjoying benefits back their
trucks up and try to get everything they possibly can autographed.

One man's day was ruined by the late withdrawal of Ricky Ponting, who has a
bout of the flu that worsened quite significantly overnight. Pigeon's day off was
now a day of toil and sweat, especially after the coin landed cruelly for the away
team's skipper. Glenn's day was made worse when, after just seven overs the
match-starved new-ball combination of Julian and Kasprowicz had earned the
groundsman's wrath – he knew he was in for some serious panel beating of the
advertising boards at the conclusion of play – while I was considering retirement
from the captaincy. The score after 35 minutes was 72 for nought was nothing
short of disastrous, and no matter how hard I tried to convince myself that the
wicket was a belter, the outfield slick, and the ground small in size, it didn't hide
the fact that we were in desperate need of a breakthrough.

Responding as he always does, McGrath gained a wicket early in his spell and,
in tandem with Warney, changed the tempo and complexion of the game. But even
with this reversal in fortunes, the West County lads still went to lunch with the
amazing return of 143 for four.

For a captain, these games are a difficult balancing act at times. Every game on
tour is played with the intention of winning, but the main priority is the Test
matches. With this in mind, you have to monitor your bowlers very carefully,
being particularly watchful of the amount of overs they're bowling. On occasions,
a bowler will want a heavy workload to allow him to settle into a steady rhythm
or to gain some match practice and confidence. However, at other times, that same
man may want a short spell, just to stay sharp or to perhaps prevent an injury that
his gut feeling suggests may be in the offing.

Today was a day where Pigeon needed a relatively brief stint at the crease, as he
knows he's in good form and his body yearned for a reduced workload. Keeping
our main strike bowler away from the bowling crease provides opportunities for
others, but it also allowed the Somerset batsmen to continue on their merry way,
scoring at around four-and-a-half runs per over.

There was, however, some joy for us as Warney continued to inflict pain on the
Pommy batsmen, creating new nightmares for fresh-faced opponents and re-
opening old wounds for those he's bowled to before.

Cricket is such a mind game. Players can sense apprehension and fear in
opponents, if they read body language with any authority. One player who is
obviously carrying some excess emotional baggage is Mark Lathwell, a guy who

made his Test debut against us back in 1993. Then he was seen as the next wonder boy. Unfortunately, his constitution wasn't quite up to scratch at the highest level and the system gobbled him up. He walked to the crease today looking as if he knew he wasn't going to last, and in Shane Warne we had the perfect executioner.

Warney ended up getting what the bowlers these days call a 'Michelle' (as in 'Pfeiffer', for 'five-for'), but disconcertingly for us we conceded 52 extras, made up primarily of no-balls, the scourge of captains and coaches. Still, Somerset's total of 284 represented a fine comeback by us and a series of wasted opportunities for the locals.

The carnage continued in the final session of play, as all our lads managed solid-looking starts without going on with the job. I was the exception, striking the ball with perhaps the most authority I've shown on tour. This was truly an amazing day's cricket, which saw 14 wickets fall, 466 runs scored, 28 no-balls bowled and 70 boundaries struck. And all in front of a capacity crowd. This sort of positive cricket will guarantee the future success of the game and must be encouraged by everyone involved with the sport.

2 August, Taunton

Somerset 284 and 147–3 (Turner 65*, Ecclestone 47) v Australia 323 (S Waugh 62, Julian 71; Caddick 5–54).

Sometimes county fixtures lack intensity and atmosphere. But not today. There was an air of excitement and expectancy about prior to the first ball being delivered, with many players having points to prove, most notably the man bowling this first over, Andy Caddick, and my partner in the middle, Michael Bevan.

Caddick had, of course, been quite amazingly left out of the English starting XI for the Test at Headingley. Judging by his impressive spell yesterday evening (three for 30), he is determined to win his place back straightaway. Bevo, in contrast, is at a stage where he needs to rebuild some personal pride and confidence, rather than worry about forcing his way back into the side straightaway. He needs to be comfortable in himself and his game before he has another crack at Test level, but once this is achieved I'm sure his natural gifts will shine through.

For me, today represented a chance to build on a solid start. However, only Caddick would have been pleased with his efforts, finishing with five scalps. Bevo and I were dismissed early on, courtesy of two pretty useful deliveries from the 'human FA Cup'. This is why the Somerset man is a dangerous competitor, for he can produce the odd unplayable wicket-taking delivery.

Brendon Julian saved us from being embarrassed on a batting paradise, weighing in with a murderous 71 which further underlined his prodigious talent. But as the immortal Jack Gibson once said, 'What has talent ever won you?' Now is the time for BJ to seize the moment, convert his natural skills into match-winning performances at the top level, and give Australia a much needed world-class allrounder. Only he can make it happen!

A lead of 39 was only just acceptable, but the speed with which we scored our runs ensured we would have plenty of time to win the game in the fourth innings.

Somerset's approach to their second innings was much more sedate than their helter-skelter attitude on Day One. However, this relative serenity was soon to change beyond anyone's expectations or wishes, and much to the distress of many people at the ground.

Warm weather, warm beer, 'soccer-type' supporters and Shane Warne at the bowling crease proved to be a volatile cocktail. With Warney's high profile and continued success, he is always going to be a target for much adulation and, sadly, some ridicule. In just about every game on tour we have seen sections of the crowd continually yelling out and chipping away at Shane, to try to put him off his game.

Mostly this comes in the form of chants such as, 'Warney ... Warney ... You fat bastard, you fat bastard ... You ate all our pies!' Or another favourite, 'He's fat, he's round, he bounces on the ground ... Shane Warne ... Shane Warne.'

This type of thing is basically water off a duck's back for Shane. For all of us. However, today the 'fans' went way over the boundary, from fun and gentle sarcasm to constant, ugly abuse. These small minorities in the crowd, which would have been limited to three groups, each with around 15 or so people, began to get way out of control midway through Shane's second over. The usual harmless fun turned nasty and far too personal, with idiotic chants being the main focus of everyone's attention – purely because you couldn't avoid them due to their loudness and crudeness.

Choruses of 'Warne takes it up the !@#$!', 'Warne is a !@##$%!' and 'Aussies, we own your country, we own your !@#$%!' became so frequent that all the players were becoming angered and distracted by the drunken louts. Our concern was shared by the umpires, and it was Nigel Plews (a former policeman, who umpired two Ashes Tests in 1989 and one in 1993) who said to me, 'This is ridiculous, they've gone way too far.'

Taunton is a small ground, which may have 'amplified' the noises from our perspective, but, whatever, what was occurring beyond the boundary was now beginning to create friction out in the middle. It finally all came to a head at the commencement of another Warne over, when the chants began again even louder than on previous occasions. As captain, I believed it to be in the best interests of the decent spectators to be able to enjoy the cricket. Of course, I was also wanted to stop Warney copping further degrading and derogatory remarks for no reason. The umpires agreed and the game duly came to a standstill.

The Somerset CC Chief Executive was summoned from the grandstands, and a conference ensued which resulted in Security being sent to the troublesome areas. We learnt later that two culprits received their marching orders.

These extreme measures quelled the brain-dead yobbos, and led to a relatively quiet last hour which was appreciated by the genuine cricket fans still at the ground.

Cricket crowds today want more for their money. This demand on the cricketers is fine, providing the stresses it creates are recognised and people realise we need some time to ourselves, particularly during breaks in play such as lunch and tea. But many cricket followers today expect players to sign autographs anytime, anywhere. 'Sorry, not now' is not an alternative. Only today, Warney was abused by a Somerset member in the committee rooms for not signing a kid's autograph during the lunch hour.

At the end of this controversial day's play, the game looked set for an exciting conclusion, particularly if the aggressive attitude of both teams continues. Inevitably, my day wasn't over even though the whites were off, as the press boys were hovering ominously outside the change room doors. There was no need for a nuclear scientist to work out their line of questioning. Some of the scribes pointed out that what had occurred was no different from what happens all over the world. But even if this was so, I argued, why should it be tolerated? Why would you bring your kids and wife to the game if you knew you would be subjected to loutish behaviour and constant swearing?

I'm not sure if they agreed with my line of thought, but I remained happy with my actions and felt I had done the right thing. That's all you can ask of yourself.

3 August, Taunton

Somerset 284 and 147–3 v Australia 323. No play.
This morning was definitely similar to what most Australians believe an English summer is like. It was grey, bleak and drizzly. You could tell by the weather that the prospects of any play were minimal, or by observing the upbeat mood around the breakfast table as the boys gathered around. Days off are precious, but to be truthful we could have done with a bit a workout today.

4 August, Taunton

Somerset 284 and 147–3 v Australia 323. No play, match drawn.
Although the weather was no better than yesterday, it was decided that both teams would venture down to the ground and wait until lunch before calling the match off, to presumably make sure that the corporate boxes were filled for the day. This was a sad end to what had been a spirited affair. Somerset must be congratulated for their approach, which was unlike that of quite a few other counties, who gave the impression that our game was no more than an opportunity to rest key players.

17
ENGLAND v AUSTRALIA
FIFTH CORNHILL TEST MATCH

Trent Bridge, Nottingham, 7–11 August

STEVE WAUGH

5 August

The grind of modern day cricket is relentless and it was in the nets we found ourselves again this morning. To their credit, our management have tried to vary training sessions as much as they can, but as Allan Border once said, 'To win cricket games you have to bat well, bowl well and catch well. There are no magic formulas.'

A normal session for us begins with a jogged lap and a few short sharp exercises, intertwined with some sit-ups and push-ups supervised by Steve Smith. Errol Alcott will then guide us through our stretching routine, which takes 20 to 25 minutes, before handing us back over to Smithy for a more intense workout – usually some sort of 'circuit work' with different activities at each 'station' (stopping point in the circuit). After this, we might take part in a game of volleyball or some other group activity, to get the energy levels up. Then it's either into the nets for the real thing or a solid fielding session, involving a couple of drills for the entire squad followed by some more specific work, such as catches for the guys who field in the catching cordon on game day.

Our efforts at practice today indicated to me that we are ready to finish off England in the fifth Test. The quality of our work was as good as we've produced all tour. The only downer was an injury to BJ, who got 'cleaned up' by an enthusiastic net bowler and needed ice on his left wrist. I hope the blow hasn't caused any serious damage, as his left arm is, of course, his bowling arm.

Tonight's team meeting revolved around what tactics we should employ against the Hollioake boys, who have been included in the English side. They've obviously been selected for their temperament and attitude. We agreed that they will be expecting a bit of chat from us, to welcome them into the fold, which more than likely will inspire them to perform at their best. So, using a bit of reverse psychology, we have decided to give them 'the silent treatment'. This can put many a batsman off, because they then know their opponents are totally focused and planning their downfall, rather than wasting their energy on talk and gestures. Hype and talk are poor substitutes for class and technique – if the Hollioakes are good enough they'll swim, if not they'll sink.

My gut feeling is that they'll be in for a bit of a struggle in the upcoming Test, especially if they think that the pressures of Test cricket are no different from those in one-day cricket. They are worlds apart.

NASSER HUSSAIN

We arrived at Trent Bridge to be greeted by our own personal copy of Raising the Standard, the Lord MacLaurin blueprint for the future of cricket in this country. So we sat down and had a look at it. There was a lot of discussion within the team, mainly because people couldn't really work out who would be playing who in the championship under the proposed three conference system and who would be in each other's conference.

Taken in its entirety the document seemed like a good idea to most people but the championship structure in particular does seem to be a compromise from what Lord MacLaurin would really like to do and what the counties will let him do. Compromise so often seems the only way forward in our cricket.

I'm pretty sure Lord MacLaurin would have liked to have been a bit more radical and I'm pretty sure he would like to have contracted England players to the ECB and provided us with fewer one-day matches but the counties would just have said no to that. The conference idea seems okay to me because the big danger with two divisions and promotion and relegation is that counties with a lot of Test players would be in danger of being penalised for it and relegated.

If this system stops us having to play big cup matches at the end of Tests then I'm all for it. That really has to be changed. You want to be giving your all for your county but it does make it difficult when you're compromised like many of us have been this year. I think Essex are broadly in favour of the blueprint but I'm sure a lot of discussions are going to take place all over the country before it is accepted. (It was later decided that the Championship will, after all, remain as a single league.)

Goochie was around in the nets with us today, so I did some throwdowns with him and he did a bit of work with Ath, too. Today we welcomed the Hollioake brothers for the first time in tandem for a Test and I'm sure they will bring the little bit of impetus and freshness that I suppose we need at this stage. Something had to be done to the team after we lost two Tests but I'm sure everyone agrees that Butch and Ealie are very unlucky to have been left out. Neither has done much wrong and they really are the victims of circumstance rather than anything they've done.

There's no doubt that having a 19-year-old about the team provides a breath of fresh air and Ben Hollioake settled in very well today. He was just his normal self.

But while he was buzzing Goughy was struggling with his fitness and there seems a real danger that we will go into this match without him.

6 August
A few of the boys went shopping after nets today – Dean was, as usual, after new clothes – but I slept all afternoon. Four or five of us ate in the hotel restaurant tonight because, being so far out, there is really nowhere else to go. Tuffers was among our number and it seems as though he's got a chance of playing this time. Ath asked me my opinion on the make -up of the team and we're both leaning towards the inclusion of a second spinner. One ball was enough for Goughy to realise that he wasn't going to make it. I kept half an eye on him at practice because he's a big gun and we wanted him in our team but I could see he wasn't right. He didn't have to say anything to us when he stopped bowling after that. We all knew the score and it's desperately disappointing for him and us.

7 August, Day 1, Fifth Test
Australia 302–3 (Elliott 69, Taylor 76, Blewett 50, M Waugh 60*, S Waugh 38*) v England.

It was a pensive mood that permeated through the team bus as we made the 20-minute journey from the hotel to Trent Bridge, where we were once again greeted by an enthusiastic full house. For England, the loss of Darren Gough through injury is a major blow, but many were hoping that this setback would be offset by the dawn of a new era, courtesy of the Hollioake boys. Adam was always going to make his debut here, but we weren't sure about Ben until they both made their way onto the ground shortly before the toss, to be presented with their first Test caps by Mike Atherton.

Mark Taylor again guessed correctly and put us in to bat. Mark and Matthew Elliott then took full advantage, putting together their most impressive stand of the tour. Except for a couple of close lbw decisions that favoured them, they were in complete control, and the lunchtime score of 84 for nought was exactly what we wanted. It is generally accepted that a scoreline of around 70 for two represents an evenly-shared opening session, so by that standard we were well on top.

Matty Elliott had eclipsed 1000 runs for the tour when he reached 31, an achievement which further confirmed his rapidly-growing status at Test level. The stand was surprisingly curtailed at 117, when the leaner of our two 'engine-room men' fell, and 43 runs later he was joined in the pavilion by our captain, not long after Mark had scored his 6000th run in Test cricket. He was only the sixth Australian to reach this mark (after Border, Boon, Greg Chappell, Bradman and Harvey), a very fine achievement from a very fine player.

Greg Blewett and Mark Waugh carried on the good work, although not convincingly early on. However, as they grew in confidence the crowd was treated to some glorious strokeplay. Ben Hollioake began nervously in his first spell at a

Test bowling crease, going for 25 from his first three overs and quickly realising that here was a much tougher assignment than the under-19s 'Test' against Zimbabwe he'd been playing in only days earlier. To Atherton's credit, the England skipper took the teenager under his wing, bowling him in short spells, and they reaped a reward when Blewett offered a lazy jab to ball pitched outside his off stump and left Stewart to do the rest.

The final session was safely negotiated by Australia's answer to the Hollioakes, leaving us handsomely placed at 302 for three. We shouldn't lose from here.

Today was probably the best I've felt all series. The feet were moving nicely, I was comfortable and at ease without being complacent, and my timing and placement were first-class. I only wished we could have continued for a couple more hours, to keep up the momentum we had developed.

Tomorrow's first session will either see England fight hard to get back into the game by way of some pro-active cricket, or we will dominate proceedings totally if they allow us to set the tone. The overriding feature of today's play was the negative body language that the England team exhibited from the very first ball. It was as if the loss of the toss had wrecked their chances of winning.

One other notable event, from my point of view, was Adam Hollioake not wearing his newly-won England cap in the opening session. Some might say 'big deal', but wearing that cap is more than a gesture.

I believe it's a mark of respect to the country you're playing for and to those that have worn the cap before you. After all, it's an elite few who get the opportunity to represent their country – I believe you have an obligation to show your appreciation by donning the team's cap with that crest upon it, at least on the first morning, as a mark of solidarity and your commitment to the cause.

NASSER HUSSAIN

The wicket looked an absolute belter this morning with just a hint of green in it. Despite what I have been saying about the need to insert this season this was definitely a bat first job and we all prayed Athers would win his first toss of the series. He even took out an Isle of Man coin as Mark Taylor always calls tails and the Isle of Man cat has no tail but a fat lot of good it did him.

It came down tails again and all of us who had batted on the spicy wickets we've had this season said 'oh no' because we were desperate to get the pads on and bat on that but, of course, Taylor had sentenced us to bowl. I mumbled bad luck to Ath when he came back but really I wanted to say 'you tosser, fancy losing another one.' Then I sat in the toilet before we went out calculating, remembering my Maths O-level, the odds on a captain losing five successive tosses. I reckon it's 32–1 against that happening.

Dev steamed in to bowl the first ball, gave it everything he had and it just hit the deck and died. I looked at Ath, he looked at me, we both looked at Thorpey and Stewie and you could see we were all thinking the same thing. 'Oh God, here we go. *This is definitely going to be a full day in the field.' Our bowlers, minus Tuffers who was left out again in the end, actually bowled very well and passed the edge often on a pretty flat wicket. We put the ball in the right areas, applied the pressure as best we could and fielded well too. I'm convinced we would have done very well batting first on this but, as it is, Australia are 302 for three with the Waughs in residence. At least Ben Hollioake has his first Test wicket.*

8 August, Day 2, Fifth Test
Australia 427 (M Waugh 68, S Waugh 75; Headley 4–87) v England 188–4 (Stewart 87).

One thing that has continually amazed me throughout this Test series is how much time the England players spend in the nets. Every day, we arrive at the ground 90 minutes before play to find the opposition in the nets endlessly bowling, facing throwdowns and taking sharp catches. On top of this, they have long fielding sessions and 'team bonding' games, which add up to a real solid workout ... even before they go into battle for the real thing. I couldn't believe they were at it again this morning, as the weather forecast predicted the sort of steamy, hot conditions where you need some extra fuel in the tank.

To the Englishmen's credit, they came out swinging in the first session and polished us off, 45 minutes after lunch, for the addition of only 125 runs. It was a superb comeback, easily the best by an England team on English soil in the past three Ashes series.

Scoring 75 was pleasing, but because I felt in such good nick it wasn't nearly enough, especially when I wasn't encountering too many problems when I was dismissed. I was taken down by Malcolm, who produced a pretty useful outswinger at good pace, but my downfall was primarily a result of me almost pulling away before the ball was bowled. I thought Devon had slipped, or lost his run-up just at the point of delivery, and switched off for a split second.

As we made our way out onto the field in single-file, I had to take a second look to make certain I wasn't imagining what I had just seen. On the edge of the ropes, inside the boundary, Andy Caddick and Dean Headley were being interviewed by a local television commentator. At the same time, the English openers were about to take the field. Quite clearly, they had not been in the dressing-room to wish their openers good luck, which to me is a very unprofessional thing to do. I interpreted their attitude as being 'I've done my job, now I can forget about the game until I'm required again.' They should have been backing up the guys involved in the immediate action.

As England were chasing 427 and needed to win this Test to keep the Ashes alive, we recognised that, from the home team's point of view, it was imperative that they got off to a steady yet positive start. Consequently, the blitzkrieg that Alec Stewart showered down upon us caught us by surprise. In the end, he fell 13 runs short of what would have been his first Ashes hundred and a much-deserved one. He'd faced just 107 balls and smashed 14 fours, and was taken brilliantly by Heals at the second attempt, which gave the world's premier custodian his 300th Test catch and his 100th Test catch against England.

Warney then dragged us back into the game with a great spell on an unproductive wicket for his art, taking 3–14 in the space of 39 balls. This return would have made up somewhat for the £100 he lost to Ian Botham earlier on in the day, after Shane failed to trouble the scorers. (At the start of the tour, 'Beefy' and Shane had agreed on the following bet – every time Warney scored more than 20, Beefy would pay him £5 for every run over 20. Every time Warney scored less than 20 Beefy would receive £5 for every run less than 20. Early on, Shane was way in front. Now, things are getting much closer.)

England's final scoreline of 188 for four, after they had been 106 for nought, was a reflection of our gutsy fightback. But it would have been even better had the third umpire not panicked and given Graham Thorpe not out before the left-hander had scored. The TV umpire was about the only person who believed the green light was the right option. But, as they say, 'the umpire's ruling is final, and always correct!'

NASSER HUSSAIN

It was really hot again this morning but there was a haze around which made the wicket a little bit wet first thing and spiced it up a bit. Consequently, it seems to have changed and is at least a yard quicker with Caddick and Headley regularly hitting the splice. We had to bowl them out quickly to get back in the game and we did so. To dismiss them out for 427 after getting just three wickets on the first day was a really good effort. Headley, Caddick and Malcolm were all pretty impressive and Dev had one exceptional spell in particular.

We were confident at the outset of our innings that we could get close to their score if not better it and it was nice to see Stewie and Ath walking out together again. They compliment each other really well as an opening pair. I really don't know how Stewie keeps wicket in heat like this and then goes straight out to open the batting. It means if he does his job well he's in the field for the whole of the five days. He's done it before and I'm sure he'll do it again but I know I couldn't do what he does.

I would have put good money on Atherton, Stewart or Thorpe scoring a hundred in this match because they all have good records here and they are all due a score, but the Aussies have just the man for the job in Shane Warne. Really, he's the only 'magician' who could make things happen on a wicket like this and just when it looked as though we were getting into an excellent position he came on and bowled a spell that has taken the initiative back to them a bit.

We were 106 without loss at one stage but Warne came on and bowled better, I think, than at any other time in this series. Ath nicked one and Stewie, having batted gloriously for his best score of the series, got an edge to a wide one that

Healy took at the second attempt before I went in. I felt in a good frame of mind, odd though that may sound as I got out for two, and ducked under a couple of McGrath bouncers while seeming to be in the right positions. They had obviously been talking about me a bit because they had a man back for me on the hook and they were chatting in the field about sticking to the plan they had for me, a plan which I took to be dig in a couple of short ones and then push it up to see if I would drive.

But I was seeing it well, playing fine and felt happy until Shane bowled me a good ball that swung in before turning and bowling me. Maybe I should have been further forward because then I could have smothered it but I can't really crucify myself for it because I think it was a pretty good one. Suddenly, with John getting out down the leg-side to McGrath, we were 141 for four and one man had made all the difference.

Any other side would have struggled to bowl us out for fewer than 400 but not Australia with Shane Warne in the side. What a joy it must be to be his captain. If things go flat you just put him on at one end and rotate three seamers at the other. For us now, at 188 for four with Thorpey still there, it's a question of trying not to fall too far behind their total.

Bit of a bombshell on the way back to the hotel tonight. Ath is in no mood to drive his car half an hour each way from the hotel to Trent Bridge during this game so I've become his chauffeur and he told me tonight that he's considering packing up as captain and that he had already told the selectors. He told me that he had always said four years would be enough in charge and that he had two or three years left as a batsman at the highest level and he didn't want his standards to drop. I just said, 'Don't do it, we need the continuity and the boys are still 100 per cent behind you.' I emphasised to him that he'd done the job well and that it wasn't his fault we were losing. I really meant it, too. He's the best man for the job. I really want him to carry on because we could win in the West Indies this winter and we've just got to appreciate that we're playing against an exceptional Australian side. Before now I was under the impression that he wanted to lead the party on tour too but now I know why Grav rang me before this Test and asked me to try to pick up Athers as he was feeling down. Ath then told me to think seriously about whether I wanted to succeed him because I would be a strong candidate. I laughed it off but I couldn't help thinking about it when I got back to my room. Most of all, though, I hope the selectors talk him out of it.

9 August, Day 3, Fifth Test

Australia 427 and 167–4 (Taylor 45, Blewett 60) v England 313 (Thorpe 53, Hollioake 45; McGrath 4–71, Warne 4–86).

The early breakthrough we so desired was not forthcoming, although it would have been except for the guy in the gully who dropped a sitter off Thorpe from McGrath's bowling.

An impressive debut knock by Adam Hollioake suggested his selection was an inspired move rather than simply speculative. However, he was out with his score on 45 and the England total on 243, as did his partner (for 53) on the same total. This double blow left the capacity crowd stunned in shock, and us well on top.

Young gun Ben Hollioake, with his laid-back approach and almost trance-like appearance, reminded me a little of David Gower at the crease. He certainly didn't look ruffled while scoring 28, in fact he looked as if he needed a good slap in the face to get him going. He also displayed a lot of talent and a dislike for leaving any deliveries at all. I'll go out on a limb and say he'll end up a better batsman than bowler.

Robert Croft walking to the wicket reminded me of a bull walking into the ring … surrounded by 11 matadors. Glenn McGrath was given first throw of the spear. Croft, realising his strength isn't against the short, fast ball, went for glory against Warne. He raced to 18 through a variety of innovative and lofted shots, but it was only a matter of time before he went down and again it was a shortish ball that brought him to his knees. He was caught by Greg Blewett, close in on the leg-side.

The English tail showed a bit of fight for the first time this series, a struggle that culminated in a thoroughly entertaining innings of 12 from Devon Malcolm which brought the house down. His three boundaries were horrific-looking strokes, but full of effort and enterprise. It's hard to hit an off drive with your eyes closed and your front foot nearly a metre outside the leg stump, but this man pulled it off, in the process showing what a class bowler and quick thinker he is.

McGrath finally bamboozled the 'wood-chopping' one with a slower ball similar to a delivery I used to produce with success in one-day cricket. He and Warne again shared the spoils, grabbing a further four well-deserved poles each.

Building quickly upon our 114-run first innings lead was what we needed. This objective was fulfilled in spectacular fashion, primarily by Elliott (37) until he fell to the catch of the series by a diving John Crawley at deep backward-square. From 51 for one, although we lost wickets at regular intervals, we kept up a healthy scoring rate to finish the day at 167 for four. Ricky Ponting and I are at the crease.

All up, it was a pleasing day's work. From a spectator's point of view, I, like many others, felt that this match has developed into far and away the best Test match of the summer. It is no coincidence that it is being played on the best wicket by a 'country mile' we've seen during the series.

A couple of interesting by-plays between members of each team occurred today. At one point, Robert Croft was admiring his straight six off Warney on the ground's huge replay screen, unaware that Shane was ready to bowl his next delivery. Finally, in exasperation, Warney called down the pitch, 'Hey Crofty, don't worry, you will be able to see the replay again in a couple of minutes … in the dressing-room.' And Shane was right!

Earlier on, the younger Hollioake had become intrigued by his own stroke play while watching that same giant monitor. As we stood silently around, someone suddenly asked, 'Is there any chance of you facing up? This isn't second XI cricket, mate.'

NASSER HUSSAIN

The Sun have a story this morning about Atherton quitting. It's been denied but from what Ath told me last night it might not be too far from the truth. Meanwhile, Adam Hollioake looked very composed in his first Test innings. I'm sure he got a lot of stick out there because of his Aussie background. For instance, I noticed Warne doing a few punching movements at the start of his run up and I presume that was in response to some press stories saying Adam was a strong lad who was going to come out punching. The Aussies are very good at picking up on press stories and using them to their advantage. Apparently Adam told Shane to take his bra off so he obviously wasn't fazed by the situation and he went on to play beautifully in company with Thorpey, who I was delighted for.

There was speculation before this match that Thorpey might be dropped which, when you think about it, is quite ridiculous. He averages 50 against Australia, scored three centuries in quick succession not too long ago and scored a century in a record breaking partnership with me in the first Test of this series. Yet now there are press men who are saying he should be dropped after one missed chance at Headingley and a couple of low scores. People were saying they were worried about his state of mind and that he may be fatigued but we're all exhausted at this stage of the season and surely it's a question of looking after him rather than dropping him.

It's staggering. English cricket has spent all this money on Graham Thorpe, sending him on four A tours before he made his Test debut and then developing him into a true Test player with an average in the forties. Instead of saying 'one of our best batsmen is tired, let's look after him' there are those who would send him back to Surrey, make him feel unwanted and let him sort himself out on his own.

I've got to the stage where I've hit the wall and am wondering how I'm going to get through the rest of the season and I've only been back in the England side for 14 or 15 months. What must it be like for these boys who have been at it for three or four years non-stop. Then look at the year we've got ahead of us after this series. In January we go to the West Indies, after that it's South Africa and Sri Lanka at home and then, almost straight after the 1998 season, we go on the hardest tour of the lot, Australia. We're going to need Thorpey at his best during that lot and dropping him at the first sign of a loss of form would not be the answer.

It's not as if you can easily miss county games between Tests. It's all very well saying we should go back to our counties and ask to be rested but I want to do well for Essex in every game and I know the other England players feel the same. Even if we were contracted to the Board, deep down you would want to play for your county at every opportunity. It's down to the authorities to ease our workload and, to be fair to Lord MacLaurin, that's exactly what he's trying to do.

So Thorpey recorded a well deserved half century and Adam never looked like getting out until he did which brought his brother to the crease for the first time in Test cricket. At 19, you have to give Ben credit for the way he played in reaching 28. It would be easy to say he needs to tighten up his game, learn to leave the ball outside off-stump more often and that he looks a bit like a one-day player. But I think it's better to say what an immense talent he is, admire his shots and his stillness at the crease and think of how he can improve on what he's got. That's the way to look at him because Ben Hollioake can only get better and in two or three years time we want him to be our leading all-rounder.

He's got all the shots and just needs to keep the ball out for long periods of time and maybe that's why he hasn't got many runs for Surrey this season. The simple art of keeping the good balls out is one that I've been working on a lot in the last year and if I'd done it at 19 rather than 29 I would have been all the better for it now. I certainly wasn't as good at 19 as Ben Hollioake is now and he could easily go on to be a world class player.

For once our tail wagged but we were dismissed for 313, 114 behind, simply because of that Warne burst yesterday. He is the difference between a good side and a great side. It would have been fascinating to see what might have happened had Shane been on our side throughout this series. It's impossible to over-estimate what he can do for them. He's certainly improved as the series has gone on. I can't imagine Shane Warne ever not being confident but maybe he has grown in confidence as the year has gone on. At Edgbaston, for instance, I can't remember him bowling many flippers but he's bowling a lot now and the flipper is the leg-spinner's confidence ball, one you only bring out if you are bowling well.

I remember bowling it in my leg-spin days and it can go anywhere and make you look very silly if it doesn't come out right. The amount of flippers he bowls is in direct proportion to how good he's feeling and now we're seeing them more and more. In 1993 I think he was consistently good. This year he bowls little spells which are as good as that but not at that level all the time. Whether that's his shoulder problem or not I don't know but he seems to have the ability to almost switch his top form on and off as needs be.

I think we got our tactics slightly wrong when the Aussies began their second innings today. I tend to think, when the wicket is flat like this, that we need to go back to being hostile and getting the ball over the batsmen's heads. That's what McGrath does. He puts two balls over your head so you only have the chance to score off four an over and the Aussies are such good technicians that I'm sure they loved it when we bowled line and length to begin with today. It made the margin for error very small.

I suggested to Ath that we stick it up them a bit and I'm sure he was thinking the same thing because he asked our bowlers to do just that soon after and we got Elliott and Blewett out that way. It's not a question of doing it all the time but just for spells to keep them on their toes and make them think they could get hit on the head.

10 August, Day 4, Fifth Test

*Australia 427 and 336 (Ponting 45, Healy 63) defeated England 313 and 186
(Thorpe 82*; McGrath 3–36, Gillespie 3–65, Warne 3–43) by 264 runs.*

On the day that English cricket was to be 'reborn', courtesy of Lord MacLaurin's
blueprint *Raising the Standard*, we had in mind a further lowering of its status.

Lord MacLaurin's proposals were to be revealed to the public during the day,
but, to me, the timing of such a document's release was very inappropriate.
Raising the Standard virtually admits that England isn't good enough to compete
at the top level and that the state of the game across the country is in chaos. Surely
such a demeaning report could have been tabled and discussed at a more suitable
time, either before the series had begun or after its conclusion? But not in the
middle of an Ashes series.

Being not out overnight almost always means a fairly light workout in the nets
before play, with not too much physical activity, because I'm hoping to save my
energy for a long stay out in the middle. Normally, I'll simply have a short net
session followed by some throwdowns from Swampy, to feel the middle of the bat
on the ball. Finally, I might receive some short, sharp catches to get my reflexes
and hand-to-eye co-ordination going.

However, today my plans for a long innings were sadly mistaken. In the day's
opening over I gloved a sharply lifting delivery from Andy Caddick to second slip,
after hitting the previous ball through the covers for four. In a situation such as
this, you find yourself back in the change rooms before you realise what has
happened, almost as if it's not true. If only I could have turned back time and
started all over gain.

England were certainly excited about my wicket, but in getting that vital
breakthrough they lost their focus. In Ian Healy, we had the perfect man to
capitalise on such a lapse, and he produced an innings of 63 off just 78 balls. The
first hour of the day produced 75 runs from 12 overs, which put England out of
the game when not so long before they had been right back in it.

Healy is a hugely frustrating player to bowl to. In one innings he looks as if he
could get out every ball, in the next he'll produce quality strokes normally
associated with the best batsmen in the game. The one constant with Healy is his
scoring rate, which is consistently the best in our side. This is a valuable attribute
for a No. 7, as it provides added impetus to an innings and more often than not
changes the course of the game.

Unfortunately, for the second time in the series, it appeared that one of our
players had been caught on the first bounce. Ricky Ponting was playing a vital
supporting role when he pushed at an Adam Hollioake outswinger, got an edge
and was scooped up by Alec Stewart behind the stumps. To be fair to Alec, he is a
very honest and admirable adversary and I have no doubt he thought he caught
the ball. However, a super-slow-motion replay, which honed in on the catch,
suggested the ball might not have carried all the way.

My point is this: A player shouldn't be blamed when such an incident occurs. After all, he genuinely believes he has caught the ball. But rather than putting the onus on the catcher, why don't we use the third umpire to judge decisions that aren't clear to the human eye. And a second thing – the way these affairs are dismissed as being part of the game (I bet the local papers don't even give the Ponting dismissal the time of day) is a little frustrating to us. I'm sure that if Ian Healy or Steve Waugh had been involved (remember the headlines my catch of Brian Lara caused in the Caribbean in 1995) there would have been an uproar.

England's momentous task began reasonably, although the early loss of Stewart virtually snuffed out any thoughts they may have had of an unlikely victory, especially as his fall came so soon after Glenn McGrath had dismissed Mike Atherton once more. A positive start had been their only chance at getting a grip on the chase that lay ahead. Then Jason Gillespie began a spell that captains dream of when they have plenty of runs to play with – Gillespie claimed wickets at regular intervals even though he was conceding a lot of runs between his successes. It didn't matter about the runs but the wickets were priceless. Jason's spell was made all the more remarkable by the fact that he was obviously suffering from back pain which had required plenty of painkillers, just to get him to the bowling crease.

After the third wicket (Hussain, bowled for 21) fell, I turned to Matty Elliott, my companion in the gully region, and stated, 'We'll win this tonight.' There was just over an hour of play remaining at this stage. These words turned out to be prophetic, as England's inexperienced and brittle batting line-up crumbled at the hands of a rampaging attack, supported by advancing fieldsmen, all sensing an historic win.

The conditions of this Ashes series stated that we could ask for an extra half-hour, if we believed we could end the Test in that time. We duly called for such an extension and Devon Malcolm obliged with a slashing cover drive that found its way into Mark Waugh's hands at second slip. Had Malcolm survived that ball, there were only seven balls left in the day. Graham Thorpe had played a great rearguard innings, remaining 82 not out at the death, but he probably should have tried to shield the strike in the last couple of overs, to try to force us back tomorrow to win the game. You never know when it might rain all day.

Our joy and ecstasy were there for all to see, as we carried on like a soccer team who had just scored the winning goal in a Cup Final. It had been a superb team performance from a great side who had dominated nearly every session of the series since the disastrous first Test. This victory meant we were the first team in Ashes history to win five series in a row. Heals, Tubs and myself are the only three Aussies to have played in all these series.

Brother Mark inadvertently gave me a nice memento of the occasion when he threw the ball in the air after taking the series-winning catch, and then forgot about it. The ball was left on the ground as the advancing crowd charged onto

Trent Bridge like the Scottish warriors in *Braveheart*. Fortunately for me, an Aussie named John Sandy swooped on the ball and then presented it to me when he saw I was after it – a fine gesture indeed!

Needless to say the celebrations were very animated, with Heals, because it was a series win, giving us three verses of 'Under the Southern Cross', our winning team song, instead of the usual two. Phone calls to Bic and Gilly were made, as these lads are still very much a part of the squad and our success, while Slats, Lang and myself made a vow to wear our green baggys for the next four days straight. Alcohol can make you do strange things! It was 4.30am before a day that we'll all long remember and be proud of for many years to come came to a close.

Boy, it was great to be part of the Aussie cricket team!

NASSER HUSSAIN

Our best chance of staying in the game and, consequently, staying in with a chance of winning the Ashes is to stay with them and our chance came this morning when Steve Waugh was out to Caddy off the second ball of the morning. At that stage, with them 171 for five, we were 285 behind. If we could have polished them off cheaply then we had a real opportunity of levelling the series because they would have had to play it very differently and set different fields to us. There's a world of difference between chasing 300 and 400.

But again we let the pressure ease and didn't make Healy feel that he had to get runs to stop them from losing. The moment was there and we didn't seize it. We ran up, bowled a few long hops and wide ones and before we knew it Healy had 60, Ponting had 40 and we were out of the game. The Aussies, without fail, always capitalise on small openings like that.

It meant, with us needing 450 to win, that we weren't sure how to play. We knew we had to be positive and play like we did at Edgbaston and that if two people could build a partnership that was our best chance. There's no point in trying to block against Shane Warne with men around the bat. It just doesn't work. If we'd done that we could have been batting at tea-time tomorrow with three wickets down and still lost the game. We had to play naturally.

We didn't really look at our target. We knew it was above 400 and that's all we really needed to know. Thorpey and Creepy were both very keen to accentuate the positive and I just wanted to play naturally which was successful for me in a similar situation at Headingley.

My philosophy was, if it's a bad ball I'm going to hit it for four and there was the added factor of knowing Taylor had a lot of fielders behind the wicket and that you were always going to get good value for your shots. It's easier to score runs when you have runs on the board and you have to look to work in pairs.

It comes down again to mental strength and that can be a collective thing. When you're bowling, for example, it's up to the bowlers to put the ball in the right place and create pressure that way while the fielders can create pressure by creating a cauldron. I'm not talking about verbal abuse, just letting the batsmen know they're in a pressure situation. The odd sledge is fine but I'm not advocating sledging per se. Some of the quietest players in Test history have had mental strength.

Individually, a lot of us have had great series. A lot of us have had our moments while a lot of their guys, people like Mark Waugh and Mark Taylor, have had relatively quiet series. But the difference is that they have been working as a well organised, mentally strong team at all times whereas when we've had our chances we haven't taken them. It's about creating an atmosphere out there which makes the batsman want to escape and get back to the safety of the pavilion and for our batsmen to say 'sod it, I want to stick around out here. I want to prove to these blokes that I can play.' That's what Steve Waugh does and that's what Ian Healy does. They make it difficult for you at all times.

All this is not meant to be an explanation of why we were bowled out for 186 today to lose by 264 runs but it is my thinking on why we have now lost three matches on the trot and with it the Ashes. We batted indifferently collectively with the exception of Thorpey, who again proved his immeasurable worth.

Me? I tried to hit the ball through the covers like I have all summer and I just tried to hit Jason Gillespie too hard. The adrenalin was flowing, I hadn't had a bad ball for a while, Gillespie ran in and I thought 'I'll show these Aussies'. I almost got a bit too fired up. I dragged it on. It was my fault. I should have punched it for four.

And so it went on with a combination of people getting out to good balls or getting themselves out. Crofty's dismissal was the most disappointing because the cauldron seemed to affect him. His idea was clearly to go down fighting but going down fighting is playing like Dean did right at the end of our innings, not how Crofty did it. Dean showed his character. That's what I mean about mental toughness. He's only played three Tests but you can tell straight away that he has the mental strength to succeed at this level. He might have bad games but you know he will come through them and do a job for you. He's always going to be the bowler asking for an extra over. Hitting Shane for six and then running down the wicket at the next ball, like Crofty did, is trying to get quick runs before getting yourself out, not going down fighting.

Before we knew it the extra half hour was being requested and it was all over. It hit me all of a sudden that the Ashes were gone. Mark Waugh took the winning catch and you could see how much it meant by the Aussies reaction. Before that moment perhaps we might have assumed that the Aussies always thought they would win this series. But their sheer joy and emotion showed that they haven't assumed anything throughout the summer and emphasised that they knew they were in for a fight after Edgbaston.

It's very revealing to see the reaction of guys who have achieved so much in the game. We've watched a lot of motivation videos this summer and I think we should keep a video of the Australians Ashes clinching catch and show it to our guys to prove how much it means to win the Ashes. People who have played 80 or 90 Tests and taken part in three Ashes winning series were hugging and kissing each other and going ballistic. They knew they were in a scrap but they pulled it round when they were down. We received a lot of letters after Edgbaston from people telling us to go on and win the Ashes. We haven't done it and we were very low.

The Aussies asked us to have a drink with them and who should be the first person to shake my hand but Shane Warne. That summed it all up for me. He winked at me and basically said that we may have had a few clashes on the field and he may have called me a few things but he respected me and hoped I respected him. It just shows how much of what he does on the field is bravado and that Shane Warne is just the same as us. We should be more like him on the field and I think the Aussies attitude is brilliant.

The only amusing aspect to our demise was when Ath realised that when he was sitting out on the balcony he was sitting near an 'exit' sign which the photographers were desperately trying to picture him with. Graham Morris, a well known cricket photographer, tipped him off about it but it gave Ath and all of us a laugh.

There was no laughing when Bumble gave us all a dressing down in the dressing room after the finish. He told us that the selectors knew we were the right blokes for the job but that we had to get tougher. He emphasised that we had played very well at times but couldn't sustain it when it most mattered and that we had to play with more togetherness and more 'affection' for each other. Of course, he was absolutely right and Bumble's been brilliant this season. He's learnt as much as anyone, I'm sure he'd admit that himself.

I'm sure he learned from last summer and from last winter's tour. All he was doing then was being natural and you should never condemn someone for that but he was so involved and so desperate for us to do well that the emotion sometimes came to the surface, like in Bulawayo and the 'we murdered em' comments. This summer he has been spot on and has said exactly the right things at the right time. We have let him down.

The selectors have got it right all summer, too. They have been spot on in every selection with the possible exception of Mike Smith but even then that was made for sound cricketing reasons and Mike had an unlucky match. The selectors have shown continuity and faith, things we've cried out for in the past, and given us everything we could have wished for. It is not their fault that we have ultimately failed. Nor the coach, nor the captain. It's the players' fault.

I was very tempted to come straight home tonight because we have our semi-final against Glamorgan on Tuesday but I wanted to do what Athers wanted. He came down from the press conference and asked me to stay up and have a few rums and I just couldn't bring myself to say that I wanted to go home. So I rang Karen and explained the situation to her.

We went back to the hotel and had a few drinks and a curry in the bar. About half the team were there, with the usual suspects – Ath, Dean, Adam, Thorpey, *myself and a few others. We just sat until about 2am discussing the series and how we can get better.*

11 August

One thing you don't want, when you've only had a couple of hours' sleep, and your head feels like it doesn't belong to you, is a succession of early-morning phone calls from the press.

I decided to attack the situation and head down to the pool for a spot of swimming. The only trouble with this plan was that the warm, muscle-relaxing spa loomed just to the left of the pool and it didn't take long for me to convince myself what the best option was.

At a special team meeting tonight, we learnt that Pistol will be heading home to be with his wife, who is experiencing some complications during the latter stages of her pregnancy.

More bad news came when we were told that Jason Gillespie has been diagnosed as suffering from stress fractures in his back and will need a lengthy rehabilitation to ensure the problem doesn't flare up again.

This makes Dizzy's effort in the second innings of the fifth Test even more meritorious. It proves, too, that he possesses great inner strength and courage by being able to play through the pain as he did.

NASSER HUSSAIN

I decided that as soon as I woke up this morning and was sure I was alive I would hit the road because I didn't want to spend half the day in Nottingham when I could be getting ready for the upcoming NatWest semi-final. When I woke I looked at the clock and saw it was 6.30am but got straight up, had a cup of coffee, freshened up and left. I didn't listen to the radio because I didn't want to hear too much about England losing the Ashes.

All I wanted to do this afternoon was put my feet up but it didn't work out that way. First Peter Edwards rang to say Prich wasn't fit for the semi-final and that I would be captain. Then Fletch rang to discuss our team and then Prich rang up for a chat about tactics.

Then I had to go to Chelmsford to do my Daily Mail interview with Brian Scovell which I thought was pretty straightforward. Scovs's first question related to exactly how I was thinking and what we have been talking about in this book. It also echoed what I had talked with Grav about at Trent Bridge. He said that Shane Warne had said in his book that English cricket was too soft and did I agree. I had to admit I did and I said that when as an England side we had won games was when we were mentally and collectively very strong. There have been other occasions when English individuals have played as well as anyone in the world but all too few occasions when we've had the collective strength to do it consistently. I include myself in that too.

We did it exactly right at Edgbaston. When we lost three quick wickets we had the strength to say 'we'll still get 400' and when Australia fought back in their second innings we had the strength to say 'if we hang on in there wickets will come' and they did. But in the last three Tests we haven't done that at the crucial moments. The difference is not ability, with the exception of Warne, it's attitude. It's like when you play squash or golf against someone who's better than you. You don't come off and say 'well, he was the better player, he deserved to win, I'll go off and play someone my own standard.' Instead you watch them play and practice, look closely at what they do to make them a better player and see what you can use from them to improve your game. The same is true of us against the Aussies.

I'm not having a go at our players or stabbing any individual in the back. I'm just saying we all need to get stronger and sit down and discuss how we can create an atmosphere that is difficult for the opposition. I'm not talking about cursing and sledging all the time. Just raising the mental stakes. I told Scovs that county cricket was very matey and lovey dovey and that it's all about a few cups of tea and maybe a Pimm's or two afterwards but that shouldn't be taken out of context. He faxed the article to me and I'm happy with it, unlike that one earlier in the season at Old Trafford. I shouldn't think it will create much of a stir.

18
THE BATTLE OF CHELMSFORD

NASSER HUSSAIN

The first surprise of an eventful day came when I turned on Sky News at 7am before getting ready to leave for Chelmsford and the NatWest Trophy semi-final against Glamorgan. The headline that greeted me on TV was 'HUSSAIN SAYS ENGLAND ARE TOO SOFT' which they had taken from my *Daily Mail* article. It had not struck me as too big a deal as I was only stating what everyone in English cricket knew.

Then, when I arrived at the county ground, David Gower came up to me and said 'I've seen your article in the *Mail*. You've come out with all guns blazing, haven't you?' I thought 'have I?' Then later on when our game was delayed by the rain Gower interviewed Goochie for the BBC and the first question he asked him was 'have you seen Nasser's piece this morning?' I thought 'what's happening here?' I suppose the attention was compounded by a live interview I gave earlier to Radio Four. I had arrived at the ground early, as is my wont, and one of the women who works in the Essex office had taken a call from the *Today* programme asking if I would be prepared to do a live interview on the prospects for the semi-final. It was no problem – until I realised I was being 'stuffed', something that hadn't happened to me since Bill Day of the *Mail on Sunday* stitched me up over an article concerning that same David Gower when he took to the skies in a Tiger Moth on tour in Australia.

This was something you do not expect from the BBC. The first question was about the *Daily Mail* piece and he pressed me, remember this is live, to name specific incidents when our game was not hard enough. I then said that when Steve Waugh was out straight away on the Sunday of the Trent Bridge Test we didn't make things hard enough for Ian Healy. Then he questioned me on sledging and I was trying to get across that I thought a few words here and there did no harm to anybody but that I wasn't advocating widespread sledging as such. I also said we needed to be a bit nastier which, with hindsight, was not the right word to use but I was under pressure and the guy asked me nothing about the semi-final at all.

I actually thought I handled a difficult interview pretty well but that word nasty came back to haunt me to a certain extent later that day. For the NatWest semi-final turned out to be the most intense and controversial game involving two counties that I have ever played in. And it was sod's law that it should happen on the very day that I said county cricket was not hard enough.

The debate that seemed to be raging over the merits of my comments – and I am happy to say that the majority of the reaction appears to have been positive – was actually the last thing on my mind when I finished talking to Radio Four. I was far more concerned about the game.

Looking at the wicket and our side, we would have been happy to be chasing 270 or 280 but Glamorgan ended up reaching 300 mainly because the amount of injuries we were carrying had restricted our bowling performance. That was made worse when Ronnie Irani tore muscles in his side before he had bowled his full allocation, a blow which cost us about 20 runs, and it was clear that we faced a hard task with the probability of bad light to contend with because an hour was lost to rain early in the Glamorgan innings. I had been involved in a bit of banter with the passionate Glamorgan supporters towards the end of their innings when I registered a direct hit to gain a run out after they had been giving me some verbal stick, offering plenty of comments about Shane Warne and asking how on earth I could be the next England captain. When I hit the stumps I turned and smiled at them, something I don't usually do with the crowd but my way, on this occasion, of easing the tension before the intensity of the run-chase.

Then , like so often this season, it was a case of me putting my pads on and just watching Stuart Law tee off. So often when with us he's made a mockery of a stiff target that you have to pinch yourself it's happening. The way he dashes along he quickly reduces a chase for 300 plus to a routine Sunday League target but you also know that, playing as he does, he's probably going to get out between 80 and 120 because he never slows down and takes a few risks. You find yourself on the pavilion urging him to steady down but he never does and one day he'll go on and get 200. More often that not he just puts us in fantastic positions before getting out.

He did get out caught at long off but not before he was involved in the first controversial incident of the day. Now, apparently, Darren Thomas had said in the Welsh papers that morning that the only way to earn the respect of Australians was to mix it with them, or words to that effect, but whether that stretched to bowling a beamer deliberately at Stuart Law we shall never know. Thomas was certainly fired up but that doesn't mean he did it deliberately. But bowl it he did and the ball hurtled towards Stuart's face before he fended it off, so Stuart was never going to just stand there and accept it. It was a ball that could have ended his career, just like a beamer from Allan Donald almost ended the career of Prich at Chelmsford way back in 1987. That ball broke Prich's finger so badly that he was out for 18 months and, it could be argued, it stopped him becoming an England player, so the stakes are high when you get a ball like that.

This was a bad one and the apology was barely forthcoming so, as far as I'm concerned, Stuart was perfectly justified in having a few words with the bowler, throwing his gloves down and calling for the physio. That's fair enough. But I can see how Stuart upsets opponents. He's the sort of bloke who, if you play against him, you can easily hate. I'm sure if I was opposing him I'd think he was the most arrogant, up himself bloke I'd ever met but if you play with him you realise that's the way he is and that his demeanor is his way of firing himself up. When you play with him you also get to know what a great bloke he is and he's very much a team man and one hell of a batsman.

I can just about see why Stuart is not in the first choice Australian Test line-up because their top six is incredibly strong but I can't see how he could have been left out of the entire Ashes party. He's at his peak now and really Australia have missed out on him. I suppose when you've got so many good batsmen there's always a danger you'll overlook one and unfortunately for Stuart he's the one of this generation. He says his attitude might count against him because he's not a great trainer or netter and just lives his life, enjoying a drink and a night out. I think that must clash a bit with the policy of Geoff Marsh, the Aussie coach, because I gather he's very big on the things Stuart doesn't relish. But Stuart and Australian cricket are the losers. I think he'll still feature in their one-day line-up but he thinks, even with a fifty on his only Test appearance, that he's missed the boat now as far as Test cricket is concerned. Let's hope not.

Few players could bat as well as Stuart did against Glamorgan. He recovered from the blow on the hand from a beamer which broke a finger to score 90, and then all we really had to do was maintain the momentum while Darren Robinson attempted to bat through the innings. Sounds easy, doesn't it? And for a while everything went perfectly to plan, with me, Paul Grayson and Robbo all contributing before Ronnie took charge. There were no panics and we whittled it down to 19 needed when it started to get darker and darker and things began to go wrong. All I said to our players was to stay out there while Ronnie was batting so well but if they wanted to come off they should. I knew Ronnie would want to stay there because he was hitting the ball like a legend but it was always going to be a different story if two new batsmen were at the crease.

Ronnie, though, was playing like a dream, an incredible effort considering he'd had three injections in his damaged side and a few pain-killing tablets to enable him to bat at all. When Ronnie's batting, especially in games like that, he gets hugely fired up and on 99 per cent of occasions he's a tremendous asset to the side. Just occasionally he loses touch with reality and, while I don't think that was the case here and while the drugs couldn't have helped his state of mind, he was extremely animated throughout his innings. It was the original gutsy knock.

When both Danny Law and Ashley Cowan came in Ronnie was seen to have strong words with both, basically reminding them of their responsibilities, but they're both such laid back characters that they probably didn't even realise Ronnie was talking to them! I certainly didn't at first because I thought Ronnie was having a go at the opposition until I realised he was swearing at his own team-mates! But give me Ronnie Irani any day. If I was captain on a long-term basis I think I'd have to sit him down and just remind him that he does go a bit over the top occasionally and that he needs to check himself while not losing his aggression, which is such a strength.

As a senior player you have to be careful how you talk to people at times. For instance, with Ashley we didn't know how he would react to being pumped up like that by Ronnie when he first went in and it's conceivable that it might have contributed to the run-out between the two. But considering Ronnie's injury is the same one which afflicted Steve Watkin and Mike Smith on A tours that I've been on and they both had to be sent home, then I think he did tremendously well.

So too did Danny, briefly, when he hit Waqar Younis for six, four, four in one over just when we were worrying that it was getting too dark. I signalled to Ronnie to do what he thought best but just at that moment a burst of sun came out so it was right to continue then. I didn't think so soon after when, in a burst of madness, the whole of our season was placed in jeopardy and we found ourselves in danger of a defeat that people would still have been talking about in 20 years time. The Norbert Phillip incident, for instance, is still legend at Essex. That was when our former overseas player threw wildly at the stumps from close range in a cup semi-final at Derby off the last ball to lose us a game we should have won. And that was 16 years ago, so heaven knows what people would have been saying about us if we had blown this.

I had sent Ashley in ahead of young Tim Hodgson after Danny and Robert Rollins had been dismissed to try to get it over with but he got involved in that run-out with Ronnie that defied belief. Not only did they end up at the same end but, in his desperation to make sure he wasn't the one given out, Ronnie started sprinting past the sawdust and towards the commentary box at the Hayes Close End. I couldn't believe what I was watching and I turned to Jim, our physio, and said 'all we need now is for Ronnie to get out and we're in trouble.' Sure enough, next ball Ronnie was given out lbw, set off for an impossible single not knowing he was out and Darren Thomas, in celebrating the wicket, landed a haymaker on Ronnie. Ronnie took his helmet off to let him know what he thought of him as he walked off and now we were in big trouble. Meanwhile, the game was becoming almost surreal.

Everybody on the balcony was in a state of shock. Stuart went into the dressing room and started punching things because he couldn't believe we were going to throw away his cup final place after the innings he played. Fletch had gone very quiet while, down on the pitch, Tim Hodgson was preparing for his first innings in the NatWest Trophy. Welcome to the big time.

This was the moment that Glamorgan chose to bring back Waqar and now, at around 8.15pm, it was very dark and, even though there was a packed house and a desire on everyone's part to get the game finished, I knew we had to come off with only six runs needed. Mark Ilott, who by this time was out there too, looked up at me and I signalled to come off. I'd cleared it with Fletch beforehand and he agreed that it was the best thing to do. Ramble (Ilott), though, didn't have time to appeal to the umpires until Waqar had bowled a ball at Hodge that he just couldn't see and which missed his off-stump by a whisker.

Then Ramble appealed to umpire David Constant, as he had a right to do because the light had got worse, and while the umpires were conferring Crofty, from mid-off, went up to Ramble and asked him what he was doing. Unfortunately what followed overshadowed everything that had gone before.

There was a fair bit of effing and blinding going on which, in the tension of the situation, was understandable. Crofty wanted to get the game over with because Glamorgan, from nowhere, were suddenly in with a chance but for Ramble to react as he did Crofty must have been particularly vociferous. He said something that wound up Ramble, calling him a coward or worse, and Ramble pointed out in the strongest terms that we had just lost two wickets in appalling light and that this was the semi-final of the NatWest Trophy, not a Sunday League match.

Up until that moment there was no problem as far as I was concerned. Verbals are not a crime and this was an intense, important match. But once people start pushing each other in cricket – and I know it happens all the time in football – then it has overstepped the mark and something has to be done. Both Ramble and Crofty laid hands on each other and, while I think Crofty started it by getting verbally involved when he didn't need to and then aiming the first push, Ramble admits he was at fault too. You can't do that sort of thing even though you can understand how it happens.

This game was meant to mean a lot. For those guys not involved in Test cricket this is as big as it gets and, after what happened to us in last year's final, it meant everything from an Essex point of view. I repeat, the game was just the sort of encounter I relish and would like to see more of before the pushing. That was when it went too far. As the teams came off Prich had a heated discussion with Crofty on the balcony asking him what on earth all that was about while Ramble was still very emotional and wanted to get a beer and sit down with the Glamorgan boys to thrash out where it had all got so heated. We told him to sit down and calm down but now we were very low.

We had Danny Law's wedding to go to the next day and we just wanted to win the match, have a good night out and relax. Then, all of a sudden, from the verge of winning we had to come back in the morning, perhaps to lose a game we had sown up, and we just sat there thinking 'what have we done?' Ronnie, meanwhile, was going around saying 'don't worry, we only need six, we'll piss this tomorrow'. Typical Irani confidence.

The atmosphere between the teams, however, was not that bad. I had a joke with Steve James and Steve Watkin, asking them if they remembered when Essex v Glamorgan matches were such friendly affairs. They replied 'wait until you come to Cardiff next month!' Crofty and Ramble are genuinely good friends, so they quickly made it up privately and went through the same thing the next day publicly to emphasize to the watching world that there were no hard feelings. A few of us went down the pub, both to let the traffic clear and because we knew there was no point rushing home because nobody was going to be able to sleep after that. Tim Hodgson wasn't among us. With the prospect of having a semi-final in his hands the next morning on his trophy debut he decided to go straight home. Down the pub Ramble kept on chuntering, saying 'don't worry boys, leave it to my cover drive'. I wasn't so sure. I was worried that if Glamorgan took one wicket quickly in the morning then it would be game over in their favour. Not because I didn't trust 'Suchy' (Peter Such), our last man, but because of the pressure of the situation. I thought that we would either get six singles with this pair at the wicket or we'd lose straight away.

It poured down all Tuesday night which made me wonder who would win if no more play was possible. That was the last thing we wanted because nobody wanted to hang around all day in our nervous state, but I was pleased nonetheless to see that we would win if the game had to be abandoned. But the day dawned bright and there was just a short delay before such a crucial passage of play.

I just couldn't watch as our batsmen took to the field. I wished Hodge luck, tried to relax him and reminded him that Ramble wasn't as quick as him, so to be careful with the running between the wickets. A run-out really would cap it all. Then I went and sat in Malcolm Field's office (the Essex assistant secretary) and listened to the crowd reaction as the match got under way.

Three cheers told me that we had scored three singles in Waqar's over which took us halfway there. But, Essex being Essex, there had to be another setback along the way and when Hodge was caught behind off Thomas at the start of the next over I really thought we had had it. I had actually come out of Fieldo's office at the end of the Waqar over but as soon as I did Hodge was out which made me wonder what on earth I had come out for. Then I walked slowly to the dressing room balcony, half watching as Suchy took strike and the first ball was a yorker which just missed his stumps. I just couldn't see where three runs were going to come from. The only way Suchy usually gets a boundary is by running to leg and flailing at it which was hardly the shot he could play in these conditions. So how were we going to get them?

Then the big moment came. Suchy, using one of Goochie's old bats for luck, made contact with a full length ball from Thomas and the ball sped through the covers. I thought 'we might get two here' but I didn't realise how well Suchy had struck it and it just carried on towards the boundary. Then I noticed that Ramble had stopped running, thinking we needed two instead of three – typical Essex that. Everyone in the ground is counting the runs down and there's one of our batsmen getting his sums wrong – so I screamed at him to run another but at that moment the ball crossed the boundary rope and pandomonium broke out on our balcony. Even Fletch was going mental and he must have been in these situations so often as a player. Suchy was hugged by everybody on his return and Gower stuck a microphone in my gob. I told the world we were all going to Danny's wedding when actually we were the surprise guests – luckily Danny was too busy celebrating to hear the broadcast – and then when Gower asked if there would be plenty of champagne I said to him 'this is Essex mate, not Hampshire. We're having beer.' I'm actually more of a wine man myself but it raised a laugh. Can you imagine what sort of wedding Danny would have had if we had lost? I think he might have been the only one who turned up for it! As it was, Ronnie, not even contemplating the possibility of defeat, had ordered four crates of beer and plenty of champagne to be sent to the dressing room at the end of play so we had an impromptu party before moving on to the wedding by 3pm.

I don't know what the bride and groom's families thought but there we were, pissed out of our heads, shouting 'surprise' as Danny walked in the registry office, but there was no bad behaviour. The only noise – but no pushing and shoving – came from Ramble's baby, who cried during the ceremony!

It was such an important win for us. Virtually the whole team are carrying wear and tear injuries and we've lost momentum in both the championship and Sunday League. Defeat here would have finished us off but now we have another Lord's final against Warwickshire to look forward to. The only sour note for me was having to sit on the disciplinary panel with Prich and Doug Insole to decide on Ramble's punishment. I backed him up as much as I felt I should but I think the fine of £1,000 was about right. Glamorgan came to the same conclusion with Crofty, so I presume there must have been a degree of collusion between the clubs. I hoped that would be the end of the matter but the ECB later decided to suspend both players for two NatWest games if they misbehaved again. I don't think they will.

For me it was just another chapter in an unbelievable season. A couple of days later I went to an Alan Lilley benefit game at Billericay and, while having lunch, a few blokes on another table shouted over to me 'we're drinking Pimm's, is that all right with you?' a reference to my comments in the *Mail* about people in English cricket sitting around with a Pimm's after a match. It was funny but it emphasized that I've been firmly in the spotlight all year. I think I might have to seek a lower media profile for a while after all this!

19
RECHARGING THE BATTERIES

STEVE WAUGH

12 August, Londonderry

It was farewell to Pistol, and goodbye to Dizzy and Hooter, too. The latter pair are heading down to London to get a further diagnosis from specialists on our paceman's injured back. It is vitally important Dizzy gets his rehabilitation right, for his own sake and for the future well-being of Australian cricket. This guy is another McGrath in the making and he's still only 22 years old!

It seems like we're never off that damn bus, and yet another hour was clocked up before we reached Manchester Airport. Once there, we underwent a very thorough and strict inspection, before beginning our trip to Belfast. Quite a few of the boys have been apprehensive about travelling to this perceived hot spot, but for most of us it has become quite normal to visit cities and countries that most tourists are advised are best bypassed.

Our trek wasn't over when we arrived in Belfast, for we still had an hour's drive to our hotel in Londonderry to endure. Thankfully, this was broken up by a pit stop at a favourite waterhole of our liaison officer. Warney was particularly grateful for the diversion, as he spotted his favourite snacks, 'Bacon Bites' hanging in their plastic bags from the wall. He was so pleased, in fact, that he relieved the proprietor of a whole strip of these snacks – 15 bags in all!

We finally reached our hotel after half a day's travelling. Half the lads were eager to get on the golf course, while the rest of us went in search of some salmon in the meandering streams just down the road. One could say the fishing expedition was a dismal failure – the only sign of success came the way of Kasper, but he let his chance of glory escape when the fish headed for the safety of the rocks and reeds before losing the hook and dashing off to freedom.

My efforts were somewhat hindered by the six stinging nettle bushes that nestled up against my arm as I threw my most impressive cast for the day. For the next 15 minutes I rummaged through the bushes, in search of a leaf that I was told would nullify the pain if it was rubbed on my skin shortly after contact. Unfortunately, I never found one, the sting didn't ease up at all, but at least I had an excuse for my lack of success on the salmon front.

13 August, Londonderry

The adulation we are receiving from the Irish is quite unexpected. We are especially pleased to learn that they are on our side, hoping and praying that the Poms are going to cop a hiding.

We had the huge honour today of playing golf at Royal Portrush. This is a course that Gary Player, the legendary South African golfer, said only last week, while winning a Seniors event, was the best links course he'd ever played. If Gary was here today, he would have been horrified by some of the atrocious tee shots that were played on the first tee. Crommo started off with two glorious cover drives, one of which scooted across the members' car park, while Tattoo looked like a dog playing with a soccer ball as he hacked his way in zigzag fashion down the first fairway.

Royal Portrush lived up to its billing, with well-thought-out holes, carpet-like greens and manicured fairways adjoined by rough that requires you to break a wrist if you want to get the ball out. Punter was again the star, carding a 75. He finished just in front of Smithy, who played only nine holes less.

The evening was spent soaking up the hospitality of these extremely hospitable people. I can tell you the Guinness hit all the right spots.

14 August, Londonderry

Australia 303–7 (Langer 57, Ponting 117*) defeated Ireland 164 (McCallan 64*; Ponting 3–14) by 139 runs.

They said it couldn't be done. Well, they didn't count on the love affair Lang has with his cherished baggy green cap. To everyone's astonishment, some four days after the Southern Comfort had done the talking in our victorious dressing-room celebrations at Trent Bridge, Lang is still proudly sporting his cap, a fact which wins him a bet neither Slats nor I could fulfil. But at least we didn't have an odour any skunk would have been proud of, or a permanent red ring around our melons from the elastic band inside the rim of the cap. This was another morale-boosting effort from Lang, who always does those little things that help bond a side together.

Today was a day in 'sheet city'. Having been excluded from the starting XI, I made the most of it – the only effort exerted came after the doorbell rang for room service or when I flicked over the pages in John Grisham's latest novel, *The Runaway Jury*.

Bad news did, however, make its way back to the hotel when an urgent message filtered through that either Pigeon or Warney was required to dash down to the ground to replace BJ, who couldn't bowl a ball during warm-ups because of that knock he received in the nets back at Trent Bridge. It was confirmed later that he has suffered a hairline fracture, thus ending his chance of a recall for the sixth Test, at The Oval, which was virtually guaranteed after the loss of Gillespie and Reiffel.

It's certainly been a tough tour for Cleo's former 'Bachelor of the Year' runner-up. First, it was a neck injury that damaged BJ's chances early in the tour, and now this. For the sake of his sanity, he must make something positive out of this setback. Like Bic, Gilly and Dizzy, he must make sure that the injury makes him hungrier when he next steps onto the field; perhaps it will increase his focus on the first game of next season.

Down at the ground Punter continued his rich vein of form with an exquisite exhibition of classy stroke-making, while the highly-impressive Darren Berry claimed five catches and one stumping in another polished display.

15 August, Canterbury

To cap off a battery-recharging couple of days, I ventured out with Warney and 'Chuck' Berry onto the hotel's golf course this morning for a game of 'skins'. The trio nearly became a duo at the fourth, after Shane lost control of our golf cart while careering down a steep fairway. He ended his descent with a wild 360-degrees spin, before safely pulling up slapbang next to his ball.

The golf developed into a titanic tussle. Walking up the 18th, Warney had five skins, Chuck, 'the burglar', had six, and I had six. You would have thought there were millions at stake the way we played the hole, such was the 'gas taking' all round, but all arguments were resolved when I rolled in a sloping eight-footer for a five (on a straightforward par 3). While the standard of golf wasn't anything to write home about, the company, atmosphere and surroundings certainly were, and it made for a morning well spent.

Shortly after it was back on the merry-go-round – bus, plane, bus and finally our arrival at what is reputably the No. 1 rated hotel in Canterbury. It may well have been highly regarded during the winter months, but now that a mini drought has hit England the absence of air-conditioners left us trying to survive in stifling, almost unbearable conditions. The absence of fresh air gives the whole place the atmosphere of a gymnasium sauna.

16 August, Canterbury

Kent 201 (Fleming 67; Kasprowicz 4–72, Lee 4–27) v Australia 207–5 (S Waugh 94*).
The St Lawrence ground at Canterbury is quite unique, in that a huge oak tree is situated on the ground inside the boundary. It's a sight that is remarkable if you haven't seen it before. I think it's great because it gives the ground a real sense of character.

Once again, a ground for a tour match was sold out. To my fellow players' dismay I lost the toss and we found ourselves in the field, on a warmish English summer's day, bowling on a wicket as good as any we've seen for the whole tour. On paper at least, this was probably the most inexperienced attack we've put on the field all tour, but the desire and commitment of these guys was first rate. Kasper troubled all the batsmen, while one of our two 'new' tourists, Shane Lee, claimed four wickets. The other 'debutant', Shaun Young, looked to be trying too hard, which is understandable considering what probably awaits him – a spot in the XI for the final Test. But he still managed to keep a tight check on the run rate.

Bowling one of the better county sides out on such a good track for only 201 was a great performance, highlighted by our best catching display of the tour. The slips cordon looked like a school of sharks eager for a feed. On such a wicket, I thought I'd be able to settle into the comfort of the change rooms. Instead, I barely had time to sort my gear out before I was facing Alan Igglesden, a former Test opening bowler, who had claimed three wickets for five runs in a destructive 11-ball spell.

As I faced my first over, I felt half asleep for some reason – perhaps because I only slept for about half an hour last night due to the unbearable heat. But once this initial settling-in period was safely negotiated, I began to feel in really good touch and with Bevo added 101 in quick time before the close of play.

17 August, Canterbury

Kent 201 and 234–5 (Ward 68, A Wells 65) v Australia 315 (S Waugh 154, Bevan 55).
It took me four balls to reach my century this morning, which was ideal after I'd had all night to think about the six runs needed to reach the landmark, and how I was going to get them. Overall, though, we were disappointing with the bat again, managing only 315 – a pretty unsatisfactory result when you consider we had Shaun Young at No. 8 and Shane Lee at No. 9, both of whom average over 40 in first-class cricket. This undisciplined display is exactly what we didn't want in the lead-up to the sixth Test and exactly what we said we wouldn't do when we sat down at Somerset to talk about how we wanted to finish the tour. Hopefully, our second innings will be a more professional effort. I was very satisfied with my 154 but slightly aggrieved to be the last man out, even though the ball I got from their Zimbabwean leggie, Paul Strang, gripped and turned out of the rough. One can only imagine what Warney would have done on this wicket. At one point, I went forward to play what was almost a half volley and ended up wearing it flush on the peak of my helmet, after it spat out of a foothole.

In Kent's second innings our fielding and bowling was top notch once more. We had no luck whatsoever early on, but gained the rewards shortly before the close of play, when two wickets fell in the last 10 overs.

Tonight gave the media guys a chance to air their 'bloopers tape' of the tour. Blunders from Healy, S Waugh and Warne featured prominently, along with some candid and sometimes embarrassing camera shots of the lads on tour. The Channel 7 and Channel 9 boys have been great company all tour and are so well known to everyone they are almost part of the squad. The Aussie journos also said a word of thanks – in general, we've had a pretty good working relationship with them during the tour. That said, I think it's important to keep some distance between players and the media. We both have a job to do and opinions are bound to vary on different issues, many of which can be personal.

18 August , Canterbury

Kent 201 and 343 (Ealham 85; Lee 4–86) lost to Australia 315 and 231–4 (Slater 47, Ponting 56*, Bevan 47*) by six wickets.

A light warm-up was all that was required before play, especially as the sun continued to shine as if trying to make up for the time lost when it deserted us all. Once the initial, crucial breakthrough was achieved in the morning session, the rest of the order succumbed under the pressure we began to exert. Shane Lee again bowled as well as he's ever done, claiming a further four wickets (which would have been his first-ever five-wicket haul in a first-class match, but for a high ball that was grassed by Slats). 'China' Young settled into a much better rhythm in this innings than he had in the first, and in doing so probably gave himself the nod for a Test jumper. Overall, it was an encouraging performance in the field and one that gives me great confidence going into our last match.

During my first-innings century my thumb problem resurfaced in a big way, and I am now struggling to hold the bat with any authority. Considering the Test is only three days away, I took on the role of McGrath and slotted in at No. 11 for the second dig. We looked a little shaky at 95 for three before tea, but in the end got home comfortably on the backs of Punter and Bevo, who overcame a few nerve-racking moments to give us only our third victory over a county on tour.

The win took longer than we had hoped. That fact, combined with the obligatory signing session for all those avid autograph collectors at the gate and a quick chat we enjoyed with the former New Zealand opener (and now coach of Kent), John Wright, meant that we arrived in London sometime around 8.30pm. After a quick feed, we hit the sack.

After all the troubles I'd had earlier in the tour organising satisfactory accommodation for my family at the Westbury, this time, now that I'm a 'single man', they've given me a penthouse suite (valued at £750 a night). No doubt this is a clerical error, but there was no way I was going to inform them of that.

20
ENGLAND v AUSTRALIA
SIXTH CORNHILL TEST MATCH

The Oval, London, 21–25 August

NASSER HUSSAIN

19 August

When I heard about our side for the Oval I was pleased for Butch. It was right to bring him back. He was unlucky to be dropped in the first place, but it was always going to a short term arrangement to open again with Alec while he still keeps wicket. John Crawley was unfortunate to be dropped. He's a class player and has made two good scores in this series on indifferent wickets, admittedly in the second innings. I'm sure the Aussies will be glad he's been dropped but, having said that, the selectors had to change things a little bit after three successive defeats and 'Ramps' (Mark Ramprakash) is a top quality replacement.

Ramps is a close friend of mine and, in cricket, me, him and Thorpey know each other as well as anyone. I'm pleased he's got this chance because, technically, he's one of the best players in the country and just has to conquer his mental problems to be a success at the highest level. He has certainly had his chances to prove he can be a good Test player. I wouldn't go along with the argument that, as he has mostly played against the West Indies, his average is an unfair reflection on how well he has done. The fact is, every Test is hard and, as Zimbabwe proved against us in the winter, you have to be at your very best to produce the goods against any opposition at this level. Ramps just hasn't been able to do that yet but I'm sure all he really needs is a piece of luck. It's up to him now.

The careers of Thorpey, Ramps and myself have often gone in the same direction but we've never all played in the same England team until now. I suppose we've all done well and badly at different times. Ramps and I got married on the same day and Thorpey got married on our first anniversary. Thorpey, in fact, was invited to both mine and Ramps weddings but turned us both down because he didn't want to let either of us down! So we all go back a long way.

It was noticeable that Ath was a lot firmer with people today. If anyone was a couple of minutes late for anything he got angry and was a lot more vociferous and stronger all round. It was almost as if he was saying 'hang on, I'm still in charge here', after all the speculation about his position. He's certainly aware of what's being said and, of course, he told me that he was considering packing it in during the Trent Bridge Test. I think he feels that if he was quiet here he could have easily given out the wrong vibes that it was all getting to him, so I sensed that he has gone the other way.

Ath didn't say anything to us about his position but he seems determined that if this is going to be his last match in charge he's going to go out professionally. That's typical of him.

One of the busiest people today was our physio Wayne Morton because a lot of us are carrying injuries. My tennis elbow has flared up again, so I spent some time with Wayne getting treatment and I was joined in there by Dean, who has a heel injury, Thorpey, who has had cortisone injections in a shoulder problem and Adam, who has a really sore hamstring. In fact, Wayne has told Adam not to play, so we'll have to see what happens.

This Test is unusual in that one of the chosen members of our squad has not turned up at any stage of preparations. Crofty was due at a disciplinary hearing in Bristol tonight along with Ramble following their altercation in our NatWest semi-final and we were told tonight that we wouldn't be seeing him because he had been released to play for Glamorgan in the championship tomorrow.

This is an area where the selectors hands are forced because they are under pressure to let one member of our 13 go off and play for their county on the Wednesday but, to be honest, it seemed unlikely that we would alter our policy at the Oval of going in with one spinner and Tuffers has earned his chance to play ahead of Crofty in this match.

Mind you, the wicket looked pretty dry when we looked at it today. All the Surrey boys said that it was a funny looking Oval pitch and Goochie said it looks as though the groundsman has taken the blades too low to it. Still, it doesn't usually turn a lot at the Oval so maybe this will prove to be a typical Oval surface.

Mosimann's restaurant in London invited us all out to a meal tonight in conjunction with Veuve Cliquot champagne and a contortionist was laid on for our entertainment. He asked Adam and Dean to help him and, to be honest, he couldn't have picked two worse volunteers. Adam had to help him put his straightjacket on and, as he tied it up through his underneath parts, he pulled it so hard that this bloke went down like a sack of shit with tears in his eyes. People thought it was all part of the act but he really was in agony for about five minutes. Then there was Dean, the great thinker, standing there scratching his head and questioning everything the bloke did in an attempt to catch him out, so I bet he loved the England cricket team by the end of it all!

20 August

There were lots of things to do today, including a promotion for Kwik Cricket. There was also the sight of Devon Malcolm appearing from the dressing room in his full whites which made me think he had got the wrong day because most players are normally seen in their training gear on Wednesdays. Then we were told he was going to bowl at John Etheridge of the *Sun* for a feature in a Rory Bremner television programme and I have to say this created a fair bit of interest among the boys. The words 'kill the bastard, Dev' could be heard emanating from our dressing room along with 'it's payback time for the *Sun*' and 'hit him hard Dev' as the balcony became more congested.

Adam and Ben went over even though they hadn't been asked to, apparently because Ethers had called Ben a medium pace dobber, or something like that, the week before and now he wanted his revenge. So we were all sat there hoping Dev and the Hollioakes would clean Ethers up but, to be fair, he actually played him quite well. The whole thing took place on a practice wicket which was a bit slow, but Dev got one to hit him quite hard and there was a bit of a cheer from the balcony!

Nets were fine today but it seems Dean's injury is worse than I feared and I don't think he's going to play. Peter Martin's been unlucky not to play for England more often than he has and he's been bowling well for Lancashire, so I'm sure he won't let anyone down.

The sixth Test was always going to be hard because it's almost a bridge too far but, however mentally tired I am, I've got to work hard to try to finish with a score.

STEVE WAUGH

Our team meeting was pretty brief. We emphasised the need for everyone to dig deep for one last effort and for each player to set himself certain goals and objectives. For the Poms, big Devon Malcolm will be playing a 'do or die' Test, while pace bowler Peter Martin, spinner Phil Tufnell and middle-order batsman Mark Ramprakash will be making their first Test appearance of the summer. Surprisingly, John Crawley has been dropped, only one game after being considered good enough to be elevated from No. 6 to No. 3. Mark Butcher comes back to open the innings on his home turf, a move which shoves Alec Stewart back down the order.

It seems to me that the English selectors have got themselves into a huge tangle. This is probably best exemplified by the dropping or 'resting' of the teenage wonder boy, Ben Hollioake, after only one game. This said, it's always a dangerous thing to pay too much attention to the opposition line-up, instead of getting your own shop in order. Our biggest danger will be our batting, as I'm just sensing that it is a little carefree at the moment – in direct contrast to our bowling, which is looking in great shape.

21 August
Day 1, Sixth Test
England 180 (McGrath 7–76) v Australia 77–2.
You could say that Australia are going to be much weaker in this final game

because of the absences of Paul Reiffel and Jason Gillespie but I don't think it's going to be too big a blow for them. Reiffel's a good bowler but I don't think the Oval was going to be his type of wicket and although Gillespie has bowled quickly and taken wickets most of us have felt pretty comfortable against him. The fact is, they've still got Warne and McGrath and most teams wouldn't need much more than that.

Ath went out for the toss with an old 20p this time – his success rate can't get any worse – and everybody in our team went out on the balcony to see what happened. You always watch to see who Simon Hughes or Tony Lewis goes up to first and when Yosser approached Ath we knew he had finally won one and there was a bit of a cheer before the realisation that now we had to make the most of it.

Ath, indeed, said that himself when he came back and urged us to bat for a day and a half. We thought that, despite its dry appearance, it had to be a normal Oval wicket so we set our sights on 400. None of the other wickets this year have actually looked like Test ones but this, devoid of grass, is more like we're used to. Or so we thought.

Butch was unlucky and Ath got another good one from McGrath before I went out there and, after about 10 minutes, I thought 'this is a lot harder than I expected.' Normally, batting at the Oval is like having an indoor net, your feet don't have to move and it doesn't seam around, but this time I never felt that I was in. The timing just wasn't right. So, after a McGrath over, I went down the wicket and tapped down where he was pitching it. I could see that the ball was disturbing the surface even then.

As usual Taylor read it well and had Shane on within the first hour and straight away he ripped two past Stewie from nowhere. Stewie came down to me and said 'this is going to be fun' and from then on it was very hard work.

I had my luck before lunch and Shaun Young came on for his first bowl in Test cricket. The Aussies, clever as always, realised that if we were going to score off anyone it would be him, so Taylor made him bowl half a yard outside the off stump knowing I would probably go after him. I did and played a couple of shots I was unhappy with but in any game you have to look for scoring opportunities and, with Shane Warne bowling on what we now knew was a turning wicket, the percentages just weren't there, so it had to be Young.

Even so, my shot selection wasn't great, but I came off at lunch thinking I'd done the hardest part and got myself in. By this stage it was now clear that this wasn't a 400 wicket at all and I was thinking more in terms of getting us up to 300. Bumble came up to me at lunch and told me I'd gone after some I shouldn't have done and to get stuck in. He was quite right, so I told myself to stay in my zone and leave those I didn't need to play at.

We lost Stewie soon after lunch and I batted for a while with Thorpey without managing to score many. The ball was reversing a bit now but I felt happy until I got out in an unusual way. McGrath tried to york me and I tried to clip it between midwicket and mid-on but I was caught at mid on. I knew the second innings was going to be hard because the wicket would be a dust bowl by then, so I was really disappointed not to cash in now. More so when we collapsed to 180, about 70 short of what I now felt wouldn't have been a bad score. After Ramps was out I gave him a bit of time to reflect on things and then went over to say bad luck. He said 'Nass, I just need a bit of arse (luck) mate' and I agreed with him. He didn't look nervous before he batted today nor wound up by the situation. He also didn't give the impression that he felt he was having his last chance. He just feels he needs the run of the ball and he'll be fine. I think he's right.

When Matthew Elliott cut the ball past me for four straight away when Australia batted I thought 'oh God, here we go again.' But when Tuffers came on and immediately turned one off the straight to bowl him I raised my eyebrows a bit and thought 'hold on a second, we've got a chance, they've got to bat last on this.' Tuffers struck again in his next over but they were only two down at the close and the feeling was that we'd let them back in the game. Bumble gave us a big kick up the arse for the first time during a Test, basically telling us that our collapses were not acceptable and that they couldn't keep on backing us as the right players for the job if this kept on happening. He was right but I almost said 'that's right Bumble but we're still in the game because it's not a typical Oval wicket' but I was worried it might become a bit of a batsmen v bowlers thing, so I kept my mouth shut. I did, though, say it to Ath in the Oval's communal bath – would you believe the showers weren't working – and emphasised that it was going to be increasingly hard work for batting and he told me that I should have piped up in the dressing room because Bumble wanted feedback.

STEVE WAUGH

The mood of the camp was a little hard to define. It hovered between focused and relaxed as we did our normal pre-match warm-up. For the first time in the series, Mark Taylor called incorrectly and Mike Atherton had no option but to bat on what looked like a wicket made for runs. It did, though, seem to be a pitch that would take quite a bit of turn – it was drier than normal for a first-day wicket. England must have been tempted to play two spinners, but such is Robert Croft's lack of form and worn-down state of mind that he was always a non-starter, even though he was in their original squad.

Complacency and thoughts of going home are our two biggest dangers in this Test (I know this from the experience of previous tours). Predictably, it was McGrath who led the way for us early, swatting aside Atherton like an annoying bee off a soft drink can. This was the seventh time he had claimed the England captain's wicket during the series. Before this, Butcher had perished to an ill-advised stroke – he must have been wishing he hadn't got a recall.

Michael Kasprowicz, meanwhile, was looking a little out of sorts. He bowled too many 'four' balls, which allowed the pressure to be released from a batsman's point of view. Into the frame stepped Shane Warne. His first ball, a vicious, spitting leg break, would have sent shivers through the home team's camp. It was exactly what they didn't want to see.

Due to a combination of Warne's almost 'unscoreable' bowling and McGrath, vice-like grip on proceedings at the other end, England found themselves going nowhere in a hurry. The lunchtime score of 97 for two didn't reflect our control over proceedings and we knew if we continued on the same path in the next session we'd reap the rewards.

Picking up a wicket with the first ball after lunch is a dream start – it offers a chance to dominate from then on. Stewart was the culprit for England, not for the first time he fell to a delivery straight after a break. The next two wickets both fell to well-conceived bowling plans. Hussain was caught at mid-on off a well-pitched-up delivery aimed at his leg stump, having been drawn across his stumps by McGrath to a point where he was overbalancing and ripe for the picking. Thorpe then had his leg stump clipped by a ball delivered from around the wicket. He, too, had been lured across his crease, a classical dismissal from a big quick's point of view.

Ramprakash went meekly, after which Caddick and Martin had a few slogs at Warne before sanity prevailed. In the end, McGrath claimed 7–76 from 21 overs of distinguished quality, while Warne went a little under-rewarded with just two wickets and Kasprowicz claimed the prize scalp of Devon Malcolm, who played the worst 'shot' I have ever seen. As always, Big Dev's bat looks as if it's allergic to his body when he grips it and seems to have a mind of its own. This could be his only explanation for an attempted sweep that crushed into his back leg just below his knee. It was a comical dismissal.

It was now time to put the boot in and make England pay for their undisciplined batting. A lead of anything over 150 should see us not having to strap the pads on again, so a scoreline of 77 for two at the close was a pretty fair effort. Taylor was looking impressively aggressive at the crease before he, like Matthew Elliott, was dismissed by Tufnell. The English spinner is already gaining appreciable turn and bounce out of the bowlers' footmarks.

Tomorrow's play will be vital to us. The wicket is showing signs of being far too friendly to the spinners, and the odd ball from the quicks is bursting through the surface, too. This sort of wicket is extremely hard to score on, as it gives the batsmen no confidence or trust to play their shots with any authority. It's just a shame we haven't got Neil Harvey in the side, as he no doubt would have made light work of the situation.

22 August, Day 2, Sixth Test

England 180 and 52–3 v Australia 220 (Blewett 47, Ponting 40; Tufnell 7–66, Caddick 3–76).

Again the ball turned from the start for the Cat today and, walking through the middle between overs, I could see that the surface was disappearing. I'm beginning to think that this is a similar wicket to the one at Southend in 1989 that cost Essex 25 championship points and it really is a mystery how bad it is. The only saving grace here compared to Southend is that the ball is exploding slowly off the surface rather than quickly. The Surrey boys have all said they've never seen anything like it here and that now they know their groundsman can provide turning wickets they'll ask for them more often in future!

From my Essex experiences I've worked closely with spinners in the field in the past and one of my jobs today was to liaise a lot with Tuffers. I'm not a huge expert on the subtleties of seam and swing but I do like to think I know a bit about spin and there are times when I can see that Tuffers is not putting his body into his action so I take it upon myself to tell him whenever I see it happening. There are other times when he's so keen that he tries too hard and he's the sort of character who likes to be reassured when he's bowling well. Tuffers values your opinion and is always asking if it's turning or how he should bowl to people. Today I told him it was the best I'd ever seen him bowl and I wasn't lying. I just kept on telling him not to change anything and emphasised how beautifully he was bowling.

Mark Waugh had made a comment in the *Daily Mirror* saying he wished Tuffers would be a bit more positive and take him on from round the wicket and there is a bit of history here. Mark and Cat have always had a healthy rivalry – on Mark's Test debut in Adelaide he kept on slog sweeping Cat and got a hundred – and Mark usually takes it on himself to get after Cat because he feels he's only half the bowler when you attack him. This time Mark had trouble getting after him because, for one thing, he hasn't scored many runs this summer and, for another, this was now a raging Bunsen. Cat won the battle this time and the fact that he wanted to go round the wicket, even to Ponting, who I felt was vulnerable from over the wicket, was a sign of how positive Cat was thinking. Tuffers had a dream day but Shane came in and slogged a few to give the Aussies a useful little lead. No batsman has reached 50 yet, so it's going to be tough from now on.

I found myself faced with an awkward little session tonight after Ath and Stewie were out because the light was indifferent and the ball was now turning square. I didn't really know what to do for the best because I got trapped up Shane's end and I just couldn't see any scoring opportunities. Even when he pitched short you couldn't get the cut going because the wicket was also two paced but that wasn't often because Shane basically bowled the best I've seen him all summer and provided me with the toughest examination of my batting that I consider I've ever had. What's worse, as the series has progressed I've realised that a technical problem has returned to my batting. I've become aware that I'm opening up again and getting front on but it's something I've had to live with because there have been so many big games I just haven't had the time and energy to get in the nets and sort it out. It really is wrong to have to try and repair these things out in the middle but at the moment I have no option.

Thorpey felt it was a bit easier for a left hander to slog sweep and he told me just to survive which I did to the close by hanging on in there. Usually I subscribe to the theory that you have to be positive against Warne and find runs from somewhere but on this occasion, with Thorpey playing well at the other end, I just didn't feel it was appropriate and ended up on two not out. It was so tough out there, though, that this could yet prove to be a vital little partnership. We had a team discussion tonight and I said that we need to be positive in the morning and that if we could all chip in with 20 or 30 then it could make all the difference. I also spoke to Ramps and suggested to him that he may be setting his sights too high in thinking that he needed 70 or 80 to get on tour and that 30 or 40 in this situation would be just as valuable to the team and could win us this game.

STEVE WAUGH

This was a day where England fought back admirably. Heading their charge was the 'artful dodger', Phil Tufnell in a display that left many wondering why he'd been sent packing down the motorway in each of the previous five Tests. Having seen England self-destruct yesterday, we should have learnt our lesson. Unfortunately, we mirrored their efforts and in doing so put them well and truly back in the hunt.

During the last four Tests he's umpired us, Peter Willey seems to have developed a liking for raising the finger in my direction. I don't think I've survived an appeal yet, although I have given him plenty of chances to get rid of me. Today's outcome, though, was one I thought might have gone the other way. Scoring 22 is a batsman's nightmare – it means you've done the initial hard work and should be now accustomed to the pace and bounce of the wicket. The job should be a lot easier. In these circumstances, I reckon that on about 90 per cent of occasions a batsman will get himself out, by premeditating a shot, thinking about the previous ball or thinking too far ahead. If you can block these thoughts out and devote all your energies to the next ball, your chances of success are greatly increased.

I think I'm a little more frustrated than normal today at getting out, because it only needed someone to go on to get a big score and the game was as good as over. Greg Blewett's 47 and Ricky Ponting's 40 were well-constructed digs, but not the big one we were looking for, while everyone felt for Shaun Young, who snared the dreaded globe on debut.

A lead of 40 was, in all honesty, no lead at all considering the wicket was deteriorating much quicker than anyone had anticipated (with the exception of Peter Willey, who mentioned to me that this is 'the driest Oval wicket I have ever seen'. Peter has been a Test and first-class cricketer or umpire for the best part of 30 years!

As we're batting last on such a wearing pitch, we don't want to be chasing anything more than 150, so it was with some relief that Kasprowicz picked up two quick wickets. This put the pressure back on England, who are in a precarious position at close, in reality 12 for 3.

The biggest downer for us is the groin strain Shane suffered late in the day, just when the scene had been set for him to run amok. The most important ice bag of the season was immediately applied to our spin-bowling champion when he entered the change rooms. One hopes it's not too serious and he'll be able to bowl to something like the standard we're accustomed to. Tomorrow, the game is there for the taking.

23 August , Day 3, Sixth Test

England 180 and 163 (Thorpe 62, Ramprakash 48; Kasprowicz 7–36) defeated Australia 220 and 104 (Caddick 5–42) by 19 runs.

Ath had a few harsh words with Cammie Smith, the match referee, this morning when we heard that one of Blewett's fours from yesterday has been turned into a six, apparently at the instigation of Ian Healy, after looking at television replays. Ath questioned how that decision could be made a day later while Tuffers was rucking about it because it added two more runs to his bowling analysis! The point from this is, where do you draw the line? How far back can you now go thanks to television replays? It's a dangerous precedent.

Goochie made the point this morning that none of us should give our wicket away and I went out to resume with Thorpey with that intention. I really did. So what happens? In the first over of the day Shane bowled me a short one, a delivery which, three or four overs later, I might easily have cut for four, but it bounced a bit and I came off the shot to try to keep it down, but I came off it far too much and cut it to point. I felt dreadful. As I walked back I thought to myself that that was the worst thing I could possibly have done to end the series. It was the worst shot I've played to get out this summer. And it came after I'd encouraged everyone to sell their wickets dearly last night and Goochie had emphasised the same point this morning. It left a real sour taste in my mouth and I thought 'if we mess up from here and lose this game I'm never going to forgive myself.' Until I get a bat in my hand in the West Indies this winter the memory of that shot will always be with me. I don't think I've given my wicket away too many times in Test matches this summer but that's what I did here, no question.

I didn't throw my gear around when I came in. I just sat there for half an hour, thinking and hoping that the boys would pull it around. Thankfully, Ramps and Thorpey played exceptionally well and Ramps got that bit of arse that he needed to give us a real chance before we went down like a pack of cards again and left them with a small target to win the match. I suppose I was pleased that Kasper got seven wickets because he's a friend, but to be honest I'd have much rather he got none for a hundred. The surprise was that Shane didn't take the wickets but that's what happens when someone is bowling very well at one end. You've got to get your runs from somewhere and the bowler at the other end benefits from it.

When any side has to chase 150, 180 or 200 to win a match they have to play properly but the Aussies knew, chasing 120 odd, that they could chance their arm and still probably get there. We knew we had to strike early but when Elliott flashed one over my head I thought 'come on Dev.' Then next ball Elliott, who has been a good judge of what to leave this year, got one wrong and was lbw. Just what we needed.

Still, at this stage I wasn't thinking that we could win, it was more a case of 'let's take a few of these bastards down with us'. The worst thing that could have happened would have been them getting the runs for two or three wickets so I wanted us to go down with our heads up. But wickets started to fall and when Mark went I thought we might have a chance. Tuffers was always going to do a job but we needed someone to do it at the other end and Andrew Caddick produced the goods.

Caddy ran in and bowled everything in the right area, keeping on hitting the patches that were exploding. When he got Steve Waugh out again the excitement began to grow and the crowd were phenomenal. I've never heard anything like it. They were even louder than Edgbaston and the defining moment of that for me came when Healy first came in and missed a drive at Caddy. Everyone jumped up, the crowd roared and the hairs on the back of my neck stood on end. When Healy finally went I really felt we were in business because both he and Warne were capable of slogging a quick 30 and winning it for them. Warne had a groin injury but had bowled all morning so Ath questioned whether he should be allowed a runner, basically playing mind games and showing Warne that we were fighting.

I knew Warne would swing the bat and he soon hit one extremely high into the air. Butch was at silly point and I was at slip. He looked at me and I looked at him. Neither of us looked at the ball. We just waited for the noise. When the roar went up me and Butch just jumped at each other and then ran towards 'Digger' (Martin), who had taken the catch. That was the key wicket. Tuffers asked me how I would get Kasper out and I said 'well, play for a run out, actually' which didn't really help Tuffers that much! Kasper, the king of the run out, almost did run himself out before Ath had one of his brainwaves to get rid of him. At the end of an over Athers said to me 'I think we'll have a man on the drive, it looks like he might put it there.' I was there for the first ball and then Adam called over to me to swap with him because he felt I would be better where he was. Then, next ball, Kasper hit straight to Adam and I thought 'thank God I wasn't in there, I might have shelled it!'.

Then all we needed to do was get past McGrath for a famous victory. When the moment came it was as if it was in slow motion. The ball was pitched up, McGrath chipped it and it lobbed towards Thorpey, a fielder who, as we've seen this season, generally takes the hard chances but can spill the easier ones. We all held our breath, the little man dived forward and when he caught it we just ran towards him as a team, ripping at his shirt. I gave Ath a hug and, when we got upstairs, the atmosphere was fantastic. Grav was in there as was Lord MacLaurin, who was clearly delighted. He was trying to shake people's hands but as far as we were concerned etiquette went out of the window and it was a case of 'Lord or not mate, you're getting a hug.'

I was also pleased for Theo, who has become so much more than our dressing room attendant. I'm not sure if he was due to be with us all summer or not, but as he was at Edgbaston he had to carry on being with us and he has seen the whole series through. Theo's a teacher by profession, so he can get the time off but he works for us for very little money and has done everything for us that we've asked of him. That included going into the Aussie dressing room and getting all their champagne from them as our celebrations begun. Then came a private moment which I'm not sure should go into the book. I asked for quiet and amazingly I got it so I suddenly felt the pressure on me to make sure I said something worthwhile. I then said that I didn't want to be considered a brown noser but that I didn't care who was in the dressing room and that this had to be said. 'here's to Athers. He's had a lot of stick in the last few weeks and we've won this game for him.'

Then the sponsors came in at the right time to stop me getting too emotional and asked us to go up for the presentations. Ath came up to me and said 'thanks for that. It meant a lot' but I told him that I just felt we owed our leader something after all he'd been through. I still don't know if this is to be Athers last match in charge but if it is it's a hell of a way to bow out.

STEVE WAUGH

We couldn't have hoped for a better start to the day. In the very first over, Hussain played an airy shot to a Warne delivery, only to see it spoon to backward point. From here, though, England fought back well. Thorpe completed the first half-century of the match – further proof of the difficult nature of the wicket and the loss of confidence of batsmen in both sides – and Ramprakash, looking to book a spot on the plane for England's upcoming tour of the West Indies, confirmed his status as the best looking and best-organised cricketer in the county system.

It's quite amazing to think that Ramprakash is averaging only around 17 per innings from 19 Tests, which further underlines that much-heard statement, 'It's a mental game.' One could see he was a little overawed in the first innings, but sometimes such a problem can be solved as simply as by getting one convincing shot through the field. That's exactly what happened this morning. The Middlesex captain punched Warne off the back foot for a couple of fours and visibly grew in stature.

With Warne courageously battling through his groin strain, but still clearly hampered to the point where he was bowling like a human, it was Kasprowicz who put his hand up and said, 'I'm the man you're looking for.' Once Thorpe and Ramprakash went, the rest of the England batting order fell rather meekly again, with Big Dev bagging one of the worst pairs in the history of the game. To his credit, though, he doesn't have any pretensions to be a batsman and always has a swing. This either results in quick runs or a quick dismissal, which at least doesn't hold the game up.

If ever there was a player deserving of success it is Michael Kasprowicz, who has worked hard all tour, even after being dropped when he did nothing wrong. Circumstances at that time worked against him. To see him take 'seven-for' was a tour highlight for me and, more importantly, is the breakthrough he needed to give him the confidence and belief that he really belongs at the highest level. From now on he will go into Test matches with a different attitude and with the self-belief that will enable him to go from strength to strength.

Chasing 124 sounds simple but we knew it wouldn't be quite that easy, particularly if we lost a couple of quick wickets. The key was reaching 50 without the loss of more than one wicket, because if we could have reached that point we felt the Poms would probably start thinking they were out of the match. However, we got off to a poor start, losing Elliott, who ill-advisedly failed to offer a shot to a Malcolm delivery that moved in and trapped him lbw. For a while Taylor and Blewett looked in control, until a fired-up Caddick trapped our captain in front. Mark Waugh quickly succumbed to his arch adversary, Tufnell, for the second time in the match. This was probably not what Mark was thinking when he mentioned before the series started that he didn't really rate 'Tuffers' as a danger. I guess it never pays to make too many statements about this game.

Blewett and I got through to tea. In the dressing-room during the break I lost my cool, giving everyone a bit of a blast because I thought we were heading in the wrong direction, that is towards a loss. I thought by doing so I might ignite a bit more passion, or trigger a more committed approach to knocking off the runs, but looking back, the move definitely backfired on me because I became too fired up to finish the job.

Back at the crease after tea, I wasn't fully in control of my game, and fell victim to a shot of poor selection which gave Caddick my scalp for the sixth time in the series, and gave further impetus to England. It was a catalogue of disasters from here on in, as we chased our target in a scatterbrain fashion, obviously getting too far ahead of ourselves rather than playing the moment. The only remaining batsman to show the spirit and application that was needed to win the game was Shaun Young, who fought hard and played each ball on its merits, even though he remained only 4 not out.

This was a weird match, won in the end by England by 19 runs. It included 10 lbw decisions and a couple of dismissals via balls that 'burst' through the pitch surface. The wicket was basically a disgrace, and again didn't allow Test cricket to be played properly. On such a poor wicket, bowlers can look better than they are and gain inflated results, while batsmen need luck to survive. This creates a situation where the good players don't necessarily influence the game as they would on a good wicket. Bad wickets, because of a lesser need for class and skill, generally bring the quality of the contest down and definitely bring the teams closer together. Having said this, the better team won this Test.

Surely, this time, lessons will be learnt from our point of view. Our record in these so- called 'dead rubber Tests' is atrocious. I, for one, don't believe the theory that 'dead' Tests don't matter as much – just pulling on the baggy green should make it a very 'live' Test.

Losing here takes the edge off our great comeback. To win 4–1 sounds and looks a lot better than 3–2, but a series win is still a great achievement especially away from home. As usual after a series, the teams got together for a drink and a chat in the change rooms, and the jovial and friendly atmosphere was in keeping with a series devoid of any real nastiness and ill-feeling.

Losing four in a row was the last thing we needed before going to the West Indies and whatever anyone says about this win coming after the series was dead, it still means an awful lot. We have stopped the rot. We have beaten Australia and the final score is 3–2, not 4–1. When we got upstairs me and Thorpey started ribbing each other about who was going to get the man of the series award but he had played really well in the last two games while I had faded so he thoroughly deserved it.

I felt particularly pleased for Tuffers, who took 11 wickets in his only match of the series. I know him well and he's desperate to go to the West Indies. He loves it there, that's where he met his wife and really he's a reformed tourist these days. He knew before this match that the left-arm spinner's place was between him and Ashley Giles, who's a better batsman, and he must have known that if he didn't bowl well in this match he probably wouldn't go. There was also talk that Australia had the voodoo on him and liked getting after him and that he doesn't turn it as much as he used to.

People forget how important a winter tour is to a cricketer and his family. One bad spell could have cost Phil Tufnell his place and it's not only the money you miss but you sit there all winter, stewing and thinking to yourself 'why did I play such and such a shot?' or 'why did I bowl like that?' I know. I've done it. Then you watch Sky and wish you were there with the lads and it churns you up inside. Just imagine, for instance, that I needed runs to go the West Indies in the last Test and then I'd played the shot that I did? It would have tortured me all winter.

Then we went into the Australian dressing room which was a fantastic way to end the series. I swapped a jumper with Shane which I was pleased about because it will be a valuable thing to put towards my benefit. I wanted his cap, too, but he wouldn't give it away because it's the first and only one he has ever had which just goes to show how much they value 'the baggy green'. I then made a point of sitting with Mark and Kasper because even though we've played it hard throughout the series they're both friends and we haven't been able to talk informally much throughout the summer.

The Aussies told us they didn't think we were as bad as our press make out and that half our problem as a team was that we believe what the press say about us and that they've played a lot worse teams than us. They also seemed to think we had a good chance in the West Indies as long as our mental approach was okay. They also thought our selections throughout the series were good but that they were happy when we left out Ealham and Crawley, which was interesting. These things are useful to know.

They also told us their batsmen were pissed off with the quality of the wickets and how bad it was that only two batsmen on each side had scored around 400 runs or more, me and Thorpey for us and Steve Waugh and Elliott for them. Warne said again that we may have had our words on the field but let's have a beer now which is exactly what I like to hear and Mark told me that a county, I can't remember which one because I was drunk, had offered Shane £250,000 to play for them next summer. I said 'what, 250,000 dollars?' and he said 'no, pounds'. I also had a good chat to Greg Blewett, not about our 'incident' but about the bats he uses because I liked them a lot. Finally I talked with Steve Waugh, the master craftsman, and asked him what I could do about opening up at the crease. He said the best thing you can do when you're worried about your own game is to walk out to bat as if you're ten feet tall, stand up straight and look completely confident because bowlers love to see a batsman looking nervous. He said 'just walk out there as if you haven't got a care in the world and that you're the best player in the world and bowlers will shrink. You can then make up for any loss of form or technical problem.' I'll remember that. You have to, of course, be a quality player, which Steve Waugh is, but you can add all these things to your game to make you a better one. It's like sitting down at school and copying someone's essay. We have to sit down and unashamedly copy Australia because everything they do seems to work.

I know there will be people reading this disagreeing and saying it's nothing to do with mental toughness and that they are simply better players than us but if anyone tells me that Steve Waugh is technically correct then they're watching a different game to me. Steve Waugh is one of the most technically incorrect Test players I've seen. Nine times out of ten when he's facing a length ball outside off stump his weight's back, he's on the back foot and he just throws his hands and bat at it. You stand there at slip thinking that he must nick it soon but he doesn't and that's as much to do with his inner belief as his superb hand eye co-ordination.

By now the beer and champagne was getting to me so I said goodbye to the Aussie guys and remembered that all summer I had meant to get some bats signed by them for various beneficiaries and charities who had asked me to and I still hadn't done it. Apparently the Aussies are doing a major bat signing at their hotel on Tuesday so Theo has volunteered to stay down until then and get them done for me.

Then followed a long night of drinking and more drinking. First we went back to the hotel and Medha Laud, the ECB's England administrator, offered to buy a round of drinks on behalf of the ECB. We all cheered and piled in and poor Medha turned white when she saw the bill. She later told Karen that it totalled £500!

Meanwhile, we were punching the air that Lord's had bought us all a drink. After that we went to a club in London called the Café de Paris and Athers was the only one they recognised so he had to vouch for us all before they would let us in. Athers got as paralytic as the rest of us but offered no hints as to whether he's going to pack it in. Time will tell. Later on the Aussies joined us and I got back to my spinning hotel room about 4am.

21

CARRY ON
CAPTAIN

NASSER HUSSAIN

You tend to make goals for yourself as a player and at the start of the summer I'd set myself the target of, firstly, playing in all six Tests and then, having heard that we were going to play on some sporty wickets, a further target of two hundreds in the series and an average of 40. I failed by five runs, averaging 39.8, so I was pretty happy with that.

A series result of 3-2? Well, I thought that if we stayed with them we could have nipped the series but we went badly wrong in the middle three Tests. When we won the one-dayers and the first Test we had a real chance but they came back really strongly which shows how good they are. There was no internal niggling on their part. They just sat down and said 'we've got to do something about this' and turned it around. To be truthful, I don't think we deserved to win the Ashes and I don't think we were good enough to. That's not being negative, simply realistic, but what was disappointing was that this was probably our best chance of beating them since the successful Gatting tour and we didn't take it

We had our chances, as Athers has said and as we all agree, but we weren't good enough to take them whereas the Aussies are so good they can afford to miss the odd chance and Warne and McGrath will win them more Tests than they lose. How good were these Aussies? A lot of people have said that they're right up there with the all-time best touring teams and, as a team, that's probably right even though I think there have been a few better individual performances from Australians in recent times.

This team were such a unit and reacted so well to pressure that there was always someone to get them out of trouble and McGrath and Warne were a classic partnership everywhere but Edgbaston. You would have to question where even the greatest players would have scored their runs against Warne. I've agreed with an awful lot that Ian Chappell has said this summer but even he was saying at the Oval that we had to get down the wicket to Warne and I can't go along with that. When the ball is turning that much it's a high risk policy to use your feet against him, so you have to try to score runs at the other end and that's how McGrath and Kasprowicz were able to get seven wickets each at the Oval.

As for me, well, I read in a few papers towards the end of the series that I had become a nought or hundred man but if it's not that then you're a Thorpey who got stick for scoring lots of fifties but not many hundreds until the last year or so. Basically, you can't win.

I've always said to myself that whether you're playing for England, Essex or Ilford, you can easily get a good one early on and get out cheaply. That happens in cricket. But if you get a start you should cash in, so if I go through my career scoring a century every five Tests but very little in between I'll be pretty satisfied. Yes, of course there's a lot for me to work on and I'm not saying everything in my batting garden is rosy but I prefer it this way rather than keep getting out in the thirties and forties.

My only real personal disappointment was to get out to such a poor shot at the Oval in a crucial situation but to average almost forty on those sort of tracks against that sort of attack is pretty pleasing. After Headingley, where I got a hundred, I scored runs in the NatWest quarter-final and then another hundred in the championship at Colchester so everything seemed rosy, but I was playing so much that a fault had crept in and now I find myself with the problem of knowing I'm opening up too much on the back foot, especially to balls leaving me, but without the time or energy to rectify it at the moment. We really do need more time between Tests to work at things in the nets but hopefully with Lord MacLaurin in charge that will come. It's simply a need for more time for self-analysis.

I've booked some dates with Goochie in November to have a look at it and I think Ath is coming along at the same time to work on things he's not pleased about in his own game. I'm sure the West Indies will have watched us this year and seen any little defect that any of us have shown so we must work at it until we correct it.

People have also pointed out that I was dismissed six times in the series by Shane Warne but it's not something I'm ashamed of or particularly worried about. If you bat at four you're going to face a lot of Warne and two of the six times he got me out was after I'd got hundreds so I'm not too dismayed about them. The four other dismissals indicate an even battle to me, certainly against someone of his class, and the only times I was really disappointed with myself was that shot at the Oval and when he got me caught and bowled for a duck at Lord's when I let my concentration slip when the match was dead.

The bloke's a genius, no question, and I just can't imagine there has ever been a better spinner than him simply because he is so accurate yet bowls so many wicket-taking balls. Accuracy and penetration is just about the perfect double I'd say. Even Waqar Younis and Wasim Akram bowl some four balls, but Shane rarely does. Probably the best answer to Shane is to play him how Geoff Boycott recommends – from the other end!

The other momentous news since the end of the series has been the decision of Ath to carry on as captain in the West Indies, a decision I'm absolutely delighted about. We all know he came close to packing it in. He told me about that at Trent

Bridge and he seemed pretty adamant that he was going to go, but what perhaps he didn't realise was just how much support he had. All the selectors and management told him he was the right man for the job and he knew he had the support of each and every player. Maybe our victory at the Oval said to him that if we can play as well as this at times why can't we do it all the time and that must have helped his decision too.

So the fact that everyone supported him would have told him that him staying would help the England team and the only question in his mind he had to answer then was if going would have helped his batting. But he's now got four months to work at that, ample time to get back to his formidable best.

I think the argument being put around that there were no other viable candidates for the job was wrong because I'm confident either myself or Stewie could have done an excellent job but Athers has my full support and always has done. He knows that. I went to Chelmsford for our game against Warwickshire and before we went on to the field on the day of Athers announcement Goochie came up to me and said 'Athers is carrying on ' and I just said 'excellent.' There was no disappointment on my part as a candidate to replace him and I'm sure Stewie feels the same. It annoys me when people make a rivalry thing out of it. Boycott wrote in the *Sun* that, like Mandy Rice Davies, we would say that we wanted Ath to carry on but we mean it.

Everyone has asked me about the captaincy but it's not a huge ambition for me. It's how you do as a player in the team that counts more. I don't understand the John Stephenson-type mentality that insists you have to be a captain to fulfill yourself. If it comes your way and people think you've got a good cricket brain, then fine, but you don't play for England just to try to become captain one day. I haven't seen Ath yet since he made his announcement but I'm going on his benefit trip to champagne at the end of September so we'll talk then and raise a few glasses.

It's also been suggested to me that I would have a better chance of captaining England when Ath eventually does call it a day if I was the Essex captain but I would never put myself forward for that job just to somehow further my own international ambitions. That's not right. I haven't got a plan. If and when Essex and Prich feel the time is right for him to step down then, as his vice-captain, I would be very keen to do the job even if it means having a full season with England at the same time but, even in these days of enlightened England selectors and real continuity, my only real target is to still be in the England side in 18 months time. If I can come through five Tests in the West Indies, five against South Africa and an Ashes tour of Australia and still have my place then I would have had a pretty good time.

I have to confess I would have been disappointed if Ath had resigned and I hadn't got it because I think I can do it. All this stuff about me still having a short fuse and being too temperamental is unfair, I think. Even if I am temperamental, I would consider that a plus in a captain because the best ones I've played under have been temperamental. They give you a rollicking when needs be and they lose their temper at times because they care and there's nothing worse than a captain who's ambivalent to everything because you wonder if he really cares.

Obviously you've got to channel that passion and I think I do channel it a lot better than I did in my younger days. My captaincy of the A tour to Pakistan in 1995 speaks for itself and I do believe that if I carry on playing well for England there's no reason why I shouldn't be captain one day. The challenge before then is to work on my batting to try to make sure I remain as an England player. That's all I really want. I hope to be vice-captain this winter and I don't see why I shouldn't be. If that's the case I'll help Ath in any way I can to try to make us a winning side more consistently. We're just too up and down at the moment. When we're good we're very good but when we're bad we're dreadful.

It certainly won't help us this winter for the press to create this imaginary battle between me, Stewie and Adam to see who will eventually replace Ath. It's just not an issue and we've got to be a unit like Australia.

One off field disappointment has been the way the fifth of my six *Daily Mail* interviews this summer was received by some. Some people, intelligent people, have taken the quotes out of all context. They include well respected writers too. I was talking about the need to be mentally tougher, I wasn't condoning sledging and I wasn't advocating nasty behaviour. I also certainly wasn't criticizing my captain nor my team-mates. I was making the general point that our whole game had to be tougher and that included all of us. One of the toughest people I've ever played with is Graham Gooch and, with the exception of one incident when he had a go at Leicestershire's Paul Nixon, I can't ever remember him getting involved in sledging. Yet you could see in his eyes how tough he was and how much he relished the battle against the world's best bowlers. That's mental toughness.

Having said that, a lot of people also backed up what I was saying and I was reassured to see Ath saying basically the same thing in the *Sunday Telegraph*. I read his article and thought 'that's exactly what I meant. Why can't the great Swanton and Woodcock see that? Why couldn't they see what I was saying in the *Mail* and, even if I was condoning sledging, why would that make me a bad captain?' The truth is I have an open mind on sledging. Each player has to decide what's best for him. If I'm on the receiving end I relish it and if I offer anything back it's usually banter – like making a joke about Shane Warne wanting to get off and have his lunch when it was approaching lunchtime – the sort of stuff, in fact, that a lot of former players use in after dinner speeches when telling stories about the legends of the game. A lot of the 'sledging' we indulge in now seems no worse to me thana lot of the banter that went on between players in the past. What was ironic was that I was completely happy with the article when it was faxed to me for approval and I didn't dream what sort of response it would get. The one that I was worried about – when my comments on Shane were embroidered – caused no hassle at all!

22
LORDING IT

NASSER HUSSAIN

A recurrence of my tennis elbow injury was not exactly what the doctor ordered in the build-up to the NatWest Trophy final against Warwickshire. It hasn't cleared up as I'd hoped and, if anything, it has got worse as the season has progressed, so the short-term solution was to nurse it before the big day at Lord's.

That meant deciding whether to miss our championship match against Lancashire at Old Trafford or, as I had not been hitting the ball well, playing and trying to get into form before the final. As ever, with a cricketing decision to make, I asked Fletch for his advice and he said the best thing was to rest and turn up refreshed at Lord's. So I missed the game, thankfully the boys won at Old Trafford so I didn't feel too guilty about letting them down, and I went on the bowling machine at my dad's cricket school. After about 30 minutes, however, the elbow said 'that's enough', so it wasn't really a worthwhile exercise and now I've got to decide, at the end of the season, whether to have a third cortisone injection and rest it again or have a small operation before we go to the West Indies. For the moment, that can wait.

The week before the final, of course, was like no other week anybody of my generation can remember. The death of Princess Diana meant that the game, which would have clashed with her funeral, was postponed a day until Sunday and the aftermath of her accident meant that a cricket match was the last thing on all our minds.

Karen and I were, like everybody, very upset about it, so we travelled down to London early on the Friday before the game, booked into the Hilton opposite Lord's and went down to Kensington Palace to place some flowers and pay our respects. Our visit happened to coincide with an appearance by the Royal Family and before we knew it they were right in front of us, talking to people and accepting well-wisher's messages. And what had I done? Left my mobile phone turned on, that's what. And what should happen as the Royals passed us? I got a phone call from Prich asking me to bring a football to the hotel so that the lads could have a kickabout at Regent's Park on Saturday afternoon. I said, 'This isn't the moment, Prich,' and hurriedly switched my phone off, acutely conscious of lots of eyes fixed on this idiot talking into his mobile phone!

The lads arrived by coach from Manchester quite early and I spent Friday night having a lovely curry around the corner from Lord's with Fletch, 'Larry' (Paul Grayson), 'Suchy' (Peter Such) and our wives. Once again, it did not feel like a big match was around the corner at all.

Saturday was a very difficult day. Most of our team and the Warwickshire boys watched the funeral on the big screens in the hotel lobby after breakfast – everybody was there for the showpiece of the domestic cricket season but there was a totally subdued atmosphere – and then we all went outside when the funeral procession passed the hotel.

Only after that did we try to think about the game, but Lord's was closed for the day so the only place we could try to practice or loosen up was at Regent's Park. The football match between us all was soon abandoned by referee Fletch when the tackles started getting too fierce and our official then conducted the bizarre scene of supervising a fitness test for Ronnie on one of the paths in the park. Obviously there were lots of people in London for the funeral and there they all were, milling around the park, while Ronnie, who had torn side muscles in the semi-final, bowled to Fletch, complete with baseball mit, on a path.

For the first few balls Ronnie just seemed to go through the motions and, so soon after an injury of this sort, I thought 'he'll never be able to bowl tomorrow.' But you can never underestimate Ronnie Irani. He had, after all, travelled to Munich three times to gain treatment from the specialist who got Jurgen Klinsmann fit in record time for the European Championship football final last year and had had something like 30 homeopathic injections in his side to try to be able to bowl for us in the final. It was a huge effort and, as Ronnie continued to bowl in front of the bemused foreigners in Regent's Park, the chances of him taking a full all-round role in the final increased.

The decision that faced us, however, when we met early on Saturday evening to talk about Ronnie, was a difficult one. He was always going to play as a batsman but, if he couldn't bowl, the whole balance of our side would have been affected. Darren Cousins and 17-year-old Graham Napier were standing by and we were thinking of bringing one of them in for Danny Law to give us more bowling depth if Ronnie couldn't do it. At the meeting Ronnie said 'I'll be okay. I can bowl.' But he is a character who will always back himself so you have to be careful with him. I had to say to him 'Ron, I've seen you in big games. You can get cramped up, your eyes go and you give 150,000 per cent. Are you sure you're okay?' Jim, our physio, backed Ronnie to get through eight overs, so we thought we could probably find the others from somewhere and decided to take the risk. It was a good decision.

Saturday night was spent in the company of Paul Grayson's brother, Simon, who plays football for Aston Villa and often comes to watch us play. We went for a meal with him and his wife at Football Football, the themed restaurant in the Haymarket, for an evening that turned into a sort of football groupies session with the fans among us asking Simon things like 'what's Ian Wright like?' and winding him up about leaving Leicester just for the money! He invited us all to watch Villa play West Ham and, after I, as a Leeds fan, told him that it was sure to be a relegation battle, we returned back to the hotel for an early night.

We decided against an official team dinner but our approach was very different to Warwickshire, who not only had a full team dinner but were decked out the following morning in their identical Cup final suits while there were 15 of us in 15 different outfits! There's a lot to be said for their approach. I suppose it must be the Dermot Reeve influence, but Warwicks have pioneered their own brand of team spirit and, while others, like Leicestershire with their huddles, have tried to copy it, Warwicks are still the masters of it. Whether it would work for us or not I don't know, because Essex have always successfully followed the Fletch method of everyone doing their job quietly and knowing when and when not to relax and when and when not to put their work in. It comes down to what's best for each individual but there's no doubt Warwickshire have turned some good cricketers into exceptional ones with their innovative ways.

We awoke on Cup final morning to be greeted by clouds and a forecast for brighter weather in the afternoon so there was never any doubt that we were going to bowl first if Prich won the toss. The lads walked over to the ground, as they had come down by coach, but I had my car with me so I drove into Lord's to be met, to my pleasant surprise, by a helpful steward who let me park near to the pavilion so that I could unload my gear.

I was the first to arrive along with Goochie, who was with us for the day and who had a chat with me about selection for the West Indies. The biggest topic of debate was whether we needed to take an all-rounder or an extra batsman and I was pleased Goochie had asked for my opinions on that and other matters.

We knew we were the firm underdogs. We hadn't played well for a couple of months and we knew that we would need to be at our very best and for luck to go our way for us to beat them. Also, Warwickshire had just thrashed us in both the championship and Sunday league. Supporting Essex must be a nightmare. If people think England are inconsistent they should watch us regularly. I never know what planet we're going to be on from day to day so there was always the danger that, even if we won the toss and bowled in helpful conditions, we would be on the wrong planet at the wrong time.

The atmosphere, meanwhile, was still subdued. Normally there is a buzz around Lord's on Cup final day and the crowd are mingling around from an early stage, but not this year. Prich won the toss and got the usual comments about it being the best thing he's done all season and the bowlers hearts missed a beat because they knew their time had come and that everything was in their favour. We all lined up for a minute's silence for the Princess of Wales – Ronnie was so busy getting strapped up and taking pain-killing tablets and injections that he missed it – before we had to try to get our minds on the job in hand.

The first couple of overs were always going to be crucial. It was weird seeing

'Knighty' (Nick Knight) opening for them as he was part of our set-up for so long. If he had got them off to a flier while our minds were elsewhere the whole picture could have changed. Suddenly our bowlers would have thought that it was not such a helpful wicket after all and heads could have gone down. As it was Ashley, who hasn't got a nerve in his body, trapped Knighty third ball and we were on our way. The crowd began to get a bit louder and it hit me that we were in a final. Meanwhile, Ashley and Ramble were bowling like a dream and the wicket did an incredible amount. Our boys kept on going past the bat time and again but their batsmen were hanging on in there and making it difficult for us.

David Hemp was just starting to play well when he was run out by dead eye Dick, Larry, and everything went our way. Dermot's policy with Warwicks was always to go after the spinner but his disciples couldn't go after Suchy because he bowled so well and took a tremendous return catch along the way. Danny Law, meanwhile, did a bit of a juggling act on the boundary but snuffled two catches and we bowled and fielded at the top of our game to restrict them to 170.

A lot of teams, though, wouldn't have even got that many on that pitch so we didn't think it was going to be easy for us. There was also, of course, the small matter of thinking back to last year during the interval between innings. In similar circumstances we had won the toss against Lancashire and kept them down to a small score, too, but then we found ourselves unable to do anything with their bowling and were dismissed for just 57. As Alan Lilley might say, this could easily have been deja vu all over again!

Something has to be done at Lord's. The wickets just seem never to be flat there anymore. It's blatantly stupid to have the showpiece 60-over final in September but the problem these days has been exacerbated by the wickets. I'm not sure that the groundsman knows what they are going to do, let alone the players, and last year's events were clearly on our minds, whatever we may have said to the contrary, going into the final.

Before we batted, however, there were performances for us to savour. Goochie had told me that morning that it was 50–50 whether Ashley would go to the West Indies and it must have been 90–10 in his favour after he took three wickets for 29 in a final. Ronnie, meanwhile, had bowled all 12 of his overs for just 22, a tremendous effort and one that is typical of the man's determination to give everything for his team's cause. Remember, also, that Ronnie and Stuart Law had been reprimanded and warned as to their future conduct a week or so before the final by Essex at the insistence of Lord's for aggressive behaviour in the cup semi-final. It could easily have had an adverse effect on Ronnie but he was back and forth to Munich and was willing to be held together by tape just to get through his bowling allocation for Essex. Fantastic.

We knew we had to be positive. Prich had said to me, after Ash had gone past Dominic Ostler's edge for the umpteenth time during their innings, that he was going to throw the kitchen sink at anything wide and I agreed that it was the best policy. We could have dug in like last year but then you can get a nick and your day's over with no reward for the graft. Attack had to be the best bet.

And attack Prich and Stuart did. We had planned to clap in the dressing room when we got past 57 but it flew by so quickly that we all missed it as Prich and Stuey rattled along. Ramble and Ronnie had insisted that none of us move from where we were in the dressing room while those two were going so well and so we stayed still watching our openers take us to the verge of victory on a wicket that was still hazardous against one of the best one-day bowling attacks in the country. Even Allan Donald was carted everywhere and, while everyone rightly talks about Stuey's influence, you have to give credit to Prich, who batted outstandingly well.

For me it was a case of after the Lord Mayor's show again. I don't usually say anything to the dismissed batsman on my way out but I had to say 'well played' to Prich as we passed each other in front of the pavilion. Really, he had taken all the pressure off us. When I met Stuey he told me they had been counting the target down in tens and that I should just take it easy. But his tens were coming in single overs and between overs he would say to me 'come on, head down, take it easy' before running down the wicket himself and charging Allan Donald! At one point I told Stuey that I would have to tape what he says between overs and play it back to him after he's hit a world class fast bowler back over his head.

He didn't have all the fun, though. I managed to hit a few boundaries and a pulled six off Graeme Welch – I went down the wicket and smiled a sort of 'I can hit boundaries too' smile at Stuey after that one – and the match was effectively over by tea. The lads just told us to see it through at tea and it was a question of not throwing our wickets away before we had won. The target quickly came down to four needed and they brought Trevor Penney on for the last rites. I knew Stuey would hit a four so I prepared to grab a stump out of the ground but when he hit Penney towards the boundary we weren't sure whether the ball would cross the rope so I thought 'Sod it, I've got to run.' Then, when it trickled over the rope, I found myself in the middle of the pitch not knowing which way to turn to get my stump. Keith Piper grabbed them all at his end and Stuey passed me to grab them at the other end so I found myself without one. Next year I'll have to find a stump from somewhere and pretend it's a NatWest Final one!

The Essex supporters were brilliant. I thought someone might try to nick my helmet as I ran off but everybody just patted us on the back before making a great noise in front of the pavilion. When I got back to the dressing room I hugged Fletch and Goochie – it means a lot to them too – and started celebrating. It must have been odd for Goochie. It was the first trophy Essex had ever won without him and if he hadn't retired unselfishly when he did he could easily have been playing in this one. I don't know what was going on in his head but he didn't look sad, just delighted for us. Everyone made sure they shook his hand and had a glass of champagne with him in the dressing room and I said simply 'thanks for everything' and went and sat with him for a while.

It was a great feeling. There has been something burning inside all of us this year telling us we had to get back to Lord's to make up for last year and show people that we're better than that. I'm sure last year you would have got long odds on us getting back to the NatWest final again 12 months later and winning it so convincingly. We were humiliated by Lancashire and people will talk about that final for years. The England boys took the piss out of me over it all last winter and me and Ronnie used to sit in Harare and Bulawayo, when he was really down about not being in the England side, talking about his need to win something with Essex if he was going to miss out on international cricket. He's done it now.

I was also delighted for our supporters. I think as a player you can sometimes forget how much it means to people and I'm sure when we slipped down both tables during the season our members would have been saying 'here we go again.' On days like this the team and the supporters come before any personal ambitions you have and players like Darren Robinson and Paul Grayson, who neither batted nor bowled in the final, were just as pleased afterwards as the likes of Cowan, Prichard and Law.

This is our first trophy for five years and my first as a senior player. I was part of the championship winning sides of 1991 and 1992 but I've grown up with this side. We are far from the finished article and need to be as rounded as the team of the eighties and early nineties if we are going to consistently win things, but winning trophies can easily become a habit and it is one I hope we get fixed on.

We all got wrecked in the dressing room and then went into town with our partners. The Sports Café, our first choice, had finished serving food so we went back to Football Football and had a quiet meal. There was no need for any massive celebrations. We can savour this all winter. The following morning we had the task of salvaging our kit from the dressing room – Darren Cousins had covered it all with all sorts of weird and wonderful things, like salmon and sugar – and had a good laugh on the coach back up to Old Trafford for the 'Sunday' league game the next day.

EPILOGUE
A SUMMER TO REMEMBER

STEVE WAUGH

It was with a feeling of acute disappointment and a nasty headache that I awoke the morning after our unbelievable capitulation in the final Test. Although there was no use dwelling on the events of that fateful third day, it is vitally important we learn from them, so that if we are faced with a similar situation in the future we can handle it in a better fashion.

The final days of the tour were very much a winding-down period, for we had been on the road for 26 of the last 29 weeks following back-to-back tours of South Africa and the UK. There were lazy afternoons in beer gardens, a team sponsor's cruise down the Thames one night, a huge team signing session that everyone in London must have heard about, judging by the amount of items stretched out in the manager's room and halfway down the corridor. In between, I had media interviews to do – mostly as a summary of the tour and how things went for myself and the team.

As a team, I thought we came back superbly after the first Test loss and the 3–0 drubbing in the one-dayers. After these setbacks we never really 'lost' a day's cricket until the final day of the tour, which in my opinion showed a lot of character and will to win. My tour was one where, along with most batsmen, I didn't really feel as if I got into the series. This was due to some excellent bowling, but also many poorly-prepared wickets, which tested everyone's confidence to the maximum. I was however, very pleased to score hundreds in each innings of the crucial Manchester Test – that will always be a fond memory for me.

We managed to pull the creams out for one last day, a six-a-side corporate tournament in London on 27 August, the day before we left England. And half a dozen of us even squeezed in an appearance at the Ian Botham Leukemia Appeal-sponsored corporate day at The Oval on the day of our departure. Then, finally, we headed for Heathrow, for the first leg of our long trek home.

Home!! A place we all couldn't wait to see.

NASSER HUSSAIN

The day of our 40-over match against Lancashire was, of course, when the England parties were announced for the forthcoming winter tour to West Indies. We heard the announcement on the coach which was just about to drive us to Old Trafford from our hotel outside Manchester. I thought Ashley Cowan would get a call from Goochie or someone telling him he was in before the announcement but when he didn't I began to wonder if he would be there. He did, actually, get a call about 10am and when his mobile rang his eyes lit up, but when he answered it was Cousins pissing about – the last thing you need on England selection day!

The first thing I listened out for when the radio broadcast the teams was the vice-captaincy and when I heard I'd retained that I was delighted. Then when Ashley's name was read out there was a big cheer on the coach and everybody piled on top of him, causing so much noise we didn't hear the other names at all. Somebody shouted out Fraser before we quietened down for the A tour party. Paul Grayson was a bit down he didn't get on that – Goochie told me that if he'd been an off-spinner rather than a slow left-armer he would have had a good chance – and Ronnie took his disappointment quietly. It's a difficult situation. I have been in a position both where I have been picked and have had to say bad luck to others and when I have been overlooked and got sympathy myself. You don't know what to say to the ones who have missed out but they are always genuinely pleased for the ones who make it.

All of us, without exception, missed the announcement that Jonathan Powell, our young off-spinner, was on the A tour. About an hour after they were read out we noticed there was a Powell there and I rang my brother, Mel, to ask him if it was the Warwickshire Powell or Glamorgan one. When he told me it was ours we were all delighted and rang him to find him struggling to take it all in after a night out clubbing. He had been hoping for an Under-19 tour, but had got the shock of his life. I'm sure a lot of off-spinners around the country will be asking what Jonathan has done to deserve this chance but I can tell them he's a player of some potential who I think may turn out to be a batsman who bowls off-spin rather than the other way around and a genuinely nice lad.

I'm sure Ronnie will come again. I've already sat down and talked to him about dropping out of the picture completely and I will do the same with Ashley about what he has now got to achieve. I told Ronnie that if he makes an England recall his be all and end all then, like I have done in the past, it will only make him more tense and will reduce his chances of gaining it. He mustn't be bitter and twisted about it, just put it to the back of his mind and concentrate on his cricket. I've also suggested to him that he goes back to the dominant batting style that was so effective for him last year rather than the more careful approach he adopted this season. It's up to him.

There were no real surprises in the main party. I don't think anyone will question Angus Fraser's presence because you know he'll do a solid job and help all the bowlers. The toughest decision must have been to leave out someone like Mark Ealham or Dominic Cork and go with an extra batsman but it would have been really harsh on Butch, Creepy or Ramps if any of them had missed out. Even so, I think I would have liked to see another all-rounder there to improve our balance.

Of course I'm a bit disappointed to miss out on the one-day trip to Sharjah but I think the trend towards different Test and one-day sides is the correct one. I've not played well on Sundays this year because, to be honest, I've found it hard to get up for the Sunday league during an Ashes summer but my record in the cup and trophy is good and I think my fielding can save us 20 runs a game. But, having said that, I could do with the extra time before we go to the West Indies to have a small operation and sort out my elbow and work on the technical fault that has crept in my game, so I'm not too despondent and I haven't given up hope yet of playing in the next World Cup. I had a chat about one-day cricket to Grav earlier in the season and I told him that I really want to be considered for that part of the game – even if I only make the World Cup squad as a substitute fielder!

Some people have said it's strange that I should be vice-captain in the West Indies and Adam be in charge of the one-day party. To me, there's nothing odd about it. It was predictable that within seconds of the parties being announced Grav was being asked about captaincy but I don't believe in this rivalry thing at all. We both have our jobs to do in support of Ath this winter.

We have a good chance of doing well in the West Indies. We must put large scores on the board and put them under pressure but it won't be easy out there. People say Walsh and Ambrose are tired and over the hill but that's nonsense. Everyone raises their game against England and, slower wickets out there these days or not, there'll be plenty of chin music for us to deal with. The challenge is a never ending one. I've now been selected for four senior tours and three of them have been to the West Indies – surely some kind of record. I just hope this time I play some Test cricket out there!

This has been the most amazing few months of my life. There have been no quiet times at all since coming back from tour. I got a lot of press after my 200, then we got out for 70 odd at Lord's, then there was the business of the Blewett catch at Old Trafford, then Goochie says to me 'don't tell anyone but I'm retiring,' then I score a hundred at Headingley, then I drop three catches but go on to be Man of the Match in a NatWest quarter-final, then Athers says to me 'don't tell anyone but I'm thinking of packing it all in,' and now we've lost the Ashes but I've been part of a side that has won the NatWest Trophy. It's one of those summers when everything has happened and I've gone from being someone who is just recognised by cricket people to being someone who is recognised wherever I go. I'm not complaining. I wouldn't have it any other way, but it's been a phenomenal summer.

STATISTICS

Nasser Hussain

First Test Edgbaston

	Score	Balls	Mins	4s	6s	Rate per 100 balls	Ct
1st Inns	207	337	440	38	–	61.14	1
2nd Inns	21	37	50	2	–	56.75	–
Series to Date	394	738	1003	62	–	53.38	6

Test Record

	Mat	Inns	NO	Runs	HS	Avge	100	50	Ct
v Australia	5	9	2	391	207	55.85	1	1	4
Overall	18	30	3	1167	207	43.22	4	3	17

Second Test Lord's

	Score	Balls	Mins	4s	6s	Rate per 100 balls	Ct
1st Inns	19	73	110	2	–	26.02	2
2nd Inns	0	5	4	–	–	–	–
Series to Date	226	415	554	40	–	54.45	4

Test Record

	Mat	Inns	NO	Runs	HS	Avge	100	50	Ct
v Australia	6	11	2	410	207	45.55	1	1	6
Overall	19	32	3	1187	207	40.89	4	3	19

Third Test Old Trafford

	Score	Balls	Mins	4s	6s	Rate per 100 balls	Ct
1st Inns	13	29	46	2	–	44.82	–
2nd Inns	1	14	15	–	–	7.14	1
Series to Date	240	458	615	42	–	52.40	5

Test Record

	Mat	Inns	NO	Runs	HS	Avge	100	50	Ct
v Australia	7	13	2	424	207	38.54	1	1	7
Overall	20	34	3	1200	207	38.70	4	3	20

Fourth Test Headingley

	Score	Balls	Mins	4s	6s	Rate per 100 balls	Ct
1st Inns	26	40	58	4	–	65.00	–
2nd Inns	105	181	253	14	–	58.01	–
Series to Date	371	679	926	60	–	54.63	5

Test Record

	Mat	Inns	NO	Runs	HS	Avge	100	50	Ct
v Australia	8	15	2	555	207	42.69	2	1	7
Overall	21	36	3	1331	207	40.33	5	3	20

Fifth Test Trent Bridge

	Score	Balls	Mins	4s	6s	Rate per 100 balls	Ct
1st Inns	2	22	27	–	–	9.09	1
2nd Inns	21	37	50	2	–	56.75	–
Series to Date	394	738	1003	62	–	53.38	6

Test Record

	Mat	Inns	NO	Runs	HS	Avge	100	50	Ct
v Australia	9	17	2	578	207	38.53	2	1	8
Overall	22	38	3	1354	207	38.68	5	3	21

Sixth Test The Oval

	Score	Balls	Mins	4s	6s	Rate per 100 balls	Ct
Ist Inns	35	114	139	4	–	30.70	1
2nd Inns	2	50	62	–	–	4.00	1
Series to Date	431	902	1204	66	–	47.78	8

Test Record

	Mat	Inns	NO	Runs	HS	Avge	100	50	Ct
v Australia–1997	6	11	0	431	207	39.18	2	–	8
v Australia–Overall	10	19	2	615	207	36.17	2	1	10
All Tests	23	40	3	1391	207	37.59	5	3	23

Results Summary   P23   W7   D8   L8

Stephen Rodger Waugh

First Test Edgbaston

	Score	Balls	Mins	4s	6s	Rate per 100 balls	Ct
1st Inns	12	20	31	3	–	60.00	–
2nd Inns	33	101	137	2		32.67	–

Test Record

	Mat	Inns	NO	Runs	HS	Avge	100	50	Ct
v England	27	42	12	1731	177 *	57.70	3	9	21
Overall	90	140	28	5615	200	50.13	12	33	66

Second Test Lord's

	Score	Balls	Mins	4s	6s	Rate per 100 balls	Ct
1st Inns	0	1	3	–	–	–	–
2nd Inns	–	–	–	–	–	–	
Series to Date	45	122	171	5	–	36.88	–

Test Record

	Mat	Inns	NO	Runs	HS	Avge	100	50	Ct
v England	28	43	12	1731	177 *	55.83	3	9	21
Overall	91	141	28	5615	200	46.69	12	33	66

Third Test Old Trafford

	Score	Balls	Mins	4s	6s	Rate per 100 balls	Ct
1st Inns	108	175	240	13	–	61.71	1
2nd Inns	116	271	382	10	–	42.80	–
Series to Date	269	568	793	28	–	47.35	1

Test Record

	Mat	Inns	NO	Runs	HS	Avge	100	50	Ct
v England	29	45	12	1955	177 *	59.24	5	9	22
Overall	92	143	28	5839	200	50.77	14	33	67

Fourth Test Headingley

	Score	Balls	Mins	4s	6s	Rate per 100 balls	Ct
1st Inns	4	12	15	–	–	33.33	1
2nd Inns	–	–	–	–	–	–	–
Series to Date	273	580	808	28	–	46.42	2

Test Record

	Mat	Inns	NO	Runs	HS	Avge	100	50	Ct
v England	30	46	12	1959	177 *	57.61	5	9	23
Overall	93	144	28	5843	200	50.37	14	33	68

Fifth Test Trent Bridge

	Score	Balls	Mins	4s	6s	Rate per 100 balls	Ct
1st Inns	75	102	68	13	–	73.52	1
2nd Inns	14	25	59	2	–	56.00	–
Series to Date	362	707	935	43	–	51.20	3

Test Record

	Mat	Inns	NO	Runs	HS	Avge	100	50	Ct
v England	31	48	12	2048	177 *	38.53	5	10	24
Overall	94	146	28	5932	200	38.68	14	34	69

Sixth Test The Oval

	Score	Balls	Mins	4s	6s	Rate per 100 balls	Ct
1st Inns	22	34	51	2	–	64.70	–
2nd Inns	6	19	21	–	–	31.57	1
Series to Date	390	760	1007	45	–	51.31	4

Test Record

	Mat	Inns	NO	Runs	HS	Avge	100	50	Ct
v England–1997	6	10	0	390	116	39.00	2	1	4
v England–Overall	32	50	12	2076	177 *	54.63	5	10	25
All Tests	95	148	28	5960	200	49.66	14	34	70

Results Summary P32 W17 D9 L6

Notes:
Became the third Australian to score a century in each innings of an Ashes Test, to equal the three by England batsmen. It was the 45th time this has been achieved in Test cricket, by 38 batsmen, eleven of whom are Australian. The centuries were his 13th and 14th in Tests and 4th and 5th versus England.

Test Career Records

Batting and Fielding

	M	I	NO	Runs	HS	Avge	100	50	Ct
NASSER HUSSAIN									
v Australia	10	19	2	615	207	36.17	2	1	10
Overall	23	40	3	1391	207	37.59	5	3	23
STEVE WAUGH									
v England	32	50	12	2076	177 *	54.64	5	10	24
Overall	95	148	28	5960	200	49.66	14	34	70

Bowling

	Balls	Runs	Wickets	Avge	Best	5W
STEVE WAUGH						
v England	1670	843	18	46.83	5–69	1
Overall	6515	2894	80	36.17	5–28	3

Limited-Over Internationals

Batting and Fielding

	M	I	NO	Runs	HS	Avge	100	50	Ct
NASSER HUSSAIN	12	12	4	155	49 *	19.37	–	–	5
STEVE WAUGH	221	201	43	5092	102 *	32.22	1	30	79

Bowling

	Balls	Runs	Wickets	Avge	Best
STEVE WAUGH	7860	5877	172	34.16	4–33

First Texaco Trophy International

Played at Headingley, Leeds on 22 May 1997
Toss: England *Debuts:* A J. Hollioake (E) and D.W. Headley (E)

AUSTRALIA

M.A. Taylor*	c Stewart b Gough	7
M.E. Waugh	b Headley	11
S.R. Waugh	lbw b Ealham	19
M.G. Bevan	run out (Thorpe)	30
G.S. Blewett	b Gough	28
M.J. Slater	c and b Ealham	17
I.A. Healy†	c Atherton b Hollioake	17
S.K. Warne	c Thorpe b Hollioake	4
M.S. Kasprowicz	not out	17
J.N. Gillespie	not out	3
G.D. McGrath		–
Extras	(LB7, W9, NB1)	17
Total	(8 wkts, 50 overs)	170

BOWLING ENGLAND

	O	M	R	W
DeFreitas	9	1	35	0
Gough	10	2	33	2
Ealham	8	3	21	2
Headley	8	0	36	1
Croft	10	1	16	0
Hollioake	5	0	22	2

Fall of Wickets: 1–8 (Taylor), 2–39 (M.E. Waugh), 3–43 (S.R. Waugh), 4–106 (Bevan), 5–106 (Blewett), 6–140 (Healy), 7–140 (Slater), 8–157 (Warne).

ENGLAND

N.V. Knight	lbw b McGrath	12
M.A. Atherton*	c. Healy b Kasprowicz	4
A.J. Stewart†	lbw b McGrath	7
G.P. Thorpe	not out	75
G.D. Lloyd	run out (Blewett)	0
A.J. Hollioake	not out	66
M.A. Ealham		
P.A.J. DeFreitas		
R.D.B. Croft		
D. Gough		
D.W. Headley		
Extras	(B1, W6, NB4)	11
Total	(4 wkts, 40.1 overs)	175

BOWLING AUSTRALIA

	O	M	R	W
McGrath	10	2	34	2
Kasprowicz	7	0	27	1
Gillespie	8.1	1	39	0
Warne	10	0	46	0
Waugh, M.E.	2	0	16	0
Blewett	3	0	12	0

Fall of Wickets: 1–18 (Atherton), 2–20 (Knight), 3–32 (Stewart), 4–40 (Lloyd).

Result: England won by 5 wickets
Umpires: R. Julian and P. Willey
Match Award: A.J. Hollioake

Second Texaco Trophy International

Played at Kennington Oval, London on 24 May 1997
Toss: England *Debut:* A.F. Giles (E)

AUSTRALIA

M.E. Waugh	run out (Croft)	25	
M.A. Taylor*	run out (Hollioake/Gough)	11	
S.R. Waugh	b Croft	24	
M.G. Bevan	not out	108	
M.J. Slater	run out (DeFreitas)	1	
A.C. Gilchrist	lbw b Hollioake	53	
I.A. Healy†	run out (Ealham)	7	
S.K. Warne	not out	11	
M.S. Kasprowicz			
J.N. Gillespie			
G.D. McGrath			
Extras	(LB8, W1)	9	
Total	(6 wkts, 50 Overs)	249	

BOWLING ENGLAND

	O	M	R	W
DeFreitas	8	0	47	0
Gough	10	3	42	0
Ealham	9	2	40	0
Giles	9	0	48	0
Croft	10	2	39	1
Hollioake	4	0	25	1

Fall of Wickets: 1–35 (Taylor), 2–37 (M.E. Waugh), 3–94 (S.R. Waugh), 4–98 (Slater), 5–211 (Gilchrist), 6–226 (Healy).

ENGLAND

N.V. Knight	lbw b Kasprowicz	4	
M.A. Atherton*	not out	113	
A.J. Stewart†	b Warne	40	
G.P. Thorpe	c S.R. Waugh b Bevan	7	
G.D. Lloyd	c Warne b McGrath	22	
A.J. Hollioake	not out	53	
M.A. Ealham			
P.A.J. DeFreitas			
R.D.B. Croft			
D. Gough			
A.F. Giles			
Extras:	(LB5, W8, NB1)	14	
Total	(4 wkts, 48.2 overs)	253	

BOWLING AUSTRALIA

	O	M	R	W
McGrath	9	1	46	1
Kasprowicz	9.2	0	58	1
Gillespie	8	1	42	0
Warne	10	0	39	1
Bevan	9	0	43	1
Waugh, S.R.	3	0	20	0

Fall of Wickets: 1–6 (Knight), 2–77 (Stewart), 3–104 (Thorpe), 4–158 (Lloyd).

Result: England won by 6 wickets
Umpires: J.H. Hampshire and D.R. Shepherd
Match Award: M.A. Atherton

Third Texaco Trophy International

Played at Lord's, London on 25 May 1997
Toss: England *Debuts:* B.C. Hollioake (E), M.T.G. Elliott (A).

AUSTRALIA			BOWLING ENGLAND				
M.T.G. Elliott	c A.J. Hollioake b Gough	1					
M.E. Waugh	lbw b Gough	95		*O*	*M*	*R*	*W*
S.R. Waugh*	c Thorpe b Gough	17	Gough	10	0	44	5
M.G. Bevan	c sub (Knight) b Gough	8	Silverwood	6	0	44	0
J.L. Langer	run out (Silverwood/Stewart)	29	Ealham	10	0	47	2
A.C. Gilchrist	lbw b Ealham	33	Croft	10	0	51	1
I.A. Healy†	c Lloyd b Croft	27	Hollioake B.	7	0	36	0
S.K. Warne	c Stewart b Ealham	5	Hollioake A.	6.2	0	35	1
M.S. Kasprowicz	not out	28					
J.N. Gillespie	c Thorpe b Gough	6					
G.D. McGrath	st Stewart b A.J. Hollioake	1					
Extras	(B2, LB10, W5, NB2)	19					
Total	(49.2 overs)	269					

Fall of Wickets: 1–2 (Elliot), 2–52 (S.R. Waugh), 3–63 (Bevan), 4–142 (Langer), 5–184 (M.E. Waugh), 6–218 (Warne), 7–228 (Gilchrist), 8–242 (Healy), 9–268 (Gillespie), 10–269 (McGrath).

ENGLAND			BOWLING AUSTRALIA				
M.A. Atherton*	lbw b Kasprowicz	1					
A.J. Stewart†	c Langer b M.E. Waugh	79		*O*	*M*	*R*	*W*
B.C. Hollioake	c S.R. Waugh b Gillespie	63	McGrath	9	2	45	0
J.P. Crawley	run out (Gilchrist/Gillespie)	52	Kasprowicz	8	1	40	1
G.P. Thorpe	not out	45	Warne	9	0	44	0
A. J. Hollioake	not out	4	Gillespie	10	0	55	1
G.D. Lloyd			Bevan	3	0	27	0
M.A. Ealham			Waugh S.R.	4	0	22	0
R.D.B. Croft			Waugh M.R.	6	0	28	1
D. Gough							
C.E.W. Silverwood							
Extras	(LB9, W13, NB4)	26					
Total	(4 wkts, 49 overs)	270					

Fall of Wickets: 1–21 (Atherton), 2–113 (B.C. Hollioake), 3–193 (Stewart), 4–253 (Crawley).

Result: England won by 6 wickets
Umpires: M.J. Kitchen and G. Sharp
Match Award: D. Gough
Series Awards: A.J. Hollioake (England) and M.G. Bevan (Australia)

First Cornhill Test Match

Played at Edgbaston, Birmingham on 5–8 June 1997.
Toss: Australia *Umpires:* P. Willey (England) and S.A. Bucknor (West Indies)
Referee: R.S. Madugalle (Sri Lanka) *Debuts:* M.A. Butcher (E)
Result: England won by 9 wickets *Man of the Match:* N. Hussain

AUSTRALIA

M.A. Taylor*	c Butcher b Malcolm	7	(2) c and b Croft	129
M.T.G. Elliott	b Gough	6	(1) b Croft	66
G.S. Blewett	c Hussain b Gough	7	c Butcher b Croft	125
M.E. Waugh	b Gough	5	(6) c Stewart b Gough	1
S.R. Waugh	c Stewart b Caddick	12	lbw b Gough	33
M.G. Bevan	c Ealham b Malcolm	8	(5) c Hussain b Gough	24
I.A. Healy†	c Stewart b Caddick	0	c Atherton b Ealham	30
J.N. Gillespie	lbw b Caddick	4	(10) run out (Crawley/Gough)	0
S.K. Warne	c Malcolm b Caddick	47	(8) c and b Ealham	32
M.S. Kasprowicz	c Butcher b Caddick	17	(9) c Butcher b Ealham	0
G.D. McGrath	not out	1	not out	0
Extras	(w2, nb2)	4	(b18, lb12, w2, nb5)	37
Total		118		477

ENGLAND

M.A. Butcher	c Healy b Kasprowicz	8	lbw b Kasprowicz	14
M.A. Atherton*	c Healy b McGrath	2	not out	57
A.J. Stewart†	c Elliott b Gillespie	18	not out	40
N. Hussain	c Healy b Warne	207		
G.P. Thorpe	c Bevan b McGrath	138		
J.P. Crawley	c Healy b Kasprowicz	1		
M.A. Ealham	not out	53		
R.D.B. Croft	c Healy b Kasprowicz	24		
D. Gough	c Healy b Kasprowicz	0		
A.R. Caddick	lbw b Bevan	0		
D.E. Malcolm				
Extras	(b4, lb7, w1, nb15)	27	(b4, lb4)	8
Total	(9 wkts declared)	478	(1 wkt)	119

ENGLAND

	O	M	R	W	O	M	R	W
Gough	10	1	43	3	35	7	123	3
Malcolm	10	2	25	2	21	6	52	0
Caddick	11.5	1	50	5	30	6	87	0
Croft	–	–	–	–	43	10	125	3
Ealham	–	–	–	–	15.4	3	60	3

AUSTRALIA

	O	M	R	W	O	M	R	W
McGrath	32	8	107	2	7	1	42	0
Kasprowicz	39	8	113	4	7	0	42	1
Gillespie	10	1	48	1	–	–	–	–
Warne	35	8	110	1	7.3	0	27	0
Bevan	10.4	0	44	1	–	–	–	–
Waugh S.R.	12	2	45	0	–	–	–	–

Fall of Wickets

	AUS	ENG	AUS	ENG
1st	11	8	133	29
2nd	15	16	327	–
3rd	26	50	354	–
4th	28	338	393	–
5th	48	345	399	–
6th	48	416	431	–
7th	48	460	465	–
8th	54	463	465	–
9th	110	478	477	–
10th	118	–	477	–

Second Cornhill Test Match

Played at Lord's, London on 20–23 June 1997.
Toss: Australia *Umpires:* D.R. Shepherd (England) and S. Venkataraghavan (India)
Referee: R.S. Madugalle (Sri Lanka) *Debuts:* Nil
Result: Match Drawn *Man of the Match:* G.D. McGrath

ENGLAND

M.A. Butcher	c Blewett b McGrath	5	b Warne	87
M.A. Atherton*	c Taylor b McGrath	1	hit wkt b Kasprowicz	77
A.J. Stewart†	b McGrath	1	c Kasprowicz b McGrath	13
N. Hussain	lbw b McGrath	19	c and b Warne	0
G.P. Thorpe	c Blewett b Reiffel	21	not out	30
J.P. Crawley	c Healy b McGrath	1	not out	29
M.A. Ealham	c Elliott b Reiffel	7		
R.D.B. Croft	c Healy b McGrath	2		
D. Gough	c Healy b McGrath	10		
A.R. Caddick	lbw b McGrath	1		
D.E. Malcolm	not out	0		
Extras	(b4, nb5)	9	(b8, lb14, w1, nb7)	30
Total		77	(4 wkts declared)	266

AUSTRALIA

M.A. Taylor *	b Gough	1
M.T.G. Elliott	c Crawley b Caddick	112
G.S. Blewett	c Hussain b Croft	45
M.E. Waugh	c Malcolm b Caddick	33
S.K. Warne	c Hussain b Gough	0
S.R. Waugh	lbw b Caddick	0
M.G. Bevan	c Stewart b Caddick	4
I.A. Healy†	not out	13
P.R. Reiffel	not out	1
M.S. Kasprowicz		
G.D. McGrath		
Extras	(b1, lb3)	4
Total	(7 wkts declared)	213

AUSTRALIA

	O	M	R	W	O	M	R	W
McGrath	20.3	8	38	8	20	5	65	1
Reiffel	15	9	17	2	13	5	29	0
Kasprowicz	5	1	9	0	15	3	54	1
Warne	2	0	9	0	19	4	47	2
Bevan	–	–	–	–	8	1	29	0
Waugh, S.R.	–	–	–	–	4	0	20	0

ENGLAND

	O	M	R	W	O	M	R	W
Gough	20	4	82	2				
Caddick	22	6	71	4				
Malcolm	7	1	26	0				
Croft	12	5	30	1				

Fall of Wickets

	ENG	AUS	ENG
1st	11	4	162
2nd	12	73	189
3rd	13	147	197
4th	47	147	202
5th	56	147	–
6th	62	159	–
7th	66	212	–
8th	76	–	–
9th	77	–	–
10th	77	–	–

Third Cornhill Test Match

Played at Old Trafford, Manchester on 3–7 July 1997.
Toss: Australia *Umpires:* G Sharp (England) and S. Venkataraghavan (India)
Referee: R.S. Madugalle (Sri Lanka) *Debuts:* D.W. Headley (E)
Result: Australia won by 268 runs *Man of the Match:* S.R. Waugh

AUSTRALIA

M.A. Taylor*	c Thorpe b Headley	2	(2) c Butcher b Headley		1
M.T.G. Elliott	c Stewart b Headley	40	(1) c Butcher b Headley		11
G.S. Blewett	b Gough	8	c Hussain b Croft		19
M.E. Waugh	c Stewart b Ealham	12	b Ealham		55
S.R. Waugh	b Gough	108	c Stewart b Headley		116
M.G. Bevan	c Stewart b Headley	7	c Atherton b Headley		0
I.A. Healy†	c Stewart b Caddick	9	c Butcher b Croft		47
S.K. Warne	c Stewart b Ealham	3	c Stewart b Caddick		53
P.R. Reiffel	b Gough	31	not out		45
J.N. Gillespie	c Stewart b Headley	0	not out		28
G.D. McGrath	not out	0			
Extras	(b8, lb4, nb3)	15	(b1, lb13, nb6)		20
Total	(8wkts declared)	235			395

ENGLAND

M.A. Butcher	st Healy b Bevan	51	c McGrath b Gillespie		28
M.A. Atherton*	c Healy b McGrath	5	lbw b Gillespie		21
A.J. Stewart†	c Taylor b Warne	30	b Warne		1
N. Hussain	c Healy b Warne	13	lbw b Gillespie		1
G.P. Thorpe	c Taylor b Warne	3	c Healy b Warne		7
J.P. Crawley	c Healy b Warne	4	hit wkt b McGrath		83
M.A. Ealham	not out	24	c Healy b McGrath		9
R.D.B. Croft	c S.R. Waugh b McGrath	7	c Reiffel b McGrath		7
D. Gough	lbw b Warne	1	b McGrath		6
A.R. Caddick	c M.E. Waugh b Warne	15	c Gillespie b Warne		17
D.W. Headley	b McGrath	0	not out		0
Extras	(b4, lb3, nb2)	9	(b14, lb4, w1, nb1)		20
Total		162			200

ENGLAND

	O	M	R	W	O	M	R	W
Gough	21	7	52	3	20	3	62	0
Headley	27.3	4	72	4	29	4	104	4
Caddick	14	2	52	1	21	0	69	1
Ealham	11	2	34	2	13	3	41	1
Croft	4	0	13	0	39	12	105	2

AUSTRALIA

	O	M	R	W	O	M	R	W
McGrath	23.4	9	40	3	21	4	46	4
Reiffel	9	3	14	0	2	0	8	0
Warne	30	14	48	6	30.4	8	63	3
Gillespie	14	3	39	0	12	4	31	3
Bevan	8	3	14	1	8	2	34	0

Fall of Wickets

	AUS	ENG	AUS	ENG
1st	9	8	5	44
2nd	22	74	33	45
3rd	42	94	39	50
4th	85	101	131	55
5th	113	110	132	84
6th	150	111	210	158
7th	160	122	298	170
8th	230	123	333	177
9th	235	161	–	188
10th	235	162	–	200

Fourth Cornhill Test Match

Played at Headingley, Leeds on 24–28 July 1997.
Toss: Australia *Umpires:* M.J. Kitchen (England) and C.J. Mitchley (South Africa)
Referee: C.W. Smith (West Indies) *Debuts:* A.M. Smith (E)
Result: Australia won by an innings and 51 runs *Man of the Match:* J.N. Gillespie

ENGLAND

M.A. Butcher	c Blewett b Reiffel	24	c Healy b McGrath		19
M.A. Atherton*	c Gillespie b McGrath	41	c Warne b McGrath		2
A.J. Stewart†	c Blewett b Gillespie	7	b Reiffel		16
N. Hussain	c Taylor b McGrath	26	c Gillespie b Warne		105
D.W. Headley	c S.R. Waugh b Gillespie	22	(8) lbw b Reiffel		3
G.P. Thorpe	b Gillespie	15	(5) c M. Waugh b Gillespie		15
J.P. Crawley	c Blewett b Gillespie	2	(6) b Reiffel		72
M.A. Ealham	not out	8	(7) c M. Waugh b Reiffel		4
R.D.B. Croft	c Ponting b Gillespie	6	c Healy b Reiffel		5
D. Gough	b Gillespie	0	c M. Waugh b Gillespie		0
A.M. Smith	b Gillespie	0	not out		4
Extras	(b4, lb4, w1, nb12)	21	(b6, lb4, nb13)		23
Total		172			268

AUSTRALIA

M.A. Taylor*	c Stewart b Gough	0
M.T.G. Elliott	b Gough	199
G.S. Blewett	c Stewart b Gough	1
M.E. Waugh	c and b Headley	8
S.R. Waugh	c Crawley b Headley	4
R.T. Ponting	c Ealham b Gough	127
I.A. Healy†	b Ealham	31
S.K. Warne	c Thorpe b Ealham	0
P.R. Reiffel	not out	54
J.N. Gillespie	b Gough	3
G.D. McGrath	not out	20
Extras	(b9, lb10, nb35)	54
Total	(9 wkts declared)	501

AUSTRALIA

	O	M	R	W	O	M	R	W
McGrath	22	5	67	2	22	5	80	2
Reiffel	20	4	41	1	21.1	2	49	5
Gillespie	13.4	1	37	7	23	8	65	2
Blewett	3	0	17	0	–	–	–	–
Warne	1	0	2	0	21	6	53	1
Waugh, S.R.	–	–	–		4	1	11	0

ENGLAND

	O	M	R	W	O	M	R	W
Gough	36	5	149	5				
Headley	25	2	125	2				
Smith	23	2	89	0				
Ealham	19	3	56	2				
Croft	18	1	49	0				
Butcher	2	0	14	0				

Fall of Wickets

	ENG	AUS	ENG
1st	43	0	23
2nd	58	16	28
3rd	103	43	57
4th	138	50	89
5th	154	318	222
6th	154	382	252
7th	163	383	256
8th	172	444	263
9th	172	461	264
10th	172	—	268

Fifth Cornhill Test Match

Played at Trent Bridge, Nottingham on 7–10 August 1997.
Toss: Australia *Umpires:* D.J. Shepherd (England) and C.J. Mitchley (South Africa)
Referee: C.W. Smith (West Indies) *Debuts:* A.J. Hollioake and B.C. Hollioake (E)
Result: Australia won by 264 runs *Man of the Match:* I.A. Healy

AUSTRALIA

M.T.G. Elliott	c Stewart b Headley	69	(2) c Crawley b Caddick		37
M.A. Taylor*	b Caddick	76	(1) c Hussain b B. Hollioake		45
G.S. Blewett	c Stewart b B.C. Hollioake	50	c Stewart b Caddick		60
M.E. Waugh	lbw b Caddick	68	lbw b Headley		7
S.R. Waugh	b Malcolm	75	c A.J. Hollioake b Caddick		14
R.T. Ponting	b Headley	9	c Stewart b A.J. Hollioake		45
I.A. Healy†	c A.J. Hollioake b Malcolm	16	c Stewart b A.J. Hollioake		63
S.K. Warne	c Thorpe b Malcolm	0	c Thorpe b Croft		20
P.R. Reiffel	c Thorpe b Headley	26	c B, C. Hollioake b Croft		22
J.N. Gillespie	not out	18	c Thorpe b Headley		4
G.D. McGrath	b Headley	1	not out		1
Extras	(b4, lb10, w1, nb4)	19	(b1, lb11, nb6)		18
Total		427			336

ENGLAND

M.A. Atherton*	c Healy b Warne	27	c Healy b McGrath		8
A.J. Stewart†	c Healy b Warne	87	c S.R. Waugh b Reiffel		16
J.P. Crawley	c Healy b McGrath	18	c Healy b Gillespie		33
N. Hussain	b Warne	2	b Gillespie		21
G.P. Thorpe	c Blewett b Warne	53	not out		82
A.J. Hollioake	c Taylor b Reiffel	45	lbw b Gillespie		2
B.C. Hollioake	c M.E. Waugh b Reiffel	28	lbw b Warne		2
R.D.B. Croft	c Blewett b McGrath	18	c McGrath b Warne		6
A.R. Caddick	c Healy b McGrath	0	lbw b Warne		0
D.W. Headley	not out	10	c Healy b McGrath		4
D.E. Malcolm	b McGrath	12	c M.E. Waugh b McGrath		0
Extras	(b2, lb6, nb5)	13	(b6, lb2, nb4)		12
Total		313			186

ENGLAND

	O	M	R	W	O	M	R	W					
										Fall of Wickets			
Malcolm	25	4	100	3	16	4	52	0		AUS	ENG	AUS	ENG
Headley	30.5	7	87	4	19	3	56	2	1st	117	106	51	25
Caddick	30	4	102	2	20	2	85	3	2nd	160	129	105	25
Hollioake, B.C.	10	1	57	1	5	1	26	1	3rd	225	135	134	78
Croft	19	7	43	0	26.5	6	74	2	4th	311	141	156	99
Hollioake, A.J.	7	0	24	0	12	2	31	2	5th	325	243	171	121
									6th	355	243	276	144
AUSTRALIA									7th	363	272	292	150
	O	M	R	W	O	M	R	W	8th	386	290	314	166
McGrath	29.5	9	71	4	13.5	4	36	3	9th	419	290	326	186
Reiffel	21	2	101	2	11	3	34	1	10th	427	313	336	186
Gillespie	11	3	47	0	8	0	65	3					
Warne	32	8	86	4	16	4	43	3					

Sixth Cornhill Test Match

Played at Kennington Oval, London on 21–23 August 1997.
Toss: England *Umpires:* P. Willey (England) and L.H. Barker (West Indies)
Referee: C.W. Smith (West Indies) *Debuts:* S. Young (A)
Result: England won by 19 runs *Man of the Series:* G.P. Thorpe (E), G.D. McGrath (A)

ENGLAND

M.A. Butcher	b McGrath	5	lbw b M.E. Waugh	13
M.A. Atherton*	c Healy b McGrath	8	c S.R. Waugh b Kasprowicz	8
A.J. Stewart†	lbw b McGrath	36	lbw b Kasprowicz	3
N. Hussain	c Elliott b McGrath	35	c Elliott b Warne	2
G.P. Thorpe	b McGrath	27	c Taylor b Kasprowicz	62
M.R. Ramprakash	c Blewett b McGrath	4	st Healy b Warne	48
A.J. Hollioake	b Warne	0	lbw b Kasprowicz	4
A.R. Caddick	not out	26	not out	0
P.J. Martin	b McGrath	20	c and b Kasprowicz	3
P.C.R. Tufnell	c Blewett b Warne	1	c Healy b Kasprowicz	0
D.E. Malcolm	lbw Kasprowicz	0	b Kasprowicz	0
Extras	(b2, lb6, nb10)	18	(b6, lb10, nb4)	20
Total		180		163

AUSTRALIA

M.T.G. Elliott	b Tufnell	12	(2) lbw b Malcolm	4
M.A. Taylor*	c Hollioake b Tufnell	38	(1) lbw b Caddick	18
G.S. Blewett	c Stewart b Tufnell	47	c Stewart b Caddick	19
M.E. Waugh	c Butcher b Tufnell	19	c Hussain b Tufnell	1
S.R. Waugh	lbw b Caddick	22	c Thorpe b Caddick	6
R.T. Ponting	c Hussain b Tufnell	40	lbw b Tufnell	20
I.A. Healy†	c Stewart b Tufnell	2	c and b Caddick	14
S. Young	c Stewart b Tufnell	0	not out	4
S.K. Warne	b Caddick	30	c Martin b Tufnell	3
M.S. Kasprowicz	lbw b Caddick	0	c Hollioake b Caddick	4
G.D. McGrath	not out	1	c Thorpe b Tufnell	1
Extras	(lb3, w1, nb5)	9	(b3, lb4, w1, nb2)	10
Total		220		104

AUSTRALIA

	O	M	R	W	O	M	R	W
McGrath	21	4	76	7	17	5	33	0
Kasprowicz	11.4	2	56	1	15.5	5	36	7
Warne	17	8	32	2	26	9	57	2
Young	7	3	8	0	1	0	5	0
Waugh, M.E.	–	–	–	–	7	3	16	1

ENGLAND

	O	M	R	W	O	M	R	W
Malcolm	11	2	37	0	3	0	15	1
Martin	15	5	38	0	4	0	13	0
Caddick	19	4	76	3	12	2	42	5
Tufnell	34.3	16	66	7	13.1	6	27	4

Fall of Wickets

	ENG	AUS	ENG	AUS
1st	18	49	20	5
2nd	24	54	24	36
3rd	97	94	26	42
4th	128	140	52	49
5th	131	150	131	54
6th	132	164	138	88
7th	132	164	160	92
8th	158	205	163	95
9th	175	205	163	99
10th	180	220	163	104

Milestones

First Test

ENGLAND
- Mike Atherton's 41st Test as captain, equalling record of Peter May.
- Mike Atherton passed 5000 runs in Tests, the 12th England batsman to do so.
- Mark Butcher became the ninth player to follow his father (Alan) into the England side.

AUSTRALIA
- Greg Blewett became the first man to score a century in each of his first three Ashes Tests.
- Mark Taylor passed 50 for the first time since December 1995, 22 Test innings before.
- Ian Healy registered six dismissals in an innings for the first time.

Second Test

ENGLAND
- Mike Atherton captained England for the 42nd time, surpassing Peter May's record, set in 1961.
- The England first innings total of 77 was the lowest at Lord's since 1974 when India scored 42. It was the third time England had been dismissed for under 100 in Ashes Tests at Lord's, the previous being 53 and 62 in 1888. The last time England failed to reach 100 against Australia was at Melbourne (92) in 1994–95.

AUSTRALIA
- Glenn McGrath's 8–38 were the third best figures by an Australian in Ashes contests, the best being Arthur Mailey, with 9–121, at Melbourne in 1920–21. They were, however, the best by an Australian at Lord's.
- Matthew Elliott compiled a maiden Test century in his seventh Test.

General
- The loss of the first day's play was the first time since 1964 that this had occurred in an Ashes Test at Lord's. The last time a complete day had been lost in any Test at Lord's was in 1991 when West Indies were the visitors.

Third Test

ENGLAND
- Dean Headley became the first third-generation Test cricketer, following father Ron and grandfather George, both of whom appeared for the West Indies.

- Alec Stewart's eight dismissals in the match were a record for an England wicket-keeper in an Ashes Test. The six dismissals in the first innings equalled those of Jack Russell at Melbourne in 1990–91.

AUSTRALIA
- Shane Warne, when he dismissed Andy Caddick, took his 249th Test wicket, passing the 248 wickets of Ritchie Benaud to become the most successful leg-spinner in Test history and also the third highest Australian wicket-taker, behind Dennis Lillee and Craig McDermott.

Fourth Test

ENGLAND
- The stand of 133 between Nasser Hussain and John Crawley was the first century partnership for the fifth wicket against Australia at Leeds.

AUSTRALIA
- Matthew Elliott became only the third batsman to be dismissed for 199 in a Test, following Mudassar Nazar (Pakistan) and Mohammad Azharuddin (India).
- Ricky Ponting scored his maiden Test century in his seventh Test. Curiously, this meant that all the first seven Australian batsmen had made their maiden Test century against England.
- Jason Gillespie's return of 7–37 was his best in Test cricket and the best by any Australian at Leeds.
- The twins, Steve and Mark Waugh were playing together in a Test for the 50th time.

Fifth Test

ENGLAND
- Adam and Ben Hollioake became the fifth set of brothers to play together for England, and the first since Peter and Derek Richardson in 1957. It was the first time this century that two brothers had made their debuts in the same Test, other than in the inaugural Test of a country.
- Ben Hollioake was the third teenager (19 yrs 269 days) to play for England, after Denis Compton and Brian Close, and the youngest since the latter made his debut in 1949 aged 18 yrs 149 days.
- Graham Thorpe, when 44 in the second innings, reached 1000 runs in Tests against Australia.

AUSTRALIA
- Mark Taylor, when 61 in the first innings, became the sixth Australian and twenty-third in all to pass 6000 runs in Test cricket.
- When Ian Healy dismissed Alec Stewart it was his 300th catch in Tests and his 100th against England.

- Ian Healy, when 31 in the second innings, completed 1000 runs against England and thereby became the third wicket-keeper and second Australian to complete the Ashes 'Double'.
- Australia, in winning the Test, retained the Ashes for the fourth consecutive series, following the recapture of the Ashes in 1989.

Sixth Test

ENGLAND
- Phil Tufnell's return of 11–93 was the best return in an Ashes Test at the Oval since F Martin with 12–102 in 1890. It was the second time he had taken ten or more wickets in a Test.
- England achieved two wins in an Ashes series for the first time in five series since 1986–87.

AUSTRALIA
- Mark Taylor lost the toss for the first time in the series and therefore equalled Ian Chappell (1974–75) and Graham Yallop (1978–79) in winning five out of six tosses in an Ashes series. Monty Noble (1909) and Lindsay Hassett (1953) both won all five in a five-Test series.
- When Mark Taylor caught Graham Thorpe in the second innings he took his tally of catches to 123 (in 88 Tests) and moved into sole possession of second place in the all-time fielding list. He had previously shared this spot with Greg Chappell (Australia, 87 Tests) and Vivian Richards (West Indies, 121 Tests). Allan Border (Australia, 156 Tests) is the leader with 155 catches.

General
- Broadcasting history was made on the first day when the Test Match commentary provided by the BBC on *Test Match Special* was made available worldwide on the Internet, via the web site at Lord's, enabling listeners with suitable equipment to hear the broadcast.

England v Australia 1997

Series Averages

ENGLAND
Batting and Fielding

	M	I	NO	Runs	HS	Avge	100	50	Ct	St
G.P. Thorpe	6	11	2	453	138	50.33	1	3	8	–
N. Hussain	6	11	0	431	207	39.18	2	–	8	–
M.A Ealham	4	6	3	105	53 *	35.00	–	1	3	–
J.P. Crawley	5	9	1	243	83	30.37	–	2	3	–
M.R. Ramprakash	1	2	0	52	48	26.00	–	–	–	–
M.A. Butcher	5	10	0	254	87	25.40	–	2	8	–
A.J. Stewart	6	12	1	268	87	24.36	–	1	23	–
M.A. Atherton	6	12	1	257	77	23.36	–	2	2	–
B.C. Hollioake	1	2	0	30	28	15.00	–	–	1	–
A.J. Hollioake	2	4	0	51	45	12.75	–	–	4	–
P.J. Martin	1	2	0	23	20	11.50	–	–	1	–
A.R. Caddick	5	8	2	59	26 *	9.83	–	–	1	–
D.W. Headley	3	6	2	39	22	9.75	–	–	1	–
R.D.B. Croft	5	8	0	75	24	9.37	–	–	1	–
A.M. Smith	1	2	1	4	4 *	4.00	–	–	–	–
D.E. Malcolm	4	5	1	12	12	3.00	–	–	2	–
D. Gough	4	6	0	17	10	2.83	–	–	–	–
P.C.R. Tufnell	1	2	0	1	1	0.50	–	–	–	–

Bowling

	O	M	Runs	Wkts	Avge	Best	5W	10W
P.C.R. Tufnell	47.4	22	93	11	8.45	7–66	1	1
M.A. Ealham	58.4	11	101	8	23.87	3–60	–	–
A.R. Caddick	179.5	27	634	24	26.41	5–42	2	–
A.J. Hollioake	19	2	55	2	27.50	2–31	–	–
D.W. Headley	131.2	20	444	16	27.75	4–72	–	–
D. Gough	142	27	511	16	31.93	5–149	1	–
B.C. Hollioake	15	2	83	2	41.50	1–26	–	–
D.E. Malcolm	93	19	307	6	51.16	3–100	–	–
R.D.B. Croft	161.5	41	439	8	54.87	3–125	–	–
M.A. Butcher	2	0	14	0	–	–	–	–
P.J. Martin	19	5	51	0	–	–	–	–
A.M. Smith	23	2	89	0	–	–	–	–

AUSTRALIA
Batting and Fielding

	M	I	NO	Runs	HS	Avge	100	50	Ct	St
P.R. Reiffel	4	6	3	179	54 *	59.66	–	1	1	–
M.T.G. Elliott	6	10	0	556	199	55.60	2	2	4	–
R.T. Ponting	3	5	0	241	127	48.20	1	–	1	–
S.R. Waugh	6	10	0	390	116	39	2	1	4	–
G.S. Blewett	6	10	0	381	125	38.10	1	2	9	–
M.A. Taylor	6	10	0	317	129	31.70	1	1	6	–
I.A. Healy	6	10	1	225	63	25.00	–	1	25	2
M.E. Waugh	6	10	0	209	68	20.90	–	2	6	–
S.K. Warne	6	10	0	188	53	18.80	-	1	2	–
G.D. McGrath	6	8	6	25	20 *	12.50	–	–	2	–
J.N. Gillespie	4	7	2	57	28 *	11.40	–	–	3	–
M.G. Bevan	3	5	0	43	24	8.60	–	–	1	–
M.S. Kasprowicz	3	4	0	21	17	5.25	–	–	2	-
S. Young	1	2	1	4	4 *	4.00	–	–	–	–

Bowling

	O	M	Runs	Wkts	Avge	Best	5W	10W
M.E. Waugh	7	3	16	1	16.00	1–16	–	–
G.D. McGrath	249.5	67	701	36	19.47	8–38	2	–
J.N. Gillespie	91.4	20	332	16	20.75	7–37	1	–
M.S. Kasprowicz	93.3	19	310	14	22.14	7-36	1	–
S.K. Warne	237.1	69	577	24	24.04	6–48	1	–
P.R. Reiffel	112.1	28	293	11	26.63	5–49	1	–
M.G. Bevan	34.4	6	121	2	60.50	1–14	–	–
S. Young	8	3	13	0	–	–	–	–
G.S. Blewett	3	0	17	0	–	–	–	–
S.R. Waugh	20	3	76	0	–	–	–	–

England v Australia Summary of Results

	Played	Won by England	Won by Australia	Drawn
IN ENGLAND				
Oval	32	15	5	12
Old Trafford	27	7	7	13
Lord's	31	5	12	14
Trent Bridge	18	3	6	9
Headingley	22	6	8	8
Edgbaston	10	4	2	4
Sheffield	1	–	1	–
Total	141	40	41	60
IN AUSTRALIA				
Melbourne	50	18	25	7
Sydney	50	20	23	7
Adelaide	26	8	13	5
Brisbane	16	5	8	3
Perth	8	1	4	3
Total	150	52	73	25
Total	291	92	114	85